Events Management

Events Management
an Integrated and Practical Approach

Razaq Raj
Paul Walters
Tahir Rashid

Los Angeles • London • New Delhi • Singapore • Washington DC

First published 2009

SAGE Publications Ltd
1 Oliver's Yard
55 City Road
London EC1Y 1SP

SAGE Publications Inc.
2455 Teller Road
Thousand Oaks, California 91320

SAGE Publications India Pvt Ltd
B 1/I 1 Mohan Cooperative Industrial Area
Mathura Road
New Delhi 110 044

SAGE Publications Asia-Pacific Pte Ltd
33 Pekin Street #02-01
Far East Square
Singapore 048763

Library of Congress Control Number: 2007943496

British Library Cataloguing in Publication data

A catalogue record for this book is available from the British
Library

ISBN 978-1-4129-2334-7
ISBN 978-1-4129-2335-4 (pbk)

Typeset by C&M Digitals (P) Ltd, Chennai, India
Printed in India at Replika Press Pvt. Ltd
Printed on paper from sustainable resources

Contents

Contents

CHAPTER 1

Introduction

<table>
<tr><td colspan="1">OUTLINE OF THE CHAPTER</td></tr>
</table>

OUTLINE OF THE CHAPTER
The historical origins of events An overview of the wide range of events that the industry covers An events industry Value of areas of the events industry in the UK The transferable personal skills of an event manager Summary Further reading

The core theme for this book is to establish a common dialogue between event managers and event specialists who consistently have a working relationship; each strand of the book will be linked to industry best practice where appropriate. New methods and strategies will enhance understanding and capitalise on the theoretical foundations.

The historical origins of events

Events are organised acts and performances, which have their origins in ancient history. Events and festivals are well documented in the historical period before the fall of the Western Roman Empire (A.D. 476). They have an important function within society, providing participants with the opportunity to assert their identities and to share rituals and celebrations with other people. People have traditionally celebrated special religious holy days – for example, Christmas and Easter – and have participated in other festivities organised by the rulers of the time. Kings and leaders have often organised events as a way of controlling the public. This was especially the case in the seventeenth and eighteenth centuries.

In modern society, it may be argued that traditional religious and national festivals are no longer viewed as the key focus for community celebrations. Modern western society instead tends to create events which celebrate *individual* milestones, anniversaries and achievements. Birthday parties, wedding celebrations and house warming parties are all ways in which we get together.

These days events are considered to make a considerable contribution to the cultural and economic development of the countries *in which they are held*. Events can have a major impact on the development of cultural tourism to the host communities. Event and festival organisers are now using historical and cultural themes to develop annual events to attract visitors and create cultural images in the host cities by holding festivals in community settings. Increasingly, larger events and festivals are not specifically designed to address the social and cultural needs of any one group but instead are often developed because of the economic benefits they will hopefully bring, primarily through tourism. Such festivals attract increasing numbers of local, regional and international visitors and thus may help to develop links with the global community.

A festival can be defined as a gathering of community or an event which is centred on some theme and held annually or less frequently for a limited period of time.

Festivals and celebrations in local communities have generally been accepted and recognised. These local festivals create entertainment for residents and visitors, but also contribute to a sense of community, building bridges between diverse community groups and giving them an opportunity to come together and celebrate their history and the place in which they live.

An overview of the wide range of events that the industry covers

Modern events vary enormously in terms of their scale and complexity and the number of stakeholders involved, ranging from community festivals to major supporting events.

Small Event
Few stakeholders
Clear objectives

Massive Event
Many stakeholders
Complex objectives

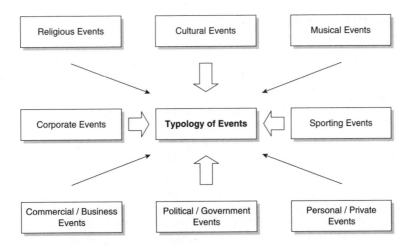

Figure 1.1   Typologies of events

The larger the event, the more objective components it will have, due to the numerous sub events and stakeholder events which comprise the whole. This is particularly true, for example, of such events as the Olympic Games (as discussed later). The typologies of events in Figure 1.1 show the different types of events that have been developed around the world, ranging from individuals to multinational organisations.

There have been considerable changes in the nature of festivals over the last decade. Where they previously tended to be associated with key calendar dates, particular seasons and heritage sites, there is now a much broader and more diverse range of festivals and events taking place all over the world. The revolution in festivals has been stimulated by commerce. The changing demand of local community groups has increased business opportunities for event organisers and local businesses.

Festivals play a major part in the economy of a city and local community. Such events are attractive to host communities, since they can promote a sense of pride and identity among local people. In addition, festivals can play an important part in promoting the host community as both a tourist and commercial destination. Events can help to develop the image and profile of a destination and may attract visitors outside of the holiday season. They can also have significant economic impacts, contributing to the development of local communities and businesses, providing support to those who pursue economic opportunity and supporting key industrial sectors.

Festivals provide an opportunity for local people to develop and share their culture. If we understand 'culture' to mean the personal expression of community heritage, we can see how festivals may create a sense of shared values, beliefs and perspectives within a local community. The peoples and communities that host festivals also offer their visitors a vibrant and valuable cultural experience. Events enable tourists to see how local communities celebrate their culture and to interact with their hosts. This not only meets their leisure needs but can increase their understanding and appreciation of the local culture and heritage.

An events industry

There is some debate as to whether an events industry actually exists. Those who work exclusively in exhibitions view themselves as part of the exhibition industry; those who work in live music might define themselves as part of the music business. Others, such as wedding organisers, may see themselves as belonging to a stand alone industry.

There are a multitude of suppliers who rely on people organising events for all or part of their business. A ticket printer's trade exclusively depends upon orders from events, be they sporting, cultural, musical or corporate. In order to prosper, a professional sound company needs contracts with event venues and event organisers, ranging from sound systems installed permanently in churches or nightclubs to those set up temporarily for a concert or conference. A printer may have a wide range of other customers, but events businesses that need posters, flyers and brochures may account for a significant part of their work. Events are merely a component of a hotelier's business, when meetings or conferences are arranged in-house. Yet business tourism is vital to the hospitality industry, especially where delegates are attending large meetings, incentives, conferences and exhibitions (M.I.C.E) events. For example, 22,000 jobs in the West Midlands are sustained by the NEC Group of venues (National Exhibition Centre, International Convention Centre, Symphony Hall, and the National Indoor Arena) alone (British Tourist Authority, 2007).

Value of areas of the events industry in the UK

Estimating the financial value of such a diverse UK events industry is a very difficult task. The typology of events presented in this text breaks the events industry down into different sectors and sub-sectors, some of which have information more readily available than others. These facts and figures, however, do take full account of the importance of events in economic and employment terms.

The British Conference Market Trends Survey 2001 estimates that conferences and meetings are worth £7.3 billion annually. Exhibitions and trade fairs are calculated to be worth £2.04 billion annually, excluding the value of business transacted at them. This means that exhibitions are the fifth largest marketing medium, attracting 11 per cent of media expenditure in the UK (British Tourist Authority, 2006). The value of the corporate events sector is estimated to be between £700 million and £1 billion annually.

Outdoor events, which are cultural and sometimes commercial, including the great County, City and Town shows and fairs, are estimated at a value of at least £1 billion a year (*The Business Tourism Partnership* (British Tourist Authority, 2007).

The music events market was estimated to be worth £613 million in 2004 (Music Concerts and Festivals – UK – August 2004 Mintel International Group Limited). Pop and rock events are the major components of this, accounting for around £458 million. Jazz festivals and concerts make a smaller contribution to the total figure, while the classical music events sector is valued at £155 million.

Sports events would merit an in-depth study in their own right, such is the range of both events and stakeholders. Given that many sporting events are part of international competitions, it can be difficult to define the boundaries of the market within the UK alone. The clearest example is perhaps Premier League Football – the UK's most popular sport in terms of spectator admissions and television viewing. The Football Association Premier League, in its last published accounts (for the 2006/07 financial year) had a turnover of nearly £598.5 m.

The most revealing figure is the increase in the value of the broadcasting rights contract value between the League and Sky broadcasting. An initial five-year deal for £200m was signed when the League was formed in 1992. The three-year contract which followed in 2007 was worth £1.7 billion (http://www.premierleague.com/page/History/0,, 12306,00.html).

There is also a core group of companies and organisations that work across these various specialist sectors of the events industry. These organisations, known as 'event support services', constitute the foundation of the industry.

Appreciation of events industry and event support services

Figure 1.2 illustrates technical sports services and how venues assist one another in the event industry.

If there is still a case for the existence of an, albeit diverse, events industry, then it is the industry's specialist support services that provide the best argument for it.

The lighting equipment creating an atmosphere at a popular music concert tour in town and city halls will, later in the year, be illuminating conference speakers and a corporate stage set. It may be shining down and helping create the 'wow' factor at a product launch or guiding models as they glide down a catwalk. Once the event is finished, it will be packed up, loaded, transported and taken to the next venue where it will be set up, used, taken down and so on.

Lighting designers and engineers are just one group of the many skilled technical specialists working within the events industry's individual support services. These range from fireworks to fire eaters to fire safety, and from waste management to welfare to web design. It is the job of the event manager to coordinate the work of all these many specialists. It may therefore benefit the event manager to have some of these specialist skills or at least a detailed knowledge and appreciation of them. However, events management also requires its own set of skills.

The transferable personal skills of an event manager

Events are an exceptionally powerful medium of communication. People may not remember exactly what was said or heard, exactly what was done

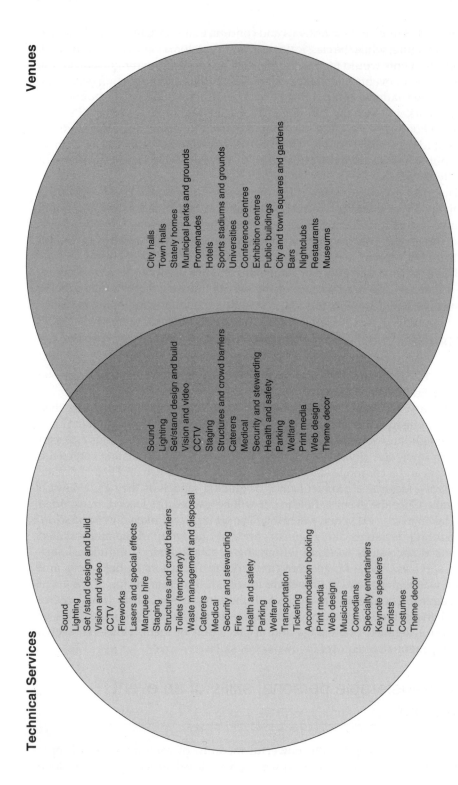

Technical Services

Sound
Lighting
Set /stand design and build
Vision and video
CCTV
Fireworks
Lasers and special effects
Marquee hire
Staging
Structures and crowd barriers
Toilets (temporary)
Waste management and disposal
Caterers
Medical
Security and stewarding
Fire
Health and safety
Parking
Welfare
Transportation
Ticketing
Accommodation booking
Print media
Web design
Musicians
Comedians
Specialty entertainers
Keynote speakers
Florists
Costumes
Theme decor

Sound
Lighting
Set/stand design and build
Vision and video
CCTV
Staging
Structures and crowd barriers
Caterers
Medical
Security and stewarding
Health and safety
Parking
Welfare
Print media
Web design
Theme decor

Venues

City halls
Town halls
Stately homes
Municipal parks and grounds
Promenades
Hotels
Sports stadiums and grounds
Universities
Conference centres
Exhibition centres
Public buildings
City and town squares and gardens
Bars
Nightclubs
Restaurants
Museums

Figure 1.2   The model for technical support services and venues in events

or seen, but they do remember how the event made them feel. This is true whether you are witnessing a major sporting achievement, a virtuoso musical performance or an inspirational keynote speaker, or whether you are attending an exciting exhibition, a well-orchestrated new product launch or your own perfect wedding.

If excellent event experiences are to be produced and the 'experiential marketing' of events is thus to be successful, then highly skilled event professionals are required. Such professionals share a set of common skills, whether they are organising concerts or conferences, meetings or matches, fashion shows or film festivals.

So what are the transferable personal skills of event managers? Having examined numerous job advertisements, descriptions and person specifications for event management posts, the following skills are invariably featured:

- Organisational and logistical skills

- Time management skills – running to a schedule

- Leadership skills – a team player / team leader

- Motivational skills – self-motivated and able to motivate others

- People skills – with a wide range of people at different levels

- Marketing skills – media, sales

- Public relations skills – generating interest, copywriting, contacts

- Communication skills – to colleagues, clients and authorities

- Presentation skills – in several forms and media

- Research skills – gathering and interpreting information

- Commercial awareness – finance, budgets and breakevens

- A positive and adaptable attitude – the 'make it happen'

- Problem-solving skills and can-do attitude

- Innovation and creativity – generating the 'wow' factor

How, then, can this prerequisite skill set be developed?

Many of these skills, especially when combined together, are those expected at graduate level and this explains the increasing number of universities and higher education institutions around the world now offering events management programmes at both undergraduate and postgraduate level.

There are also professional development initiatives within the industry. These often bring together diverse aspects of the industry, for example, the Events Sector Industry Training Organisation (ESITO). ESITO is officially accredited by City and Guilds in the UK as the assessment centre for the

Events National Vocational Qualifications (NVQs). Events NVQs apply to virtually anyone in the events industry, particularly those involved in organising events, working at event venues, exhibiting and supplying goods and services for events.

The Events Sector Industry Training Organisation is supported by 12 leading organisations. They are:

ACE   Association for Conferences and Events

ABPCO   Association of British Professional Conference Organisers

AEO   Association of Exhibition Organisers

BECA   British Exhibition Contractors Association

EVA   Exhibition Venues Association

ITMA   Incentive Travel & Meetings Association

MIA   Meeting Industry Association

MPI   (UK) Meeting Professionals International

MUTA   Made-Up Textiles Association

NEA   National Exhibitors Association

NOEA   National Outdoor Events Association

TESA   The Event Services Association

ESITO is involved in projects seeking to identify the common skills, knowledge and understanding required by international events organisers and managers. They are undertaking this research in the Czech Republic, Germany, Portugal and the UK.

The Association of Conferences and Events (ACE), which was the original founder of ESITO, created the first Careers Fair aimed purely at the conference and events industry in 2003.

SUMMARY

The chapter has discussed the way in which events and festivals have changed over the years. In the past, festivals were associated with key calendar moments, linked specifically to particular seasons and heritage sites. Events and festivals have been revolutionised to meet the commercial needs of the market in response to the changing demand of local community groups and increased business opportunities for event organisers and local businesses. Local authorities are now using events as a major tool to promote their town or city and are justifying their bids for large-scale sporting

---

events on the grounds that they form part of their regeneration strategies. Events and festival managers are now using historical and cultural themes to develop annual events to attract visitors and create cultural images in the host cities by holding festivals within community settings. Such events provide an opportunity for local people to develop and share their culture, enhance their own values and beliefs and promote local culture to visitors and tourists.

FURTHER READING

Getz, D. (1991) *Festivals, Special Events Tourism*. New York: Van Nostrand Reinhold.
Getz, D. (1997) *Event Management and Event Tourism*. New York: Cognizant Communications Corporation.
Hall, C. (1994) *Tourism and Politics: Policy, Power and Place*. Chichester: Wiley.
Yeoman, I. et al. (2004) *Festival and Events Management*. Oxford: Elsevier Butterworth Heinemann.

CHAPTER 2

Types of events

Technical definitions of events management

This chapter introduces the reader to the concept of different types of events that exist within the events management industry. The chapter will analyse and specifically discuss a range of events and their implications on the events industry.

Introduction

In order to understand more fully the large array of events that take place today it is important to begin by examining their objectives. Any dictionary definition of an 'event' will include a broad 'something happens'.

The word 'event' also has specific meanings in medicine, philosophy or physics. In such sciences we are concerned with happenings or incidents beyond the will of man or woman. When we couple this term with the concept of 'management', the definition of which includes words such as 'organisation', 'administration' and 'control', we begin to see an 'event' as a purposeful human creation. For events to be managed, they must therefore involve other people and have a predetermined purpose and a location.

A definition of event management is thus:

Event management is the capability and control of the process of purpose, people and place.

It follows that events are 'happenings with objectives'.

The prime objective for an event can be strictly defined. An objective may be quantitative and financial, for instance to sell tickets and produce a profit. There may also be less tangible, qualitative objectives relating to the thoughts, feelings and emotions, during and after the event, of those attending it. These would be key objectives for a wedding or a private party.

Further consideration of event objectives and in particular their role within the event planning process takes place in the next chapter. In this section, however, we will explore the way in which 'event objective components' can help us to analyse the full range of international events currently being staged.

'Event objective components' are the building blocks of event objectives. They are divided into the three categories derived from our earlier definition of event management: purpose, people and place. These 'event objective components' are best represented diagrammatically.

We can thus attempt to classify events by their objective components in order to understand the range of events. This process produces so many permutations and overlaps, we must conclude from it that events cannot be precisely classified. One positive conclusion though is that all events involve a community. This community can be local or international; it may be a certain business community or a cultural community.

If we look at events ranging from the individual to the global in scale, a private and personal event such as a wedding anniversary or birthday will involve a community of family and friends on a particular calendar date in an individual's life for the purposes of a celebration. Culture and community are both expressed and enhanced through the social interaction of the event.

At the global end of the scale, an Olympic Games such as Beijing 2008 or London 2012 will probably involve every possible component somewhere in its tiered objectives and stakeholders. This is due to the complexity of our planet's premier event, which is actually a whole series of events in one. Looking at our event object components diagram (see Figure 2.1), we can identify the culture, carnival and celebration of the opening and closing ceremonies; the many competitors; the corporate elements; and the positive change the event brings to citizens, communities, city and country.

Community or communities are thus the most important of the 'event objective components'. Communities include the international track athletics or football community; the expatriate and descendent communities such as a city's Irish or Caribbean communities who come together to celebrate

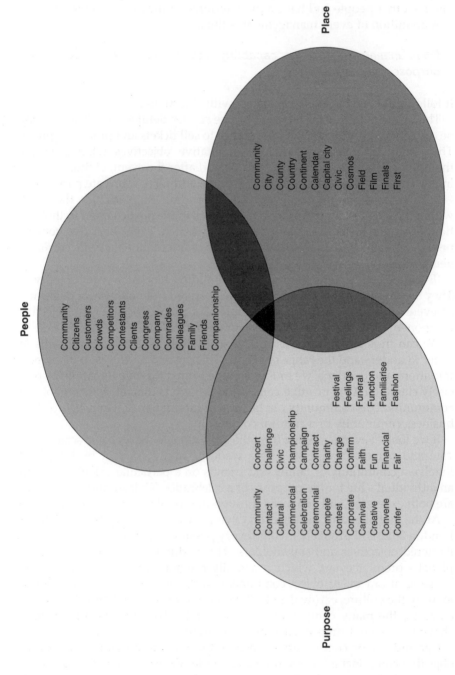

Figure 2.1 Event objective components – the 'C's and F's' of events

St Patrick's Day or Carnival; or any field of commerce, such as the UK utilities industry business community. Events are all about the vast and varied communities of people of the world. Events are where people commune!

Different types of events

Religious events

The largest event in the world in terms of actual attendance is the Hajj in Makka, Saudi Arabia. This annual event is a pilgrimage, which is sacred to the Muslim faith; it is the fifth and final pillar of Islam and is undertaken by approximately 3.4 million people each year (The Saudi Arabia Information Resource, www.saudinf.com, is the Saudi Ministry of Culture and Information website and Official News Agency of Saudi Arabia). This figure not only includes the world's largest number of 'religious tourists' who fly in from all over the world, but also the large numbers who converge upon Makka from within Saudi Arabia and neighbouring countries. Papal visits within Roman Catholicism are another example of large religious events. When John Paul II visited Ireland and the United States, he said mass to a million people in Dublin, New York and Boston.

These enormous gatherings of people share the objective components, drawn from Figure 2.1, of faith and feelings, culture and community, ceremony and contact.

The date of such religious event experiences becomes etched in the memory of the people attending, alongside their feelings and emotions. The same is also true of individual religious events such as Bar Mitzvahs. A Jewish male automatically becomes a Bar Mitzvah after his thirteenth birthday. The popular Bar Mitzvah celebration is a relatively modern innovation and the elaborate ceremonies and receptions that are commonplace today were unheard of as recently as a century ago. The Bar Mitzvah is a celebration of the Jewish faith by friends and families, and the local Jewish community.

A Bar Mitzvah takes place on a Saturday shortly after a boy's thirteenth birthday. Saturday is the Jewish Sabbath, a day of rest and spiritual enrichment. He is called upon to lead sections of the weekly service at the synagogue. This may be as simple as saying the blessing but can often involve much more and vary from congregation to congregation. The boy then often makes a speech which, tradition dictates, begins with the phrase, 'Today I am a man'. His father responds by reciting a blessing, thanking God for taking the responsibility for his son's sins from him (www.barmitzvahs.org).

The religious service is nowadays invariably followed by a reception and celebration. It is this event which is also a cultural and indeed a personal event. However, this celebration would not take place without the religious ceremony. Bar Mitzvahs have the function of convening a community to celebrate their faith. They can rival weddings in terms of size and scale and are consequently significant to the events industry.

Cultural events

Some cultural events have a religious aspect and some may be held for commercial reasons. However, the primary purpose of such events is the celebration or confirmation of culture. Cultural events, such as concerts or carnivals, incur costs. They also create important economic opportunities and impacts, though a district, town or city may not directly benefit on a festival's balance sheet. For example, Liverpool's Matthew Street Festival is held every year at the end of August at a cost to Liverpool City Council, yet the event generates £30 million for the local economy (Liverpool Culture Company).

At one level, cultural events facilitate the integration and inclusion of smaller communities of families and friends within the wider community. On another level, they allow outsiders and tourists from different cultures to join and share in the process. For example, St Patrick's Day's parties are held not only in Dublin and Belfast but also in New York, Boston and around the world. While these events are a celebration of Irishness, they also give anyone that wishes to the opportunity to enjoy Irish food, drink and music.

Musical events

Musical events range from the Glastonbury or Roskilde Music Festivals to the Last Night of the Proms in the Royal Albert Hall and all manner of concerts and performances in between. Musical events are often commercial in purpose but they are also about culture and fashion. They can even be concerned with change or charity and they are a celebration of creativity. A concert is about a shared feeling, fun with friends and new companions. Music festivals in particular promote a sense of belonging to the crowd.

An example is T in the Park, which has become Scotland's leading music festival. The first festival was at Strathclyde Country Park on the outskirts of Glasgow in 1994. However, in 1997 T in the Park moved to a more central location at Balado near Perth. This larger and more easily accessible site enabled T in the Park to grow. The event now features hundreds of musicians from many countries around the world. They perform a wide range of popular music on four different stages to a combined audience of over 60,000. This takes place every year on a weekend in early July. In 2005, 40 per cent of people buying tickets for T in the Park came from outside Scotland, making the event one of Scotland's larger annual tourist attractions.

The event is strongly supported by the local council and surrounding communities and thus does not experience the licensing problems of some comparable events in England. In 2004, Party in the Park became the only festival in the UK to have been awarded a three-year licence for the second time. T in the Park has a large number of stakeholders with different objectives. For the organisers, DF Concerts, and the title sponsor, the Scottish lager brand Tennants, the event's purpose is commercial. Yet to its audience, it is a celebration of music and specifically of the Scots' love of music and partying, which they wish to share. This is what gives the event its atmosphere.

The event is about country but it is also about fun; it is *the* date on the calendar for the popular music community of Scotland. The event's objectives now go beyond the commercial ones it began with. Scotland's First Minister, Jack McConnell, when attending T in the Park in 2003, said: 'It is great to see so many young people enjoying themselves. The festival is very valuable to the Scottish economy and it symbolises the modern Scotland we want to portray' (www.tinthepark.com).

Sporting events

These range from the largest of international events to local leagues and competitions for communities and children. Their purpose is contest, challenge and competition but they also involve companionship, camaraderie and colleagues. They can often take the form of a championship, where there are displays of differing skills or prowess depending on the sport. Examples range from the US Open Golf Tournament or the Formula One Grand Prix Drivers' Championship to a city's schools' swimming gala and countless others, both large and small.

As professional sports men and women are often very well paid and as some sports attract large numbers of spectators, including huge global television audiences, there is invariably a strong commercial purpose in any large sports event. The success of teams or individual sports men and women from a community, city, county or nation is often a cause for great celebration, particularly if not expected. A perfect example is Greece's victory in the 2004 European Football Championships in Portugal. This had a very positive impact upon Greek national pride, which continued throughout and after the Athens Olympics. Sports events may therefore have political significance. With so many stakeholders and such high stakes, sports events require a high degree of professional events management.

Personal and private events

Personal events are celebrations of special occasions with friends and family. These could be viewed as a subsection of cultural events but then they are cross cultural. The format of weddings or funerals may vary, but the celebration of the union of two people or the mourning and respect at the passing of a life are the oldest and most widely practised events. Many other life stage celebrations occur, linked either to age or achievement, including birthdays, anniversaries, graduations and homecomings. These events concern family and/or friends and their purposes are celebration and feelings.

Political and governmental events

From annual political party conferences and trade union conferences to events held by specific government departments, these events may be commercial in that they can be costly to organise, but the profit they seek is not financial but political change. As the media play a major part in such events, some – especially the party conferences – have become contests. This ranges from subtle internal contests, played out virtually behind the scenes, to blatant competition for public opinion and future votes between opposing parties on a stage provided by the attendant media.

Commercial and business events

These often involve a whole section of an industry or business. Exhibitions tend to be the most complex type of event within this category since each stand can be regarded as a sub event, particularly where new products or services are being presented. Every stand has its stakeholders and all are competing for customers or clients. These events are key points on the calendar at which an industry convenes or confers in order to coordinate campaigns, make contacts and agree contracts. The overriding purpose is thus commercial.

Major exhibitions such as motor shows or, the largest of all, air shows are such spectacular events that, alongside bringing together the crucial business buyers and manufacturers, they also attract many thousands of members of the general public who pay for tickets. A good example of this is the British International Motor Show. By 1978, the motor show had outgrown the London exhibition facilities and was moved to the then new Birmingham National Exhibition Centre (NEC). Attracting around 700,000 visitors annually, The British International Motor Show ranks alongside similar international motor shows in Detroit, Brussels and Turin. From 2006, it will be back in London running at Excel (www.britishmotorshow.co.uk).

Business Events also include 'association events' – the annual conferences of a very wide range of professional and business associations. From dentists to banking, ocean technology to e-marketing, all spheres of human industry and endeavour have at least one association conference.

Corporate events

Events of this type involve just one single business, company, corporation or organisation. They may include annual conferences; product launches; staff motivation events; or awards ceremonies. They draw their audience from within the organisation and often include an 'incentive' element in their choice of venue or location. Their purpose may be to give colleagues the space and place to confer in order to create change within the organisation. Key tasks may include considering competitors, clients or customers; reviewing the challenges faced by the organisation; and generating creative solutions to them.

Special events

The term 'special events' is used to describe events that are first-class or extraordinary in terms of the widespread public recognition they receive.

Special events enrich the quality of life for local people and attract tourists from outside the area on account of their uniqueness.

Special events sometimes become synonymous with and dependent on the place where they are held. For example, the annual Edinburgh International Festival, which is a prime example of a special event, would not hold the same prestige should individual festival organisers ever decide to move any of its components to another city.

The primary goal of special events is to develop recognition for the local community and festival organisers. Examples of such events include Notting Hill Carnival, Bradford Mela, Berlin Love Parade, Toronto Street Festival and Britain's Queen's Jubilee celebrations. Such events create images for the tourism market and attract visitors to the location. A city wanting to upgrade its infrastructure or its political image may also use a large-scale event as a tool to generate funds from corporations and higher levels of government.

The host community benefits from special events both socially and economically.

Yet special events are also typically dependant on the large outlay of public monies, which may arise not only from hosting them but also from bidding to host them in the first place. Despite the enormous costs and benefits for host communities, the full impact of special events, socially and environmentally as well as economically, is rarely calculated.

Special events can range in size from small community fairs to large-scale sporting events. Community and local festivals can be classed as special events, since they can create a cultural and social environment for tourists who are attending the event. Major cities will use special events to celebrate the city and highlight what it has to offer in terms of sport, music, culture and art.

Leisure events

Large-scale leisure events are capable of attracting substantial numbers of visitors, gaining global media coverage and reaping vast economic benefits for the hosts. There is generally a competitive bidding process to determine who will host such events, which include the Olympic Games, the FIFA World Cup, the Commonwealth Games and City of Culture.

Events on this scale are extremely important for the host community, not only because of the number of visitors, but also because they create legacies, which may continue to have an impact on the host community long after the event has taken place. The bids for large-scale sporting events often incorporate urban regeneration goals into their strategies in order to justify the high costs of such events to all stakeholders, especially the local community. Large-scale leisure events are linked to government funding programmes, which enable the construction of facilities and infrastructure, and the redevelopment and revitalisation of urban areas. This process creates a physical, economic and social legacy, which may have long-term benefits for the local communities.

Leisure events can act as a tool for urban regeneration, since through them host cities are given the opportunity to present new, or promote existing, images of themselves and thus enhance their profile on a global scale. Improving the image of the location as a destination will attract tourists to the area and hence generate future local employment in the tourist industry.

Crucially, leisure events provide an opportunity to acquire funding to regenerate cities and develop new facilities. The planning for these events should include a legacy plan to ensure that local communities continue to benefit from the event and associated investments in the future. This should consider the urban regeneration and social impacts of the event on host communities, identifying any adverse effects and ensuring that benefits to the surrounding communities are not squandered. How new facilities are utilised once the games are moved out of the host city is of great importance, as improper planning can mean they may not be used to their maximum potential. The facilities for the Commonwealth Games 2002 in Manchester were fully utilised, since it was agreed at the planning stage that the main stadium would be handed over to Manchester City Football Club and that the athletic village would be passed on to the local authority to provide accommodation. In this century, with competitive bidding for large-scale sporting events by local authorities, countries and cities, it is no longer acceptable to stakeholders for central and local governments to host a large leisure event without developing a comprehensive strategic plan for the post-event.

There has been much discussion over who benefits most from large-scale leisure events and whether the costs and benefits are shared equally by the different stakeholders. It is clear, for example, that the games can produce tangible benefits for governments and businesses, especially within the tourism industry. The non-tangible benefits for the community are less self-evident, aside from the privilege of participating in the mega-event in one way or another.

Community festivals now play a significant role in generating income for local businesses and attracting tourists to the local area. These economic impacts have increased considerably over the past decade as the festivals have grown in size. The expansion of information technology and media networks has contributed to the development of these events and the industry which promotes and runs them. The festival organisers now utilise these new communication tools to advertise their events to wider audiences. Festivals now attract visitors from all over the country and from other countries, not only for the duration of the festival but also possibly as a result of the media attention attracted by the event in the longer-term. A festival can however bring both positive and negative associations to an area; but if the positive impacts are stronger, it can help to develop a sense of local pride and identity. Examples of this include Glastonbury, Reading Festival and The Edinburgh Festival. These events have all taken the host community's name and have therefore reinforced the relationship between event and host community.

Local authorities' events strategies

Many local authorities are using events to position their destinations in the market, and thus to support their cultural, tourism, and arts strategies. Over the last decade, local authorities' strategies have begun to state the importance of festivals in promoting tourism and developing the social and economic cohesion, confidence and pride that connect local authorities with the communities they serve. Through events, councils can secure political power and influence among local residents and businesses. Local authorities undertake the development and direct delivery of festivals to pursue specific economic and community development objectives. Given their responsibility for public spaces, they have some advantages in presenting outdoor public events.

Local authorities in the UK are developing event-led strategies in cities and they want events to serve as a marketing tool to boost the national and international profile and image of their cities. There are many public and private companies and agencies working in the UK events sector at present to deliver successful events and festivals. Local authorities are increasingly promoting awareness of the events industry and the role it can play in providing inspiration and ambition to local communities to deliver large festivals and events on an international stage. They see events as a means of building an international profile and image for their city, so as to attract hundreds of thousands of visitors every year.

Although not all local authorities have an explicit event-led strategy, many can be seen to use events and festivals as marketing tools to achieve some of their goals and objectives. The events and festivals can promote urban regeneration and enhance the profile of the city. The international hosts of major sporting events have all experienced positive benefits in terms of their economic and social development. For example, the Athens Olympics in 2004 and Sydney Olympics in 2000 had major impacts on the local economies and on the two cities as a whole. Greece is now seen as the most popular country in Europe compared to before the games. — International

Corporate events strategies

The corporate events sector has been the fastest growing industry in the UK over the last decade. Corporate events are used by companies to attract and maintain customer loyalty; to raise their business profile; and to increase the motivation level of their workforce to maintain high standards. Over the last decade, companies have become increasingly strategic in their planning of corporate events so as to maximise their impact on their business profile. They may, for example, hold a team-building activity at a unique time of year or link their event to a specific ritual, ceremony or large-scale sporting event.

Corporate events can be broken down into many two main types:

- Large-scale events

- Corporate hospitality events

Large-scale events may include sports events such as the Olympics; the Commonwealth Games; Royal Ascot; the Grand Prix; and the FA Cup Final. They also could include cultural and lifestyle events such as the Notting Hill Carnival; the Berlin Love Parade; the Chelsea Flower Show; and major music festivals.

Corporate hospitality can be defined as events and activities organised for the benefit of companies who want to entertain clients, prospective clients or employees at the company's expense. A variety of options for entertaining are available, including evening receptions and dinners with a private view of current exhibitions.

Corporate hospitality events are a form of non-financial reward to employees and are increasingly being used by companies in order to motivate staff, foster team spirit and secure employee loyalty in the long term. Corporate hospitality events may include cultural, team-building and sporting events. The increasing demand for high quality and high profile corporate hospitality events has enabled the expansion of events management companies around the world who specialise in organising them. Corporate events are big business within the UK market. The Keynote Report 2004 estimated the industry's value at £912m in 2003, compared to £740 million in 2000.

Community festivals

The concept of 'community' has complex social, psychological and geographical dimensions and there are divergent views as to what constitutes 'a community'. Traditional views of 'community', as defined by the parameters of geographical location, a sense of belonging to that locality and the mix of social and economic activities within the area, have been supplemented with greater degrees of complexity by analysts. 'Interest communities' rely not on the focus of place, but are anchored by other characteristics, such as ethnicity, occupation, religion, etc. This type of community thrives on social networks and social/psychological attachments. Britain has always been a multicultural society and people with diverse histories, beliefs and cultures have settled here. People from South Asia, Africa and the Caribbean initially arrived in the UK after the Second World War to help meet labour shortages. These multicultural communities now play an important role in enhancing the cultural diversity of Britain. Multicultural communities are spread all over the British Isles, with approximately 30 per cent settled in the sub-regions of Yorkshire and Humberside.

Clearly, while some communities might have a shared locality and common interests, there are underpinning complexities which have ramifications for public policy making, particularly in terms of community development goals. A misconception of what 'community' is, or a lack of precision or under-standing regarding some of these elements, can lead to imprecise and ulti-mately unsuccessful and wasteful policy initiatives.

Community festivals now play a significant role in income generation for local businesses and create tourism for the local area. The expenditure in the local economy is more likely to *support* supplier jobs in tourism-related sec-tors of the economy than *create* new jobs; however, many other factors will also have an impact.

Community festivals or cultural events are those produced primarily for the community and only secondarily as a tourist attraction. There are various reasons for organising community events, including a celebration of religious festivals, such as Diwali (Festival of light). Community events can be part of regeneration schemes aimed at giving communities a sense of involvement and community spirit. Community events are organised by members of the community; community leaders; and professional event managers or festival producers. These events are often seen by government and community leaders as a way of improving communication between various sections of the community.

In addition to creating community cohesion, such festivals and events have the potential to improve the economic life of the host destination, by developing employment, trade and business; investing in the infrastructure; and providing long-term promotional benefits and tax revenues. Events and festivals not only generate significant economic benefits, they also provide host destinations with the opportunity to market themselves nationally and internationally, bringing people from diverse backgrounds to the destination for the duration of the event or festival. As a result, they have the potential to provide host destinations with a high-status tourism profile and may enhance the links between tourism and commerce. Events may do this by improving the image of a place; generating economic impacts, such as the development of local communities and businesses; providing a tourist attraction, which may overcome seasonality; and supporting key industrial sectors.

The economic impacts of events are the most tangible and therefore the most frequently measured impacts. Economic impacts can be both positive and negative. The positive effects may include visitor expenditure, invest-ment in infrastructure and increased employment. Examples of negative economic impacts may include price inflation on goods and services to cashing-in on the influx of visitors, or local authority-funded events which run at a loss leading to an increase in local council tax. The latter occurred fol-lowing the 1991 World Student Games in Sheffield.

Cultural tourism through festivals

The term 'culture' has been debated intensely over the last two decades and no clear definition of the concept has yet been accepted by the community as a whole. Culture, in modern day terms, is largely seen as a product of governments, large organisations and individuals who are aiming to develop their own standing in the given market. Culture is closely linked to our national identity and the importance that individual people place on local and national social organisations, such as local governments, education institutions, religious communities, work and leisure.

Cultural tourists visit heritage, religious and art sites and take part in cultural activities in order to develop their knowledge of the way in which other communities live. There is a very wide range of cultural tourist experiences, including, for example, performing arts; festivals; and visits to historic sites and monuments, museums, natural heritage sites and religious festivals, as well as educational tours.

SUMMARY

This chapter has demonstrated the breadth of the events industry, both in terms of the types of events and their objectives. The typology of events, presented in the first chapter, has been thoroughly examined and many examples of diverse events have been discussed. Our focus in this review has been on the objectives of these different events, or to be more precise, the components that make up their objectives, in terms of people, place and purpose. We identified the most fundamental of these objective components as being that of 'community' in all its many applications.

The various sectors of the events industry have been introduced. These include both specialists who organise a huge range of different events and the core event support services who are sub-contracted to work across these different events.

Discussion Questions

Question 1

Why do event managers target communities to host festivals and events?

Question 2

Critically analyse and discuss the role festivals and events play within the tourism industry.

Question 3

How might strategic event management be able to integrate the various components of the people, place and process model to augment value adding throughout the lifecycle, i.e., prior to, during and after the event or festival?

FURTHER READING

British Tourist Authority (BTA) 2001 [Internet] Available from www. visitbritain.com.

Glasson, J. et al. (1995) *Towards Visitor Impact Management: Visitor Impacts, Carrying Capacity and Management Responses in Europe's Historic Towns and Cities*. Aldershot: Avebury.

Goldblatt, J. (2002) *Special Events Best Practices in Modern Event Management*, 3rd edn. New York: Thompson.

Hall, C. (1992) *Hallmark Tourist Events: Impacts, Management and Planning*. Chichester: Wiley.

Raj, R. and Morpeth, N.D. (2007) *Religious Tourism and Pilgrimage Management, An International Perspective*. Oxford: Cabi.

Tribe, J. (1999) *The Economics of Leisure and Tourism*, 2nd edn. Oxford: Butterworth-Heinemann.

Tomlinson, J. (1992) *Cultural Imperialism: A Critical Introduction*. Baltimore, MD: The Johns Hopkins University Press.

CHAPTER 3

Planning for festivals, conferences and events

OUTLINE OF THE CHAPTER
Key stages within the planning process
Planning for festivals
Planning for conferences
Planning for events
Case study
Summary
Discussion questions
Further reading

The purpose of this chapter is to explain and discuss the planning of festivals, conferences and events. The chapter will present an integrated model for the successful planning of events. This in-depth integrated analysis will be illustrated with practical examples, presenting different types of events that have a regional, national and international perspective. These case studies will illustrate the academic and industrial perspectives on each topic area. This process will be a prelude to the presentation of a successful event plan, constructed around seven key stages.

Introduction

The chapter will refer to legislation, regulation and guidelines, where they have universal application, and we will also draw upon the relevant industry working documents. Before we deconstruct and reinvent suitable integrated planning mechanisms this chapter will present the author's approach to planning as a generic subject area.

Watt (1998, p. 9) sets out seven stages within the planning process:

1   idea and proposal;

2   feasibility study;

3   aims and objectives;

4   implementation requirements;

5   implementation plan;

6   monitoring and evaluation;

7   and future practice.

Once an organisation has been asked and decided to plan and deliver an event, it must first consider the reason for the proposed event, therefore establishing its idea and proposal. Watt has highlighted the need for a feasibility study, in which research into the external and internal environment is conducted.

This investigation is then followed by an idea and proposal, which will necessitate looking at customer demands and the client's plan. Watt (p.9) has taken a customer led and strategic approach to setting ideas and proposals, and this particular approach is discussed in stages 2 and 3. Feasibility study/ aims and objectives are the next stages of the process, which cover marketing, budget, resources and availability. Although these areas will have been covered in stages 4 and 5, this stage also looks at the economic effect of them on the business, event and the wider environment. *Implementation plan* develops the logistical relationships and partnerships associated with the event. This part of the plan is integrated in stage 3 and 4. Watt's final two stages involve *monitoring and evaluation* and *future practice*.

This chapter will use and consolidate Watt's seven key stages to allow the event planner to integrate business and event planning approaches.

The planning process, mechanism or system that an organisation employs to realise an event is, in part, embedded in past experience, and before we deconstruct and reinvent suitable integrated planning mechanisms this chapter will introduce an integrated reinterpretation.

One should not totally disregard prior knowledge and understanding. However, development and integration will be the driving force behind this chapter.

Key stages within the planning process

Stage 1 of the planning process will look at the aims and objectives (according to Watt) presented by the business, client or key stakeholders. With clear aims and objectives in place, the organisation can set specific benchmarks and a process for developing an event. This stage is also vital if the event is to be evaluated meaningfully at the end of the process, since the overall success and outcomes can only be determined if it is clear what the event was intended to achieve.

Stage 2 involves accumulating data on all the key areas that support the event, business and existing sector. Armed with that information, stage 3, the feasibility study, will have a definable focus. The feasibility study should examine and conclude whether the event is viable within the economic climate or business constraints, taking into account internal and external relationships and partnership arrangements. Stage 4, the business risk development plan, will measure all financial risks to and other possible impacts on the business from the event. It should also investigate the likelihood of both positive and negative effects on the external environment.

Stage 5 identifies the key stakeholders and will ascertain in what way and at what level they affect the planning process or event. They may, for example, be linked to the event by sponsorship, partnership arrangements, financial investment or they may be participating directly. Once their level of commitment has been determined, the role of the stakeholders can be integrated within the planning process. Stage 6 is the detailed operational, *project management and implementation period*. The key concern here is how best to manage the event within the constraints that exist around it, in order to meet its key objectives. The *event evaluation at stage t 6 is vital if the* organisation is to learn, develop and build upon the failures and successes of the event. The evaluation of an event from a business perspective must draw from the aims and objectives, the feasibility study and the key stakeholders. *Customer evaluation* would be undertaken at stage 6.

Planning for an event is systematic of the knowledge base within an organisation. The planning process is ultimately determined by the resources and type of events for which one is planning.

The term 'festival' will be defined to allow us to use this type of event as a practical illustration.

We can define a festival as an event that celebrates culture, art or music over a number of hours, days or weeks. Festivals require all emergency services that need access to the event to be represented within the planning process. Apart from the emergency services, a number of agencies should also play a significant role within this process. These may include the borough council, local authority or London authority and associated departments (Scotland has a different legal precedence and process).

Festivals, by definition, are a collection of events, which may be held in outdoor spaces, indoor venues or a combination of both. They are therefore bound by legislation and regulations. These legislative and regulatory frameworks will be presented as a guiding thread as we outline the planning process. The business administration, such as financial marketing, advertising and promotion, can also have a limiting impact on the process if it is not fully integrated within the process.

In order to understand the planning of an event we will identify the fundamental elements of the planning process and work through them in a logical order. We will incorporate business planning alongside these main elements in order to develop an integrated approach.

The area of planning that is under investigation and reinterpretation does not align itself to organisational planning, which is concerned with the strategic process and the positioning of the overall organisation and all of its business operation.

We can establish some of the generic elements present within the majority of planning processes, regardless of the type of event which is being planned. We will identify these generic elements first and will then build upon our model to explore additional parts of the process that may be required when planning particular types of events.

Before starting to plan for events, it is vital to ascertain who the key stake-holders are, and to undertake sufficient research to establish the intended nature and aims of the proposed event. Within the research process, it may be necessary to make a business decision to undertake a feasibility study. Such a study would analyse the current market and organisational constraints in order to give an economic profile of the sustainability of the intended project.

A conference has a number of distinct differences within the planning process, compared to festivals and other events. Although the first, prepara-tory, stage which we have set out in the last paragraph should be present in all event planning processes, the development of festivals is strongly influ-enced by the type of licence required. The structuring of a conference, on the other hand, will be greatly influenced by the building or location in which it will be held. The planning of other events may be constrained to varying degrees by licence, location and building factors.

Once the aims and objectives have been established and the research and feasibility study has been undertaken, event planners need to select the appropriate personnel to head up the process and to ensure the integration of its elements.

Planning for festivals

We will start by considering the planning of a festival. Most outdoor festi-vals are held on civically controlled park land, national heritage grounds or private land. A suitable site or sites should have been identified and researched before embarking on the licence application.

In selecting the site, the organisation will need to determine whether it is likely that a licence can be obtained, and whether the location is appropriate for the audience, facilities, and external infrastructure. The selection and design of a site by the event manager must take into consideration all of these components if the event is to be successful. As part of this process, the event team should assess the services and utilities available on the proposed site. This assessment should consider, for example, whether the external lighting on site will be adequate for safety and security, and whether the type of roadway is accessible to emergency vehicles, customers and contrac-tors and is likely to remain so for the duration of the event. This particular aspect must be assessed in all weather conditions and should take account of predicted attendance levels throughout the event.

As part of their assessment, the event team should identify external power conduits to be used by contractors and the event production team. Direct feeds can be connected where external power outlets are operational. An on-site communication network can be established using the landline supply service if a connection is accessible through underground network cabling. This can also be a contingency in the event of a power failure during the event, since communication can be re-established. Such eventualities should be covered by the emergency procedure plan, which is drawn up by the event team in association with other agencies.

Within the planning process, the movement of people within the site boundary must be clearly defined. To maintain control and safety, it is vital to identify the areas where contractors can obtain access, both prior to, during and after the event. Those attending the festival must be allocated sufficient space for movement at any given time throughout the event, taking into consideration the health and safety issues arising at different times of the day and night and from all possible weather conditions. In planning the site layout, overspill areas for customers should be identified, and where these may impact on the safety of customers, it must be indicated within the emergency plan.

Early consultation with the relevant authorities is vital. The accessibility of the site to emergency vehicles will determine whether the licence agreement is granted and renewed. The event team should therefore consult the local emergency services (fire, police and ambulance) on the choice of site and its layout before applying for a licence.

Where hazards in and around the site have been identified, sufficient measures should be put in place to reduce the risk of harm or injury to contractors, emergency agencies, customers and other personnel working on site. As the planning process develops, so too must the risk assessment document, if the event planners are to ensure that such hazards can be assessed and managed according to health and safety regulations. However, hazards arising from the *construction* of the site need to be assessed before a full licence agreement will be granted for the event. An initial assessment of anticipated hazards must be presented before a full licence is granted. It is also necessary for the event organiser to produce a written document outlining the site rules and regulations. Contractors must be given a copy of this before commencing any work on site.

As part of the licensed agreement, and especially where the event site is located within a populated area and/or is likely to have an adverse effect on the local environment, the planning process must consider the potential impact of the event. Under the licensed agreement and in accordance with the 2003 Licensing Act, the local community must be informed via a local newspaper and information posted in and around the local environment for a stated duration, prior to the provisional licence being granted. It is therefore prudent to consult the local community before applying for a licence to gauge the degree of support and anticipate any likely opposition that could be presented at the licence hearing.

Investing in consultation with the local community can produce a number of cost benefits for event planners. Such consultation can help to establish a long-term licence agreement with the local authority, which means that the event can be held on a regular basis. Marketing, sponsorship and financial budgeting can thus be planned strategically over time. Securing the support of the local community should also shorten and simplify the application process, thereby reducing the cost of legal representation.

A significant number of outdoor festivals are sponsored by commercial organisations, including V-festival and Carling Festival Leeds. The allocation of sponsorship monies and deals requires long-term planning; however this type of arrangement guarantees sustainability and longevity.

Before a licence is granted, the event planning team will be required to prepare and present a number of documents, in line with industry guidance, legislation and regulations. For example, when constructing outdoor events, demountable structures will generally be required and The Temporary Demountable Structures Guidance will apply. Published by the Institution of Structural Engineers, this guidance provides a benchmark for procuring, erecting, maintaining and dismantling temporary structures.

The local authority planning and building control department will give guidance and make safety checks on the structure(s) during construction and/or on completion. The Fire Safety Officer from the local fire department operates under the Fire Precaution Act 1971 and the Guide to Fire Precaution in Existing Places of Entertainment and Like Premises. The Fire Service will issue the event with a fire safety certificate to cover temporary demountable structure(s), where the event requires the structure to be accessed by the general public, contractors or event personnel.

Further documentation will also be required by the local authority. This includes a risk assessment under the Health and Safety at Work Act 1974, which should be presented with the licence. The licence application and the fire safety certificate state that a risk assessment must be undertaken, and an emergency evacuation plan should also be written and presented alongside the fire safety certificate.

In preparing for their planning meetings with the local authority, emergency services and contractors, the event team must acquire and develop an appropriate plan of the site and surrounding areas. This site plan will be an essential tool in designing the site layout and facilities. It is also a requirement of the application process. The plan also gives the event manager/ licensee a clear visual sense of the event and hence enables their strategic control of it.

The scheduling of performers and performances is a key task for all event planners. This must reflect the type of venue, the audience, the theme of the event, the intended impact and the profile of the performer/performance. These factors should be documented alongside the proposed schedule for the event and presented within the licence application.

Once the event team has undertaken adequate consultation with outside agencies, the local community and the emergency services and has obtained a provisional licence for a site under the 2003 Licensing Act, they should

consult the *Purple Guide*. This is an industry document endorsed by the Health and Safety Executive and used by many local authorities, emergency services, contractors and associated organisations. *The Purple Guide* also has an international reputation as the definitive guide for outdoor festivals and similar events.

The *Purple Guide* provides detailed guidance for on-site services, management and operation, both prior to and during the event. It also describes the regulations that may impact on various aspects of the event, making particular reference to health and safety guidelines. The document gives direction on suitable site design and the layout of amenities and basic services. It directs event planners to the other guidance documents, legislation and regulations that they need in order to manage an outdoor festival.

Planning for conferences

Although there will be similarities to the processes used in festival planning, there are also specific issues to be considered when planning for a conference. Such an event clearly focuses on the key speaker(s) and delegates. A conference may also be described as a 'destination event', since the location is an integral element, which can shape the entire planning process. We shall begin this planning process without directly relying upon the location to dictate the entire planning process.

As with planning for a festival, it is prudent to estimate the financial cost of delivering a conference. This can be done by undertaking the seven-key planning stages as outlined by Watt (1998).

The overall cost of a conference is likely to include staff, marketing, the venue and a number of other areas. These costs must be anticipated and covered by the charge to delegates for attending the event.

A conference has many similar characteristics to other events and this section will outline the common characteristics within the planning process. The conference organiser should first undertake research and conduct a feasibility study. This process, as highlighted in the previous section, will examine the nature of the business and its ability to hold this particular type of event. An organisation should always undertake this aspect of the planning process before starting to plan all new or existing events. Alongside the feasibility study, a business risk development plan should highlight potential adverse effects for the overall business and assess the level of risk for each.

There are a number of specific factors which must be taken into account when planning a conference. A conference must cater for an agreed number of delegates; it should be housed at a location that is easily accessible to the intended guests; and the event may include an overnight stay tied into the proceedings or offered as an option to delegates. Sufficient research should be carried out and the feasibility study should explore cost, availability and quality. Many conference facilities have developed an all-in-one package for conference organisers. These typically include venue and equipment, hotel, hospitality, labour and external entertainment. Where such a package is offered, it remains the responsibility of the organiser to research every element independently to assess operational levels of service quality.

If the financial business risks of the conference is directly associated with the number of delegates and cost of attending, it must be factored into the equation to cover all costs to the organisation developing and delivering the event. The overall cost of all external facilities that will contain the event for the given period must be included.

A cost benefit analysis should be conducted, where the financial risks to the organisation of failing to attract sufficient delegates is high. This analysis should incorporate all costs associated with the event, including the cost of services provided in-house by the organisation and those purchased from external contractors. Where external operators are required, there may be additional costs due to transportation, seasonal cost variations, or fluctuations in currency and these must also be fully investigated, if relevant. Only after these areas have been priced accurately can the charge for delegate places be set. This must, however, also reflect acceptable price levels for this type of conference. The overall cost of the conference cannot be met by the total projected income from delegates' fees.

Many conferences have business-to-business relationships attached to the theme, therefore most conferences are paid for in full by the company or companies that host them, since they act as a promotional exercise for their business. However, some conferences require publicity to encourage participation. In The City international music conference, which is held annually in Manchester, England, attracts approximately 2000 international delegates. In 2005, the cost to each delegate was £575 + VAT. For an event of this scale, the planning process must include continual marketing, including the production and distribution of promotional information from the previous event. Marketing can influence the number of delegates who attend this type of conference and the marketing strategy should identify and use effective communication platforms to transmit information across international boundaries. Since the conference has a yearly timetable of delivery, researching and targeting both existing and new customers will be a key and continuous part of the strategy.

Commercially driven conferences, apart from relying on delegates who pay to attend, can also get financial assistance with overall costs from sponsors. This is the case for the international music conference within the planning process; key stakeholders must play a significant role in determining the aim and objectives. This will be more apparent where key stakeholders contribute to the event directly, for example, by supplying free or reduced cost venues and equipment. If a conference is a not-for-profit event, economic assistance may sometimes be allocated from local authorities if the event meets the basic criteria for the area. Where financial assistance is factored into the event planning process, event planners must ensure that the event's aims and objectives are linked to the criteria for assistance and must demonstrate this within their evaluation of the event.

As highlighted previously, delegate registration does not always include accommodation and hospitality and this cost must then be borne by the delegates. In developing an overall package, deals should be negotiated with hotels to allocate a block booking for the number of delegates at a reduced cost if possible.

As in the case of festivals, conferences have legislative requirements that can determine the scope of the event. The building in which a conference is to be held must have a licence, though it is the responsibility of the venue operator rather than the organiser to apply for this. The venue operator and the organiser are however jointly liable for fire safety, risk assessment, insurance and health and safety. The venue or location must always meet the operational requirements of each Act of Parliament. All regulations, be they European or UK, including the health and safety regulations and the British standard on fire retardant materials, must be cross-checked with the insurance risk assessor, the venue risk assessment and the fire risk assessment. All the documentation pertaining to risk and health and safety must be easily accessible to all the organisations and individuals concerned.

If an event is to be successful, the business must allocate adequate resources to the planning process. For example, where the feasibility study and business risk development plan identify tasks such as financial accounting and marketing as significant, the organisation should provide appropriate human and financial resources to support these areas.

The Association for Conference Organisers produces guidance on the planning and delivery of conferences and can direct event planners to other sources of support. The British Association of Conference Destinations plays a major role in the area of venues and locations for conference organisers.

Planning for events

The chapter so far has demonstrated the first seven key stages within the planning process. This seven stage model can provide a starting point for the planning of festivals, conferences and events. It has been shown that each stage is integral and must be fully integrated with the day-to-day operational business of the organisation. If you are developing a type of event that falls outside of those discussed here, the seven stage model can be used as a template.

All seven stages must carry equal weight when developing and planning the process. Where issues are presented that can affect the business or event, appropriate measures must be instigated to reduce the risk of failure or of a negative impact on the business. Where other organisations, contractors, or the emergency services play a major role in the licence application, it is a good idea to involve a representative from each organisation within the planning process.

If a significant level of entertainment and hospitality is included within the event or is required by customers it is necessary to ensure that the facilities can sustain these demands and that the location is accessible for the duration of the event. Again, where sponsors are crucial to the overall event, they should be identified and involved at an early stage in the planning process and their aims and objectives for their sponsorship of the event should be established.

Seven stages of the event planning process:

Stage 1   Idea and proposal

Stage 2   Feasibility study

Stage 3   Aims and objectives

Stage 4   Implementation requirements

Stage 5   Implementation plan

Stage 6   Monitoring and evalution

Stage 7   And future practice

Once the seven key stages have been explored plus developed the conference is entitled 'function' or 'event'. Each step along the process requires continual correlation with the stages and should remain ever present.

CASE STUDY

IN THE CITY: THE UK'S INTERNATIONAL MUSIC CONVENTION AND LIVE MUSIC FESTIVAL

This case study will describe an event that has to take a dual approach to planning, in that it is both a conference and a music festival. In addition to the 2000 international delegates that attend this industry conference on an annual basis, an area within the event is also open to members of the public who wish to attend the unsigned live music acts. The case study will demonstrate how stages within the planning process become an integral integrated business approach.

The 2005 In The City music event, (ITC) was supported and sponsored by The North West Development Agency, Radio 1, Lastminute.com, Manchester City Council, Manchester City Music Network and England Northwest. As part of the event, the city hosted 500 bands in 50 venues over five days. It is estimated that over 100,000 people attended the five-day live music event.

The conference is primarily for industry professionals, who attend various workshops, interviews and discussions presented by specialist panels. These meetings and discussions are scheduled within a one-day programme at the main venue, which for 2005 was The Midland Hotel in the city centre. Due to the number of people attending this event, a selection of hotels within the city offered reduced rates to registered delegates.

(Continued)

(Continued)

In The City could be described as a 'destination event' for Manchester. Manchester City Council, in association with Marketing Manchester and the Tourist Board of Greater Manchester, uses events as a way of furthering the city's key objective to be seen as a culturally diverse and creative environment. The target for this particular objective is to raise Manchester's profile from a regional and national to an international destination location.

In The City music convention has a 12 year history. It is an annual event that was initially launched in Manchester and has subsequently travelled to Liverpool, Dublin, New York and Glasgow. In recent years, it has been held in Manchester City Centre and is scheduled for late September.

An event of this magnitude requires a significant amount of planning, logistical operation and control, given the number of artists and venues. The event is a commercially driven venture and is sustained by vital sponsorship. Therefore, the key stakeholders are not just circulating around the sponsors; the 2000 registered delegates will dictate the style and content of the convention, along with the level of service quality and venues that will support this event.

Integration of the planning process

It is essential for the In the City event to have a distinct commercial aim and objectives at the heart of its planning process. The event's aims and objectives are:

- to bring together industry professionals from all over the globe and create business to business opportunities
- to promote new and unsigned artists to the music industry and a wider audience
- to share knowledge for the advancement and sustainability of a rapidly changing global music industry.

Some of the aspects of the event that require a significant amount of research include: venues; hotels; potential or previous sponsors; travel arrangements; panellists/speakers; and interesting and relevant topics for sessions, e.g., new technology for the industry.

The feasibility study should assess all the information accumulated at the research stage. It will look at hotel costs and availability; venue cost; scheduling and contra sponsorship deals; informative and current/explorative areas for workshops, interviews and discussions.

The business risk development plan will assess the business, the event and the wider environment. The majority of data presented will be financial. The business must determine the overall cost of the event and assess market trends in relation to pricing for delegates. It is vital to identify the break-even point in order to set the correct pricing structure. Where there is a projected shortfall in income the remainder must be acquired by sponsorship/contra deals. The business must also assess the likely financial impact and human resource implications of the event's planning process on it. For example, human resources may be required for web development, press and public relations and regional, national and international promotional advertising. There are a number of important and external factors that may have a negative impact on the event. Scheduling of the event must take into consideration other events that may reduce hotel availability and participation from the wider audience at selected venues.

Stage 6, project management and implementation, becomes the litmus test; the success of this stage will depend on how well the first five stages have been carried out. A great deal of logistical and operational management is required throughout the entire event. Therefore, appointed individuals that are fully briefed should deliver the event schedule, with room for flexibility where sudden changes are deemed necessary.

Stage 7, event evaluations. Quantitative and qualitative feedback can be collected from ITC delegates at the point of contact. Business evaluation will also be necessary due to organisational changes; these may include human resource issues or the acquisition of new business opportunities. This can be carried out with information obtained at stage 4.

This case study has presented the seven key stages of the planning process as they apply to the ITC event. It has shown that planning must be an integral part of any business when undertaking a new or existing venture. It has also set out clear and distinct stages that need to both be understood and realised, by the organisation planning the event. Effective leadership of the planning process is therefore vital and a strategic view of all constituent parts and their impact on the process should be monitored continually.

SUMMARY

This chapter has demonstrated that planning for an event is a logical, systematic, yet fluid process. Developing a generic planning process that integrates not just the event but the business and sector that supports it should enable the event planner to gain a clearer understanding of the event, the business and the impact of each on the other.

We have also seen how the research and feasibility study is connected to outcome and success. Where a business undertakes a new type of event, the business risk development plan can ascertain the level of financial impact on the business in sustaining the process and delivery of the event. The process has shown the stakeholders' contribution and their relationship to the outcomes highlighted in the aims and objectives.

The chapter has also made reference to recent events that have a national and international profile in order to illustrate the issues pertaining to planning and to give a greater understanding of the organisation supporting the planning process and event. We have explored this from a financial perspective and looked at the expertise and resources required to sustain delivery.

Planning can be a long and arduous task even with all factors taken into consideration.

Discussion questions

Question 1

Within the event planning process why should event management clearly identify goals in relation to critical success factors and measures?

Question 2

Within the planning process, outline why is it necessary to undertake a feasibility study?

Question 3

Outline some of the positive cost benefits (to an organisation) that can be derived from community consultation when planning an event.

FURTHER READING

Dogan Gursoy, Kyungmi Kim, Muzaffer Uysal (2004) 'Perceived impacts of festivals and special events by organizers: an extension and validation', *Tourism Management* 25: 171–181.

Notting Hill Carnival: A Strategic Review (2004) Published by Greater London Authority www.london.gov.uk

---

CHAPTER 4

International and legal requirements for event organisers

OUTLINE OF THE CHAPTER
Legal structure for limited companies
Public liability and health safety requirements for events organisers
The Licensing Act and permits for events / festivals
Consumer Protection Act 1987
Security industry authority
Contracts and their legal complexity
Summary
Discussion questions
Further reading

Events have continually toured throughout the world, legal structure for limited companies and licensing act has significant financial impact on international revenue. The relationship of an event and its direct obligation to European and international legal requirements will be discussed. Licensing, copyright, performing rights will be introduced from a UK perspective drawing conclusion to international law on contracts and their legal complexity.

Introduction

The purpose of this chapter is to give an overview of the standard legal requirements for event organisers. The chapter will present in the first instance a number of statutory legislations under UK jurisdiction. The focus of the chapter circulates within the UK, however, it will include the legal requirements within the market of purchasing, procurement and the sale of products or services. The context to which this approach is driven will ultimately stem from the UK. The European market and the wider international business environment will be introduced to alleviate confusion on operating procedures and legal jurisdiction.

To give a complete understanding on the issues and complexity of various legislation, this chapter will make reference to a number of authoritative websites to obtain further advice and guidance. This approach is important as not all aspects related to each individual piece of legislation presented in this chapter can be covered in their entirety. Areas such as amendments, clauses, exemptions and notification etc., will be contained within each document.

Legal structure for limited companies

To operate as an event organiser within the UK, no formal registration or licence is required at present. Each individual business should look at registering the business through Companies House under the Companies Act 2006. This particular legislation has direct lineage from the 1989 Company Act. The 2006 Act covers limited and unlimited companies, private and public companies, companies limited by guarantee and having share capital and community interest companies. The most popular type of company registered by event organisers in the UK is companies limited by guarantee. Formal registration of a limited company can be done by an individual but a chartered accountant is required for submitting year-end business accounts to Companies House under Company Law. A company with share capital may require the assistance of a solicitor who specialises in company law and drafting articles for share holders.

Registering a company not only gives direct access to particular operating company procedures but also allows your organisation to have credible prominence in its particular market. From a consumer perspective, it demonstrates legitimacy and accountability for consumers. Investors will be given protection under company law along with shareholders. Outside contractual relationships with suppliers, agencies, partners and other companies, and a legal framework to establish sustainable working relationships when operating outside of the UK, organisations must have legal protection for employees and contractual disputes. Company annual accounts can be accessed via the gate keeper (Companies House) for a nominal fee by any interested individual or organisation. This information could help in determining the type of business relationship that could be entered into by any outside organisation.

Once your company is registered with Companies House there are a number of legal requirements to undertake before the business can become operational. It is not a legal requirement to register your business with the Health and Safety Executive (HSE) or the local authority. However, various types of organisations may require permits or certificates from the local authority including the Health and Safety Executive before commencing a business operation. From an event perspective, it is advisable to register with the local authority through the HSE website. Where your event has a construction build as part of the event planning process it is necessary to complete a HSE 'Notification of Construction Project Form', which is available from the HSE website. As many outdoor event organisers work with suppliers who have health and safety regulations attached to their particular type of activities, it is advisable to access the HSE website and equip oneself with the necessary information that will enable the event organiser to interpret, manage and sign off, where required to do so, work carried out by outsourced companies.

Public liability and health safety requirements for events organisers

Food hygiene falls under local authority control: the environmental health department within the local authority will take full responsibility for the issuing of a Food Hygiene Certificate along with the procedures for checking that each establishment or temporary catering unit(s) continually meets the legal requirements. Where an owner of premises or a manager has responsibility for food production, storage and consumption they must comply with; Food Safety Act 1990; Food Premises Registration Regulation 1991; Food Safety (General Food Safety) Regulation 1995; and Food Safety (Temperature Control) Regulation 1995. Further advice and guidance can be obtained from The Food Standards Authority. The environmental health department is also responsible for issuing closure notices and legal proceedings for the contravention of food hygiene law and regulations. Further advice and guidance can be obtained from the HSE or your local authority.

The Health and Safety at Work Act 1974 states that if you have five or more employees, a health and safety policy must be in operation with a clear health and safety certificate displayed at a location visible to all employees. The employer, apart from developing a health and safety policy, is also required to undertake a full risk assessment of the working environment for all employees. Consideration should also be given to employees where working conditions may endanger their health. Therefore, an occupational risk assessment could be part of the health and safety policy. The Health and Safety at Work Act 1974 has direct links with UK and European regulations; this area will be highlighted later within the chapter. Once a full health and safety policy has been developed and introduced to all employees and a risk assessment has been carried out the organisation can seek insurance.

Under the Employers' Liability Compulsory Insurance Act 1969 employers' liability insurance is compulsory for all businesses with employees. If your organisation has employees based abroad they must also be covered by your company insurance. Company insurance should be obtained from authorised insurers. The Financial Services Authority (FSA) maintains a register of authorised insurers in the UK. Your insurance company may undertake their own risk assessment or ask for a copy of yours. This will determine the level of insurance liability required for any particular type of business. In general the minimum level of insurance cover for any UK business is £5–10 million. However, insurance liability may fluctuate on the type of business event planned, managed and delivered. If your organisation has witnessed previous insurance claims, it may affect the overall premium. Therefore, it is the requirement of each organisation to seek further advice and guidance from their insurer on each event if it has not been included in the organisation's insurance policy.

Public liability insurance is different and voluntary; it covers against claims made by the general public. As an event company that may manage, produce and deliver events in many guises to the general public, it is considered essential to obtain public liability insurance. This particular cover is mandatory by many local licensing authorities when applying for a Temporary Event Notice for outdoor events open to paying or non paying members of the general public.

Under a Temporary Event Notice the maximum number of people that can attend at any one time is 499. The holder of a personal licence can apply for a Temporary Event Notice up to 50 times in one calendar year. Someone who does not hold a personal licence can only apply five times in one calendar year. Under a premises licence the number of times that a Temporary Even Notice can be given is 12 times in one calendar year. Further clarification, advice and guidance related to this specific notice should be obtained from the Department for Culture, Media and Sport (http://www.culture.gov.uk/aclchol_and_entertainment/default.htm) or from your local licensing authority.

As a company you have a legal responsibility to inform and display a copy of the employees' liability insurance certificate. This certificate must be displayed where all employees have access to it. There are some exemptions to employers' liability and one area is where family members are employed.

For further advice on employee insurance, contact a registered insurance company regulated by the Financial Services Authority (FSA). Further advice can be obtained from the HSE and the Department for Work and Pensions. Self-employed people, regardless of the contractual status between the organisation and the person(s), can also be covered by your employees' liability insurance. This would depend upon the nature and relationship of the control that you have with that individual while they are working for your organisation. Within the events industry there are a number of activities by outside individuals or an employee of your organisation that may require an individual insurance cover to support their type of work. 'Riggers' by definition undertake very high risk-intensive operational procedures, therefore it is essential to ensure that any rigger has full insurance cover that allows them to carry out this type of work. In some local authorities within the UK it is a requirement to obtain a permit before a rigger can undertake their activities.

Once your event company has been registered with Companies House along with notification to the Health and Safety Executive (HSE) and your local authority and a health and safety policy has been drafted with a risk assessment attached, and your employees have been assessed as to the level of fitness and competence to carry out their work, and employers'/public liability cover has been granted and displayed where all employees can see it the organisation is close to becoming operational. Many organisations today have a legal remit to register their company with the Information Commission under the Data Protection Act 1998. The Data Protection Act was brought into existence based on a number of issues; one of the principles was to protect individual personal data held by organisations. It also has a remit to allow individuals to have access to their personal data. The Information Commission can provide training courses to staff and assist organisations in developing data protection handbooks and policy.

Where an event company stores personal data on employees and in particular where a Criminal Records Bureau (CRB) clearance is required the Information Commission must be notified. The vast majority of event companies actively partake in direct marketing. Therefore, personal information held by a company can only be used once authorisation has been obtained from each individual. Websites that have an option to collect personal data must protect individuals' rights.

Once an organisation has undertaken these operational and legal requirements, it is then the responsibility of the company to issue employment contracts that reflect and meet UK and European legislation on employment rights. Minimum wage, human rights, disability discrimination, equality and race discrimination should be given full representation when selecting employees and during staff development/training and awareness.

Once the business has secured an office location it can begin to 'trade'.

Apart from the initial start up and legal requirements to that process, the business may need ongoing legislative adherence. This, however, will be reflected in the type of events developed and delivered by the organisation and while the organisation expands. To provide a full picture of the various legal issues and requirements, it is necessary to present a particular business situation.

When an event company negotiates with a venue for the purpose of delivering an event, there are a number of regulations and statutory requirements to meet before the final contractual negotiation. It is the responsibility of a representative from the event company to ascertain if the venue has all the legal requirements and documentation that are legally required. The Regulatory Reform (Fire Safety) Order 2005 came into effect in October 2006 and replaced over 70 pieces of fire safety law. This applies to all non domestic premises in England and Wales under the order, and a responsible person must carry out a fire risk assessment and implement and maintain a fire management plan. This legislation may have representations as to the use of materials within the venue, such as curtains or drapes, and the requirement of those materials to meet British Standards on fire retardant capability. A separate fire certificate will also be required for any material that is brought into the venue that does not meet British Standards on fire retardant materials. Therefore, venues and event manager operating outdoors must now undertake an independent fire risk assessment. The venue must present a recent and full risk assessment of the venue, including a health and safety policy indicating a full emergency and evacuation procedure. A premises entertainment licence denoting the type of entertainment granted by the local licensing authority with any restrictions associated to the said licence should also be presented along with a full alcohol licence and the associated certificate which should be displayed at the venue. The event company has a legal responsibility to relay the health and safety and evacuation procedures presented by the venue to all employees of the event company, suppliers or outside contractual staff working within the venue. This information must be presented and understood prior to any outside employee commencing work within the venue. To accompany any health and safety policy an event organiser must have an understanding of the different type of regulations that will have an impact on the event, staff and venue. The most common group of regulations are known as the 'Six Pack' and were developed by the EU and represented into UK law. The requirement for an event organiser to understand and implement these regulations will go far in the effective management and delivery of an event through the staffing, contractors and facilities acquired for the intended purpose.

As mentioned earlier, the Disability Discrimination Act as written and made law in 1995 has had a far reaching impact on event organisers and venue operators. Local authorities, educational establishments and their facilities had specific inclusion and amendments made to the 1995 Act for the 2006 amendment. We now operate within a climate whereby all individuals within society should be given an equal chance without prejudice or discrimination.

Entertainment venues, exhibition halls, conference venues and outdoor spaces have a legal remit to demonstrate an effective approach to meeting the requirements within the amended Act.

The Licensing Act and permits for events/festivals

The 2003 Licensing Act was introduced to modernise and meet European standards and control places of entertainment. It also extends to temporary event notice entertainment licences along with the sale of alcohol. The 2003 Act only has jurisdiction for England and Wales. In Scotland, entertainment is governed by the Civic Government (Scotland) Act 1982. All applications for entertainment, renewals and alcohol licences in Scotland must be sent to the local authority. For entertainment in Scotland where no fee is charged for admittance an entertainment licence is not required. In England and Wales the entertainment requirements were previously regulated by the Local Government (Miscellaneous Provisions) Act 1982. The new changes are broad and far reaching. Administratively, the 2003 Licensing Act is now controlled and administered by the licensing authority department within each local authority. The licensing Act requires the issuing of two licences, one for the event or building and a separate and national licence for the individual. A personal licence is valid for ten years and can be obtained from the local authority where the person resides and may only be renewed at the end of the ten year period by the same local authority. This enables a person to sell or authorise the sale of alcohol. A Premises Licence under the new Act is valid indefinitely unless it is revoked, or the business decides not to continue in its current form issued under licence.

There are four clear objectives within the Act that must be translated into practical operational duties for purveyors of this licence:

- the prevention of crime and disorder

- public safety

- the prevention of nuisance, and

- the protection of children from harm.

If the local authority or appointed agencies charged with the responsibility for upholding these four objectives obtain evidence that a breach of these objectives has occurred they have the power to enforce closure of an establishment or to use the full legal due process available.

Alongside that, each holder of an entertainment premises licence must produce what is known as an Operational Document. This document should set out the full operational duties related to the event or venue, including substantial information about all the regulatory documents that support any particular activity. The document should act as a footprint for any agency, authority or contracted service and above-line management will be charged with the responsibility for a particular aspect at the event or building. The document should also clearly specify the roles and responsibilities for all the parties involved.

Apart from the legislative requirements, each local authority has the opportunity to produce supporting conditions for obtaining and operating a temporary event notice licence within the local authorities' jurisdiction. The condition to the licence, as it is usually known within the industry, carries enormous influence on a successful application and continued use of the licence for the agreed length of time. The cost incurred by an organisation for obtaining an entertainment licence will be an internal matter for each organisation. However, each local authority will charge an administration fee for processing an application and each licence will relate to a sliding scale in relation to costs and customer capacity under each licence. Another aspect to the application process is the requirement for the organisation applying for the licence to place an advertisement in the classified section in the local newspaper for a period of one month.

The full legislation as passed by parliament can be accessed at the Department of Culture, Media and Sport's website. Not only is it possible to read the full document but a copy of the guidance document associated with the Act is also available.

As part of the event planning experience an organisation may wish to obtain a road closure around a building or site which may be in a residential, commercial or non residential location. For this to take place an organisation or representative must make an enquiry to the local police in the area where the event is taking place. The permit for a temporary road closure order is regulated under the Road Traffic Regulation (special Events) Act 1994 and the Town Police Clause Act 1847 section 21. This type of arrangement is generally enforced at outdoor music festivals, sporting and cultural events and should be completed early on in the event planning process. Where disruption to daily traffic flow is considered to be outside of the norm for that location, consideration as to public safety and emergency vehicle access must take precedence.

When there is a need to obtain an entertainment licence or temporary entertainment licence with singing and dancing attached to that licence, further legal consideration must be given if live or pre-recorded music will be part of the event or will be played within the facility.

Under the Copyright, Designs and Patents Act 1988 events or venues that provide live music performances to the public will be subject to the requirements of the Act to safeguard writers and music publishers, therefore an application to the Performing Rights Society (PRS) must be made for a music licence. The PRS has over 40 different tariffs for premises and types of performance. Where your venue or event would like to play original sound recorded music it is essential that a (PPL) Licence is obtained. Phonographic Performance Ltd represents the record companies who own the copyright for recordings.

Alongside the PRS and PPL there is also the Mechanical Copyright Protection Society (MCPS). The main remit of the MCPS is to collect and distribute royalties. These will be levied against anyone who wishes to record music for television, radio, websites, feature films and so on.

The guiding principle for the use of live or pre-recorded music at events and venues, where the music will be played to the public, is that there is a cost/tariff and a licence will be required.

As previously mentioned in relation to other legislation presented thus far there are also exemptions regarding the obtaining of a music licence. For further clarification and guidance it is essential to access the MCPS-PRS alliance website, link 3, for a more conclusive discussion.

A Video Performance Ltd (VPL) Licence is needed for the public playing of music videos. VPL represents the companies who own the 'film' copyright in the music videos themselves. Contact VPL through the PRS and MCPS.

What is discussed in this next section is not considered to be a legal requirement under UK law. However, to protect the individual identity and integrity of your company, product or event and to secure the merchandising rights, this particular process would be a necessary requirement. The UK Patent Office is where all UK trademark registrations can be applied for and held. This process protects the intellectual design/logo given to a company or event. Registering that design, name, logo or sound gives your organisation immediate protection once the application has been successful.

Upon receiving notification from the trademark office it is a simple process of filling in a form supplied by the Patent Office at no cost for the merchandising rights.

Obtaining the merchandising rights and the licence to produce items could potentially be a huge income generator for many events as they increase in size, and frequency and become successful. This also allows a company to sell the merchandising licence to an agency for the production of official merchandise. With that licence an organisation can also franchise the event/product to any interested party. Further trademark registration must be taken out in each separate country/tertiary if you consider that your event has an international reach, audience profile and locations.

Registering with the Patent Office is not a straightforward process and it can take up to a year to receive a final application notification. Therefore, a considerable amount of pre-planning in the formulation of a business idea to the intended market is essential.

Not all applications sent to the Patent Office will be approved. There are some names and designs that will never be approved – such as the five rings for the Olympic Games. It is necessary to contact the office with any queries concerning trademark registration. Trademark registration is held within the UK office and has a renewal date of every ten years. (Glastonbury Festival was first registered in 1999 at the UK Patent Office, and was in the market since 1970. It was first licensed as an entertainment event in 1983.) Upon receiving full trademark registration there is no legal requirement to place the official trademark logo on company letter-headed paper or on any communication materials, products or associated items that fall under trademark law.

Consumer Protection Act 1987

Consumer protection is essentially a piece of government legislation that protects the rights of consumers. Trading Standards are the authority that will act on consumers' behalf when their rights have been infringed. Alongside the Trading Standards, the Financial Services Authority also has powers where unfair terms and fairness are under represented in consumer contracts.

Within the event management selection process for contractors and subcontractors who will supply goods and services at events, it is imperative that every contractor has all the legal requirements associated with their particular task or activity before commencing work or supplying a service. If the products that are supplied, sold or used at events are found to be defective when in contact with the consumer, product liability under the Consumer Protection Act will enable a person to request a refund or an exchange of goods and, in some cases, to sue for damages. The latter will only come into play when that consumer's rights cannot be resolved via the normal channels of negotiation.

Where an event organiser imports goods into the UK, including the EU, the liability will rest with the first importer. By placing a company name on a product that gives the impression to the consumer that they are the producer, liability will rest with the company.

Within this type of business arrangement it is vital that the event organiser places great care in selecting products and service providers who meet with all the regulatory requirements under Health and Safety law, including all regulations which support their particular activity. This will ensure that consumer rights are protected at events, thus avoiding refunds, defective products/services or possible litigation.

Security industry authority

The Security Industry Act (SIA) entered on the statute book in 2001. The implementation of this legislation came in 2006/07. The main purpose of this legislation was to remove/clean up the rogue security companies that permeated the leisure and entertainment industry. It also had a further remit linked to seven other licensed activities.

When an organisation approaches a venue for the purpose of securing it for an event, it is vital to ascertain the legality of all security personnel employed at that venue. A full list of all licensed security operatives should be logged with the SIA, the local authority. The local police may also have a copy of the same information. If security checks on operatives are required by event organisers the SIA website has a full list of all licensed individuals and the local police can assist with that process. It is an offence to employ security staff who have not been trained and security staff who have been investigated by the police or who do not have the appropriate licence to carry out a task. Stewards at events, as titled, have a different operational remit and do not require a licence to undertake their designated operational task. Working within a football stadium, stewards will fall under different licensing requirements and certificates and must be regulated accordingly. The sports industry had made a representation for exclusion from the SIA. This was presented on the basis that sporting facilities are governed by the Safety of Sports Ground Act 1975 and the Fire Safety of Places of Sport Act 1987. The representation was not successful and sporting events remained bound by the requirements of the SIA. Adequate training must be given to stewards before permitting them to work.

Contracts and their legal complexity

Another area within the event management remit is to construct contracts which are fair in their content and expected outcomes. Contracts by definition form legally binding agreements. Event managers will ultimately encounter many type of contracts while producing events. Apart from the terms and conditions attached to a contract a service agreement could also be one addition. It is necessary to have an understanding of the different levels of contracts available.

Contracts are formulated to ensure that all parties' rights and obligations are not infringed and if breached they can be enforced in the civil courts, usually with the outcome of an award of compensation to the aggrieved party. Contracts can be divided into two main areas: contract by deed or simple contracts. The majority of event managers will work under simple contracts. These can be written, delivered orally or they may be implied by general conduct.

Another way of classifying contracts is according to whether they are 'bilateral' or 'unilateral'. Bilateral contracts generally relate to the sale of goods whereas unilateral contracts are used where an offer is made not to a specific party but to anybody. A unilateral contract can best be explained where a competition is promoted to anyone via a website. When producing an event and working with suppliers a simple contract under a bilateral agreement will be the standard approach. An event provider promises to make available access and an area on the site for the safe erection of a temporary structure. The company supplying the temporary structure promises to deliver and erect the structure within an agreed time frame that meets all the regulatory requirements and to hand this over upon the completion of all safety checks.

It has become standard practice for many event providers and suppliers to include alongside the contract what is termed a service agreement; the two may have similarities but are different in their general style and approach. As stated earlier, a contract is written from the standpoint that rights and obligation must be upheld. A service agreement is written from a position regarding the delivery of the service or product and all its associated complexities. The service agreement gives a greater understanding to the level of service or product that could be supplied and its intended use throughout its lifetime at the event. Therefore, any disagreements as to service delivery or product defects have a direct point of reference.

In the early contract negotiation stage there are a number of elements to consider before signing a contract. A legally binding contract must posses an offer, an acceptance of that offer and due consideration to promise to give or do something for the other. The parties must be legally capable of entering into the contract, and must knowingly have the capability to carry out the given task or provide the product/service. Consent to deliver on the contractual promise must be without duress or undue influence. On the whole, contracts should be drafted by a legal representative with sufficient knowledge of this particular area associated to the law. Mistakes in contracts, even down to the name of an individual, can render a contract void.

A breach of contract can occur if one party does not uphold their side of the bargain as set out in the original contract. A claim for unfair contract terms may come about at a later stage if one party believes that the original draft had expectations far beyond the scope that was required.

SUMMARY

This chapter has outlined many of the regulatory requirements for event organisers to undertake. In order to keep updated on the changes in legislation and regulations, one should register their organisation with the HSE website, which will provide regular updates on the new legislation and regulations associated with particular activities and organisations. Apart from this there is a requirement for the operational deployed staff at events to have undertaken training courses in key areas such as health and safety, demountable structures, crowd management and licensing law. It is essential here to advise the reader to embark upon extensive investigations on all legislation, regulations and areas of concern highlighted within this chapter. The full breadth and depth of each topic presented does not give a full 360 degree approach and in particular the area related to the HSE and the many regulations that have a direct impact on the event industry.

This type of approach will help to ensure that events are planned, organised and delivered within the confines of the law and operational procedures. Apart from UK legislations, regulations, policies, procedures and benchmark standards one must also take into account the international marketplace. Many companies within the event sector have a long history of delivering events across international boundaries. Operating outside of the UK brings with it many new challenges and obstacles. Exporting goods to another destination could render the entire operation redundant if the paperwork pertaining to said operation is inaccurate. Where one has opted for a handler to collect goods on arrival and store these at a secure location, if appropriate use a reputable company that has been fully investigated.

For employees who travel, work and reside within a different international jurisdiction for a month or a year and beyond, it is essential to ensure that your insurance covers their stay and the activities they undertake doing their job. If further insurance is required due to the nature of the location, political situation or potential instability, environmental or otherwise, then seek further advice from your insurance company. Most insurance companies allow for cover outside of the UK but this must be negotiated and continually risk assessed.

One must understand that operating an event business requires not only business acumen in setting up a business, it also necessitates that a vast number of operating policies and procedures are adhered to while delivering an event. Knowledge of those will help to remove difficulties as and when they are presented. This is more the case when supported by contractors and business partners/stakeholders. Setting the appropriate business 'tone' is essential for future growth and long-term partnership development. To develop this area of partnership, the Department of Trade and Industry (DTI) has been working in the business community for a number of years to pioneer this formula.

Discussion questions

Question 1

Under the 2006 Company Act, name three different type of companies available for registration through Companies House and indicate which company requires the assistance of a solicitor for the administration and formal registration process.

Question 2

State which particular Licensing Act was in use in England by local authorities and event providers, prior to the 2003 Licensing Act for England, now represented on the government statute book.

Question 3

Outline your understanding of the two types of business cover from an insurance company, and why event companies should consider them before trading commences.

FURTHER READING

Published by the Security Industry Authority (October 2007) *Security Industry Authority, Get Licensed SIA licensing Criteria*. A definitive guide by the organisation responsible for regulating the new licences under the 2001 Act.

Opening the Doors to Better Security – Case Study. Published by the Security Industry Authority Luminar Leisure Ltd.

Meeting the Security Challenges, Channel 4 Case Study. Published by the Security Industry Authority. www.the-sia.org.uk

The 'Six Pack' Usdaw Guide to the 1992 Health and Safety Regulations. Published by the Health and Safety Executive.

Security at events SIA Guidance on the Private Security Industry Act 2001 (updated May 2007). Published by the Security Industry Authority.

Guidance issued under 177 of the Licensing Act 2003 and Guidance of Police Officers on the operation of closure powers in part 8 of the 2003 Act. Published by the Department of Culture, Media and Sport.

CHAPTER 5

Human resource management

OUTLINE OF THE CHAPTER

Types of organisations

Human resource planning process

Human resources strategy

Policies and procedures

Recruitment

Training and professional development

Supervision and appraisals

Retaining personnel in event organisations

Termination of employment

Evaluation of the process

HRM theories

Summary

Discussion questions

Further reading

This chapter aims to provide an overview of Human Resource Management (HRM) for festivals and events. The theories of Human Resource Management (HRM) will be discussed in order to identify the prime methods and techniques which would help event managers to develop the necessary skills and attitudes to deal with employees in the workplace.

Introduction

Over the last 100 years HRM has become a distinct feature in organisations as people are now considered a vital resource. Its development grew from the studies of Japanese firms by American academics due to the development of the Japanese manufacturing industry. They discovered that Japanese personnel policies revolved around performance, motivation, flexibility and mobility (Blyton and Turnbull, 1992).

This discovery meant that Japanese firms were using people as a key resource within their strategic plans. This change in attitudes to employment resulted in the increase in quality of Japanese products and business practices, allowing them to challenge for industrial dominance. What the Japanese lessons suggested was that people were the key asset of any organisation and that the management of people has to be at the heart of the strategic issue, rather than a necessary inconvenience.

Human resource (HR) management is the process of organising and effectively employing people in pursuit of organisational goals. Dessler (2000, p. 2) has stated that human resource management refers to:

> **The policies and practices one needs to carry out the people or human resources aspects of a management position, including recruiting, screening, training, rewarding and appraising.**

According to Krulis-Randa (1990, p. 136), HRM involves the following characteristics:

- A focus on horizontal authority and reduced hierarchy; a blurring of the rigid distinction between management and non-management.

- Whenever possible, responsibility for people management is devolved to line managers; the role of personnel professional is to support and facilitate in this task and not to control it.

- Human resource planning is proactive and compounded with corporate planning; human resource issues are treated strategically in an integrated manner.

- Employees are viewed as subjects with a potential for growth and development; the purpose of HRM is to identify this potential and develop it in line with the adaptive needs of the organisation.

- HRM suggests that management and non-management have a common interest in the success of the organisation. Its purpose is to ensure that all employees are aware of this and committed to common goals.

Whatever the characteristics of the human resource management in event organisations, the planning process for human resources needs to be carried out carefully in order to fulfil the needs of the different types of event organisations.

Types of organisations

Flexible organisations

A pulsating organisation is one whose workforce increases and decreases with demand. This means that the organisation must be flexible with a core of permanent workers and a periphery of other staff. Due to the peripheral nature of temporary workers they will raise their own management issues.

The amount of temporary staff used means a corporate hospitality organisation will be pulsating and so therefore flexible. Flexibility can be placed into two distinct areas; functional and numerical flexible labour (Goss, 1994).

Functional Flexibility

Functional flexibility allows employees who are multi-skilled to perform various jobs and roles whereas numerical flexibility accounts for the employment and dispensation of different forms of labour.

Corporate hospitality will operate both functional and numerical flexibility due to the fluctuations in its labour demands. The functional flexibility could refer to an organisation employee who, in the events lead time, was responsible for the logistical operations but during the event is required to perform as a section manager due to their prior role being completed.

Numerical flexibility

Numerical flexibility in terms of corporate hospitality will refer to the many agency staff employed solely for the events' duration. This is numerical flexibility because they are not required before and after the event.

The fact that numerically flexible staff are employed for short periods raises issues of how to achieve maximum output from them, build relationships and have high service levels.

Human resource planning process

Several models exist for the human resource management process but the model proposed by Getz (1997, p. 184) perhaps best represents how this process works within the event industry.

Human resources strategy

In this stage of events many activities are involved including job analysis, job descriptions and job specification.

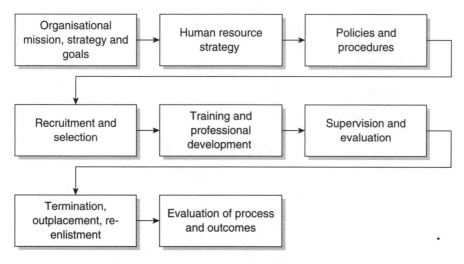

Figure 5.1   The human resource planning process for events

Source: Adapted from Getz, D. (1997) *Event Management and Event Tourism*.

Job analysis

Job analysis is a very important part of this stage of the HR planning process. It includes defining a job in terms of specific tasks and responsibilities and identifying the abilities, skills and qualifications needed to perform it successfully. Stone (1999) states that the following questions can be answered by this process:

- What tasks should be grouped together to create a job or position?

- What should be looked for in individuals applying for identified jobs?

- What should an organisational structure look like and what interrelationships should exist between jobs?

- What tasks should form the basis of performance appraisal for an individual in a specific job?

- What training and development programmes are required to ensure staff/volunteers possess the necessary skills/knowledge?

The level of the job analysis process will be different event to event. However, some small-scale events that depend on volunteers may simply attempt to match people to the tasks in which they have expressed an interest. Under these conditions, it is still nevertheless important that consideration should

Figure 5.2   Typical elements of a job description

be given to factors such as skills, experience and the physical abilities of the
volunteers.

Job description

This is another element of the job analysis process which event managers
need to be familiar with if they are to effectively match people (both
employees and volunteers) to jobs. A job description is a statement identifying why a job has come into existence, what the holder of the job will do,
and under what conditions the job is to be conducted (Stone, 1998).

Allen et al., (2002; p. 131–132) summarise the aspects of a job description
which include:

- *Job title and commitment required*   This locates the paid or voluntary position
  within the organisation, shows the functional area where the job is to be based and
  states the job duration/time commitment (e.g., one year part-time contract involving
  two days a week).

- *Salary/rewards/incentives*   Each is associated with the position. For paid positions a
  salary, wage, or hourly rate will need to be stated, along with any other rewards such
  as bonuses. For voluntary positions, consideration should be given to identifying benefits such as free merchandise (e.g., T-shirts, free/discounted meals, free tickets and end
  of event parties), all of which can serve to increase interest in working at an event.

- *Job summary* A brief statement describing the primary purpose of the job. For example, the job summary for an event operations manager may read:

  > Under the direction of the event director, prepare and implement detailed operational plans in all areas associated with the successful delivery of the event.

- *Duties and responsibilities* A list of major tasks and responsibilities associated with the job. Furthermore, it may be useful to express these in terms of the most important outcomes of the work. For example, for an event operations manager, one key responsibility expressed in outcome terms would be the preparation of plans encompassing all the operational dimensions of the event, such as site set-up and breakdown, security, parking, waste management, staging and risk management.

- *Relationships* These are with other positions within and outside the event organisation. Questions that need to be answered in this regard include: What positions report to the job? To what position(s) does the job report? What outside organisations will the position need to liaise with in order to satisfactorily perform the job?

- *Skills/knowledge/experience/qualifications/personal attributes* These are required by the position. In some cases most deficiencies in these areas may be overcome quickly with training. However, for more complex jobs individuals may need to possess experience, skills or knowledge before applying. A distinction is often made between these elements, with some described as essential while others are viewed as desirable. In addition formal qualifications are now being recognised as important and are becoming desirable for event managers in event management. Personal attributes, such as the ability to work as part of a team, to be creative, to work to deadlines and to positively represent the event to stakeholder groups, may also be relevant considerations.

- *Authority* This is vested in the position. What decisions can be made by the position without reference to a superior? What expenditure limits are there on decision making?

- *Performance standards* These are associated with the position. Criteria will be required by which performance in the position will be assessed. If duties and responsibilities have been written in output terms, as discussed previously, these can be used as the basis of an evaluation.

Job descriptions for paid positions often involve most, if not all, the information noted previously, while voluntary positions are often described in far more general terms. This is the case because they often (but not always) involve fairly basic tasks.

Policies and procedures

Policies and procedures are required to provide the framework in which the remaining tasks in the HR planning process take place, including recruitment and selection; training and professional development; supervision and evaluation; termination, outplacement, reemployment; and evaluation. Stone (1999) states that policies and practices serve to:

- reassure all staff that they will be treated fairly (e.g., seniority will be the determining factor in requests by volunteers to fill job vacancies)

- help managers make quick and consistent decisions (e.g., rather than a manager having to think about the process of terminating the employment of a staff member or volunteer they can simply follow the process already prescribed)

- give managers the confidence to resolve problems and defend their positions (e.g., an event manager who declines to consider an application from a brother of an existing employee may point to a policy regarding employing relatives of existing personnel if there is a dispute).

The event manager needs to make sure that policies and procedures are communicated to staff and that they are applied. Furthermore, resources will need to be allocated so that the policy and procedure documents can be stored, accessed and updated/modified when needed.

Recruitment

Recruitment is about making sure that the right staff are taken on to do the right job. For large events, more than likely, there may be a budget for this purpose in order to cover costs such as recruitment agency fees, advertising, the travel expenses of non-local applicants and the search fees for executive placement firms. In reality, for smaller events, event managers will have few resources to allocate to the recruitment process. Even so, according to Allen et al. (2000; p. 135), through a variety of means event mangers can still successfully engage in this process by:

- using stakeholders (e.g., local councils, community groups, sponsors and event suppliers) to communicate the event's staffing needs (voluntary and paid) to their respective networks

- agreeing with a sponsor that they are required, as part of their agreement with the event, to provide temporary workers with particular skills, e.g., marketing

- identifying and liaising with potential sources of volunteers/casual staff, including universities and colleges (projects and work placements may be specially created for these groups, particularly if they are studying festival, exhibition and event management), job centres, and religious groups

- identifying who the volunteers are and what their motivations are and using this information as the basis of further targeted recruitment

- making use of local and specialist media (e.g., radio, television, newspapers, specialist magazines) in communicating the event's human resource needs

- targeting specific individuals within a community with the specialist skills to sit on boards or undertake specific tasks

- registering with volunteer agencies.

Once the right staff are recruited event organisations need to provide the appropriate training and professional development.

Training and professional development

The prime motive for an event manager should be to treat individuals as vital assets and enable them to make the maximum contribution to the organisation. This can only be done if the individual is educated and fully trained on the job. Training is the most vital tool to motivate and enhance knowledge within the workforce.

Therefore, it is important to help new and current staff to develop new skills that will allow them to contribute to the overall event organisation's goals. Training courses and workshops for staff can be set up which will address different skills and areas of development and enhance staff knowledge for the future. The training programmes should include:

- work shadowing

- mentoring

- leadership

- team development

- education courses.

If an organisation addresses its training and staff development issues it will also have satisfied employees and reduced rates of staff turnover, which is notorious within events.

Boella and Goss-Turner (2005) have stated that an employee needs to develop and effectively achieve their role with:

- knowledge required for the job

- skills developed over the years

- attitude towards the job.

The authors describe how these can only be improved on by effective training and clear mentoring to achieve the required task. By providing clear and effective training to a workforce it helps an organisation to achieve the set tasks quicker and more effectively.

Mullins (1999) describes how training is a key element in the ability, morale, job satisfaction and commitment of staff, which will lead in turn to improved levels of service and customer satisfaction.

The events and festival industry is very complex and changes in line with the nature of the event. For this reason, it is important for the event's organisations to offer on-the-job training and appoint individuals according to their skills and knowledge. To support this the US Department of Labour has stated:

> In an effort to enhance morale and productivity, limit job turnover, and help organizations to increase performance and improve business results, they also help their firms effectively use employee skills, provide training and development opportunities to improve those skills, and increase employees' satisfaction with their jobs and working conditions. Although some jobs in the human resources field require only limited contact with people outside the office, dealing with people is an important part of the job.
>
> http://stats.bls.gov/oco/ocos021.htm

The importance of training is unquestionable but it is not always sustainable within events due to the short period of time that staff are required and the flexible nature of the organisation. Due to the strong customer focus of both the events and hospitality industry, much of an employee's time will be spent at the customer interface. This means that a great deal of training may be considered 'on the job' (Boella and Goss-Turner, 2005). In the context of corporate hospitality at large scale events this may place extra pressures on a manager who themselves may be unfamiliar with the event.

The need for orientation at events is evident, due to the large amount of staff on site and their temporary nature. Within a permanent sustained corporate culture orientation takes the form of socialisation and can be described as acquiring a firm's cultural perspective and an understanding of others' expectations and their personal role boundaries (Foote, 2004). If this understanding is not reached then it may lead to misconceptions and a dysfunctional organisation.

This poses the question; how does a temporary employee who is arriving at an event on the morning it goes live become orientated?

Supervision and appraisals

According to Allen et al. (2000), a general rule is that the bigger and more complex the event, the greater the need for staff/volunteers to perform a supervisory function. This function may be carried out through a variety of means, including having potential supervisors shadowing an existing supervisor, developing a mentoring system, or encouraging staff to study professional courses.

One of the main tasks of supervisors and managers is that of performance appraisal. This task normally involves evaluating performance, communicating that evaluation and establishing a plan for improvement. The main outcomes of this process are a better event and more competent staff and volunteers.

Allen et al. (2000, p. 145) further suggest that once an appraisal has been conducted there should be a follow-up review discussion in which the supervisor/manager and the staff member/volunteer together review job responsibilities, examine how these responsibilities have been done, identify how further improvements can be made to the performance, and carry out, review and revise the staff member's/volunteer's short- and long-term goals. The interview process should be a positive experience for both parties. Therefore it is important to consider making training available to the managers/supervisors involved in this process so that they understand and follow certain basic practices, such as preparing for the interview by reviewing job descriptions and previous assessments, and being constructive and encouraging discussion.

Part of the appraisal system also involves rewards, which in the case of paid staff come in the form of salaries, bonuses, profit sharing, promotion to other jobs or other events, and benefits such as cars and equipment usage (e.g., laptop computers). A range of options also exist to reward volunteers for their efforts. These include:

- training in new skills

- free merchandise (e.g., clothing, badges, event posters)

- hospitality in the form of opening and closing parties, free meals/drinks

- certificates of appreciation

- opportunities to meet with celebrities, sporting stars and other VIPs

- promotion to more interesting volunteer positions

- public acknowledgement through the media and at the event

- free tickets to the event.

Discipline also needs to be considered by managers. Thus it is useful to have in place specific policies and practices that reflect the seriousness of different behaviours/actions, and these should be communicated to all staff (paid and voluntary). These are likely to begin with some form of caution and end with dismissal. It also needs to be noted that many of the approaches to disciplining paid employees (e.g., removing access to overtime) are not applicable to volunteers. Approaches that may be applied to this group include reassignment, withholding rewards/benefits, and simple admonition by a supervisor (Allen et al., 2000).

Retaining personnel in event organisations

Retention of staff is a fundamental issue in generic organisations. But this is a specific problem for event organisations because they are different from other organisations in the way they pulsate. These organisations often transform their structure overnight, expand personnel by significant numbers for an event, and then reduce to their original size in a matter of weeks. This pulsating feature places unique and specific demands on event managers in relation to retaining personnel. For example, for major sport event organisations, there are three quite distinct stages in the operating cycle and there are different elements that need to be taken into consideration by managers in each stage. The three stages are: lead up to the event, during the event, and post-event (Hanlon and Jago, 2004).

In the lead up to the event stage, an event can be put at risk if key personnel depart. Since in many events most personnel are seasonal, minimal notice is required before such staff can leave, which has the potential to pose problems. During the event itself, loss of staff can be unfortunate. Many part-time personnel involved in events will generally begin to look elsewhere for employment in the concluding stages of an event. Finally, some personnel may even leave during the last days of an event. Having these three stages requires more complex and tailored retention strategies at major sport event organisations than at generic organisations. Hanlon and Jago (2004) recommend that in order to overcome these problems organisations should have a guide illustrating the retention practices, which will recognise what strategies are required for various personnel categories at different stages of the event cycle. This would assist event managers to optimise performance. In addition they suggest that the proposed strategies are made available to all personnel.

Termination of employment

Occasionally, event managers will be faced with the need to terminate the services of an individual – whether employing staff on contract or as permanent employees. This may be necessary in circumstances where an employee violates the employment contract (e.g., repeatedly arriving late at the workplace) or under performing.

This need may also arise when the economic or commercial circumstances of the organisation conducting the event are such that it needs to let staff go (e.g., insufficient revenue due to poor ticket sales).

Getz (1997, p. 195) suggests that the following approaches may be applied in terminating voluntary staff:

- Make all volunteer appointments for a define period. Volunteers should then apply and go through another screening process.

- Use job descriptions and performance appraisals to provide evidence for taking appropriate actions.

- Use other volunteers to exert peer pressure for a resignation.

- Find them an alternative position somewhere else.

- Move them into positions of less value and attractiveness and hope for their resignation.

Getz argues that the last three approaches to volunteer termination may be classed as 'backhanded' and present both ethical and public relations problems.

Outplacement is assisting terminated employees, including volunteers or even those who choose to leave the event organisation voluntarily, to find other employment. In doing so, the event organisation is providing a benefit to employees for past service, and at the same time maintaining and improving its image as a responsible employer (Allen et al., 2000).

With repeating events, such as annual festivals, opportunities often exist to re-enlist for paid or voluntary positions. For example, many staff from the Sydney Olympic Games took up positions within the organisation responsible for the Athens Olympics (Allen et al., 2000). According to Getz (1997, p. 196), in order to maintain contact with potential volunteers and past staff between events a variety of approaches can be employed including:

- sending newsletters to all former volunteers

- calling them once a year

- offering them an incentive to re-enlist

- giving support and counselling

- providing data base development.

Evaluation of the process

A regular review is necessary to see how well the process is working. To carry out such a review it is necessary to obtain feedback from the relevant supervisory/management staff and from organising committee members in the case of a voluntary event. A specific time should be set aside to analyse the extent to which the process and its individual parts achieved the objectives. Once the review has been done, revisions can then be made to the process for subsequent events.

: motivates staff and how can they be encouraged to pursue excellence? ᴗᴗᴗ e staff may be motivated by empowerment, others may be motivated by promotion, while still others may be motivated by a pay rise. These questions can be answered by understanding the various theories of human resource management.

Empowerment

Knowing your job roles leads to another management issue: empowerment. This can be described as permitting staff to undertake duties and accept responsibilities which were previously practised by management (Mullins, 1999).

This description is consistent with the HRM idea that empowerment will increase efficiency by removing unnecessary layers of management. In the live event context empowerment is associated with the art of delegation.

Delegation involves the passing on of authority and responsibility throughout the structure of an organisation (Mullins, 1999). It can be conducted at an organisational or individual level.

Empowerment may concern management as it could lead to various control failures due to a more remote management style (Boella and Goss-Turner, 2005), but will it lead to a more positive and committed workforce due to them having more control over the way in which their roles are performed?

Commitment

The next HRM issue to consider when managing temporary workers is the theory of organisational commitment. This is a contentious issue as its main purpose is to develop an employee who is committed to the organisation and its work.

This line of thinking originated with early theories on motivation, with the assumption being that a committed worker – in a similar vein to a satisfied worker – would be more productive (Blyton and Turnbull, 1992).

This assumption stands to reason: if you are committed to an organisation and believe in its objectives and goals it is likely you will perform for them. To be committed to the organisation what must it first deliver to you? In relation to events an employee may not be committed to the organisation itself, but might be committed to the event or the work they are responsible for, so it is therefore the organisation's responsibility to enhance and maintain this commitment.

To develop commitment an organisation must first satisfy its employees' needs (Mullins, 1999). This will be a hard task to achieve as each employee will be different and will have different needs; they will also have different expectations regarding the psychological contract.

Diversity

This leads to the issue of workplace diversity. Diversity can be defined by the following quote

> Valuing everyone as individuals – as employees, customers and clients.
>
> (CIPD, 2007)

The Chartered Institute of Personal Development places diversity into three separate types. The first is social diversity, which relates to demographic differences such as age and race.

The second type is informational diversity: this acknowledges the differences in people's background such as knowledge, education and experience.

The third type is value diversity; this refers to the difference in people's personality and attitudes and is also known as psychological diversity.

Diversity will become a parallel issue with the other HRM theories and practices. It is an element that needs managing simply because it is the make-up of an event's workforce. An employee's background, age, experience and 'racial origins' may have impacts on their motivation, commitment and your ability to achieve the maximum output from them.

Kandola and Fullerton (1998) describe various ways whereby managers as individuals can help with the issue of diversity. These are listed below.

1   Examine their own behaviour styles, beliefs and attitudes

2   Consider their own feelings and reactions to people

3   Be curious; get to know staff

4   Try to see things from other people's perspective

5   Be honest with staff

6   Examine their personal communication style

7   Look at how flexibly they treat their staff

8   Take care to make sure everybody feels part of a team

9   Act as a role model.

Motivation

Motivation is one of the key factors that exist in every individual and contribute to their daily life. It is important to understand that motivation is key for an individual or workforce to perform their duties. For this reason

Table 5.1 **Maslow's Hierarchy of Needs**

Type of Need	Examples
SELF ACTUALISATION	Developing self confidence and fulfilling individual potential capabilities
PHYSIOLOGICAL NEEDS	Develop self satisfaction of hunger, food, shelter and sex
SOCIAL (SUPPORT)	To care for others, love and be loved by others, developing social activities and friendship
SAFETY AND PROTECTION	Look for security and stability, feel secure and safe for future
SELF ESTEEM (RESPECT)	Admiration, self-respect, good opinion

employees level of work performance is determined by their ability and through their motivation, which has been developed through job satisfaction and individual needs. Theories of motivation are commonly described by carrying out studies in the workplace.

Motivation is a very complex concept. Carrell et al. (2000, p. 127) define motivation as:

> **The force that energizes behaviour, gives direction to behaviour, and underlies tendency to persist, even in the face of one or more obstacles.**

Maslow (1943) provides a theory of individual development and motivation. The idea behind this is that people want better living standards and job satisfaction, and they will always desire more. This desire is dependant upon what they already have. Maslow suggests that this desire can be arranged into a hierarchy and called *the hierarchy of needs*. This is shown in Table 5.1.

This model shows how each need or level has to be satisfied for the person to be motivated in order to progress to the next level. The first three levels are seen as deficiencies. They must be satisfied in order to fulfil a lack of something. In contrast, satisfaction of the two higher needs is necessary for an individual to grow emotionally and psychologically.

The problem with this model is, however, that when applied to a work situation many of the needs could be considered personal and are not necessary for motivation at work. It should be noted that Maslow's theory relates to individual life and not just to work behaviour (Mullins, 1999). Furthermore, it has been argued that Maslow proposed his model in 1954, and thus it does not incorporate modern thinking on managing the organisation.

Nevertheless, it is important to understand that an employee in any organisation will attend work in return for an agreed salary or wage in advance. The level of effort from each employee will be different, because it will depend on an individual's motivation. In addition, Maslow's model has implications for human resources managers in that if the organisation can give individuals competitive wages or salaries according to national requirements and can also provide workers with a safe and clean working environment, this will satisfy the basic level needs of individuals.

Therefore, it is important for events managers to address the needs which have been identified in Table 5.1 and encourage individual members of staff to fulfil their needs through the workplace.

Expectancy

Maslow's model is about motivating individuals rather than a work system. To fully understand motivation at work there needs to be a discussion on expectancy theory.

Expectancy theory is about the need to link performance outcomes to rewards valued by employees. Expectancy theory is really a framework for performance management (Mabey et al., 1998).

Its main premise is that the motivation of an employee is determined by the perceived strength of the link between the following points (Mullins, 1999).

- effort expended

- performance achieved

- rewards obtained.

Figure 5.3 shows these points and the relative links between them.

Expectancy theory when linked with Maslow's Hierarchy of Needs provides a strong theoretical base for motivating factors when discussing temporary staff.

The social aspect to work

Mullins (1999) describes how interactions with others and supporting working relationships can be strong motivating factors. This ties in with both Maslow's Hierarchy of Needs and the Expectancy Theory of Motivation.

The social elements at corporate hospitality events will have a bearing on motivation, whether it is workforce-to-workforce interaction or workforce-to-customer interaction. Figure 5.4 shows the links with the hierarchy of needs.

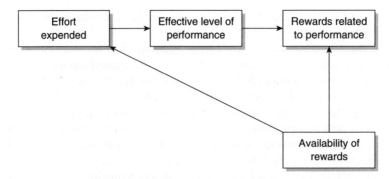

Figure 5.3   Expectancy theory

Source: Adapted from Mullins (1999, p. 326) *Management and Organisational Behaviour*, fifth edition. Reprinted with permission from Pearson Education Limited. © Laurie J. Mullins 1999

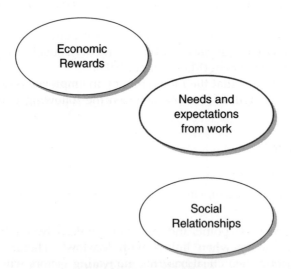

Figure 5.4   Needs and expectations model

Source: Adapted from Mullins (1999, p. 314) *Management and Organisational Behaviour*, fifth edition. Reprinted with permission from Pearson Education Limited. © Laurie J. Mullins 1999

SUMMARY

Human resource management is a process of staffing and organising the right kind of people who will benefit both the organisation and the event. Managers should understand that this is a process of integrated activities, including human resources strategy, policies and procedures, recruitment, training and professional development, supervision and evaluation, termination, outplacement and reenlistment, and evaluation. Why are these activities and techniques so important? Perhaps it is easier to list the personnel mistakes that managers need to avoid. For example, hiring the wrong person for the job, both paid and volunteer; experiencing high turnover; finding that staff are not performing to their best; wasting time with useless recruitment and allowing a lack of training to undermine the organisation's effectiveness.

The final part of the chapter discussed the issues of empowerment, commitment, diversity and motivation. The latter examining the theory of Maslow's Hierarchy of Needs for understanding what may motivate an individual and expectancy theory for understanding motivation at work.

Discussion questions

Question 1

What is HR management and how does it relate to the management process?

Question 2

Why is it important for an event company to make its human resources into a competitive advantage? How can HR contribute to doing so? How can HR contribute to integrating various functional processes into an integrated bundle of event/festival celebration?

Question 3

What items are normally included in a job description? What items are not usually shown?

FURTHER READING

Getz, D. (1997) *Events Management and Tourism*. New York: Cognizant Communication Corporation.

Hanlon, C. and Jago, L. (2004) 'The challenge of retaining personnel in major event organisations', *Event Management*, 9: 39–49.

Maslow, A.H. (1970) *Motivation and Personality*, 2nd edn. New York: Harper and Row.

Shone, A. and Parry, B. (2001) *Successful Event Management: A Practical Handbook*. London: Thomson.

CHAPTER 6

Events tourism

OUTLINE OF THE CHAPTER

Events tourism

Cultural tourism

Developing communities' culture through events / festivals

Case study

Managing visitors for events

Cultural and economic impacts

Summary

Discussion questions

Further reading

This chapter introduces the reader to the concept of events tourism. Events tourism and tourism destinations are extricably linked. Cities and regions throughout the UK and the European Union have developed strategic policies for encouraging tourism when this is associated with festivals and events. Festivals attract culture tourists to local community events and promote enriching exchanges between tourists and residents.

Introduction

Festival organisers are now using historical and cultural themes to develop annual events to attract visitors and create cultural images in host cities by holding festivals in community settings. The desire for festivals and events is not specifically designed to address the needs for any one group. The hosting of such events is often developed because of the tourism and economic opportunities and for social and cultural benefits. Many researchers have agreed that local communities play a vital role in developing tourism through festivals.

Governments now support and promote events as part of their strategies for economic development, nation building and cultural tourism. These events, in turn, are seen as an important tool for attracting visitors and building image within different communities. According to Stiernstrand (1996), the economic impact of tourism arises principally from the consumption of tourism products in a geographical area. According to McDonnell et al. (1999), tourism related services, which include travel, accommodation, restaurants and shopping, are the major beneficiaries of such events.

As far as events and tourism are concerned, the role and responsibilities of the government, private sector and society in general have significantly changed over the last decade. The situation has altered; whereas previously the state had the key responsibility for tourism development and promotion, now the public sector is obliged to reinvent itself by relinquishing its traditional responsibilities to the provincial, state and local authorities. This indicates the growing influence on the behaviour of government and business for the development of the event and tourism industries. This suggests that festivals impact on the host population and stakeholders in a number of ways, including social, cultural, physical, environmental, political and economic factors. All of which can be both positive and negative.

The case studies within this chapter explore the development of cultural tourism and multicultural festivals and events within the UK, and the positive contribution that these events make in solidifying community relations with the development of cultural tourism.

Events Tourism

Events and festivals are found in all societies, and are seen as a unique tourist attraction for the organisers, constituting one of the most exciting and fastest growing areas within the tourism industry. The phenomenon known as 'events tourism' originated in the 1980s. Events and festival organisers recognised the opportunity to enhance the development of events tourism as a brand to attract consumers and also to ensure tourists that they would get the promised benefit from the chosen destination. Getz (1997, p. 16) describes events tourism in two approaches as:

> The systematic planning, development and marketing of events as tourist attractions, catalysts for other developments ... event tourism strategies should also cover the management of news and negative events.

> A market segment consisting of those people who travel to attend events, or who can be motivated to attend events while away from home.

Getz (1997) believes that many countries and destinations fail to recognise the advantages of events, mainly due to being unable to manage negative images and publicity. Getz also states that due to rising competition, tourist regions and communities should strategically plan in order to achieve their environmental, social and economic objectives.

Events have the potential to generate a vast amount of tourism when they cater to out-of-region visitors. Although definitive data on the impact of event tourism is not available due to the complexity and diversity of the industry, Key Leisure Markets (2001) claim that day trips in England are now worth more than domestic and inbound tourism combined. Festivals play a major part in cities and local communities. Festivals are attractive to host communities, because they help to develop local pride and an identity for the local people. In addition, festivals have an important role in the national and host community in the context of destination planning, enhancing and linking tourism and commerce. Festivals have become more and more part of the tourist attraction, which has great economic impact on host communities. The event industry has developed over the years, due to the expansion of information technology and media network. Festival organisers now utilise these new communication tools to advertise their event to a wider audience.

Community events are developed to create cross-cultural diversity within the wider community and to enhance the economic value for the local ethnic minority communities. Events such as African and Caribbean carnivals and Asian melas have given the local communities a sense that they are of long-term cultural benefit to the host city. Such events can promote cross-cultural understanding and social integration among local communities and visitors.

Cultural tourism

Cultural tourism is defined by international Cultural Tourism Charter professionals as

> Domestic and international tourism continues to be among the foremost vehicles for cultural exchange, providing a personal experience, not only of that which has survived from the past, but of the contemporary life and society of others. (www.icomos.org/tourism/charter.html)

The culture is an identity and the importance that individual people place on local and national social organisations, such as local governments, education institutions, religious communities, work and leisure. Cultural tourism describes tourists who take part in cultural activities while away from their home cities. The purpose of cultural tourism is to discover heritage sites and cultural monuments on their travels. Keillor (1995), in an address to the

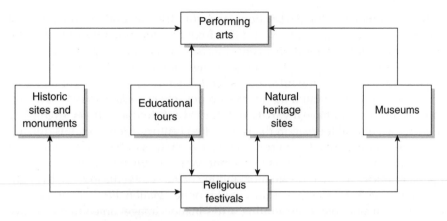

Figure 6.1   Types of cultural tourism

White House Conference on travel and tourism, best described cultural tourism by saying,

> We need to think about cultural tourism because really there is no other kind of tourism. It's what tourism is ... People don't come to America for our airports, people don't come to America for our hotels, or the recreation facilities ... They come for our culture: high culture, low culture, middle culture, right, left, real or imagined – they come here to see America. (www.nasaa-arts.org/artworks/ct_contents.shtml)

The theme of culture has grown over the last two decades but no clear definition of culture has been accepted by the community as a whole. Culture in modern day terms is seen as a product by governments, large organisations and individual people that develops their own standing in the given market.

Moreover, cultural tourism relates to those individual groups of people who travel around the world, individual countries, local communities and individual events to experience heritage, religious and art sites and to develop their knowledge of different communities' way of life. This can include a very wide range of cultural tourist experiences, for example performing arts, visits to historic sites and monuments, educational tours, museums, natural heritage sites and religious festivals (see Figure 6.1).

The model in Figure 6.1 shows that culture tourism is driven by visitors being attracted to different destinations and famous heritage sites. Therefore, it is important for the government to control and enhance the development of cultural tourism.

The future of events tourism in developing cities or countries relies significantly on governments developing clear and effective events tourism strategies.

It is also important for destinations and countries to understand potential tourists' needs and expectations and to introduce a consumer decision-making process for events. In addition, events tourism can be encouraged by developing complex and extensive planning strategies for the future. Relying on events to generate tourism in the future is difficult. Therefore, it is essential that governments and other related authorities do not rely on certain events to attract tourists, but instead have a variety of future events tourism strategies in place to increase cultural tourism in the twenty-first century. Moreover, it is difficult for some countries or cities to control negative images of their destination and events through the media. It is important for governments to avoid negative media publicity for their destination and to encourage events tourism by highlighting the cultural element of the country or destination. Festivals and events can play a major role in generating a destination image; amending negative images of a country can be important both economically and socially for the host community.

Strategic decisions made by a variety of governments in the past have resulted in poor support from local communities. Despite this, it is important for governments to work with local communities to attract visitors to cultural and heritage sites. Transport, accommodation and food facilities in tourism areas might need improvement. Governments might consider providing tax breaks for those companies who cater for the local and international tourists who come to their destination.

Events tourism allows locals to become independent. Government laws allow locals to make and sell handicrafts, rent rooms in their own houses as well as cook for tourists. This is an advantage both to the local community as well as the country's economy. Government strategies, with support from locals, can involve regular improvements to heritage buildings, such as museums, churches and large sports facilities. They can also provide facilities for visitors, which ensure that the locals are not disturbed during their time in the area. Events can be used to develop community pride and self-sufficiency as well as intercultural communication.

Developing communities' culture through events and festivals

Festivals have changed over the years, as previously these were associated with key calendar moments, linked specifically to particular seasons and heritage sites. However, over the last decade these have been changed and developed and there is now a broad and diverse range of festival events taking place all over the world all year around.

The revolution in festivals has been stimulated through a commercial aspect to meet the changing demand of local community groups and increasing business opportunities for the event organisers and local businesses. Festivals play a major role in cities and local communities. Festivals are attractive to host communities, because they help them to develop a local pride and identity. In

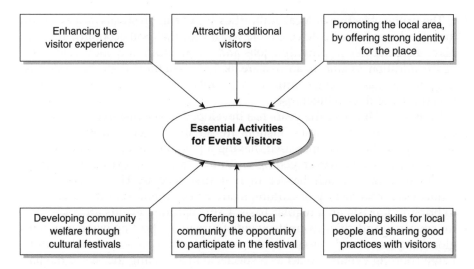

Figure 6.2   Essential activities for events visitors

addition, they are vital in the national and host community in the context of destination planning, and enhancing and linking tourism and commerce. Some aspects of this role include: events as image makers, economic impact generators, and tourist attractions; overcoming seasonality; contributing to . the development of local communities and businesses; and supporting key industrial sectors.

Festival organisers are now using historical and cultural themes to develop annual events to attract visitors and to create a cultural image by holding festivals within community settings. Festivals provide an opportunity for local people to develop and share their culture, which creates a set of values and beliefs held by the individuals in that local community. They provide tourists with the opportunity to see how local communities celebrate their culture and help these visitors to interact with the host community, thereby allowing them to enjoy and meet their leisure needs.

Festivals also provide opportunities for visitors to enjoy and experience local illumination and culture, also allowing support to those who pursue economic opportunities related to sharing community culture with the broader world. UNEP (2002) suggest that cultural tourism is boosted by the development of festivals and events. Tourism can add to the vitality of communities in many ways. One example is that events and festivals of which local residents have been the primary participants and spectators are often rejuvenated and developed in response to tourist interest. Local authorities in the UK and other countries have provided grants and support for local festivals to add additional activities to cater for visitors. In addition, priority is given to those events and festivals which include some of the themes listed in Figure 6.2 in their events.

The prime objective of local authorities supporting festivals and events in their local area is to create economic wealth for the local economy. Tourism plays a crucial role in providing jobs and income for many local communities. In addition, visitors to an area are likely to visit more than one place: visiting more than a single attraction creates more revenue for the local community and local businesses.

Events tourism over the years has developed into a massive income generator for local communities. Visitors are staying longer in urban areas and spending per head has increased, having a positive effect on local communities (Raj, 2004). However, getting visitors to stay for an extended period in an urban area is much harder than it first sounds. Unless the area is renowned for its history or culture, many cities do not have the credentials to bring in tourists on a regular basis. Large sporting events are a key area for countries and cities to create events tourism. A sporting event generates global exposure and raises interest from local and international visitors. Large sporting events can act as a spectacle in attracting the world media's attention and in concentrating their focus on a particular city during a short but intense period, enabling the hosts to showcase their destination on a world stage and highlight the key attractions and activities on offer. Large sporting events are extremely beneficial for cities to promote themselves as tourist destinations and to enhance the visitor's experience.

CASE STUDY

DEVELOPMENT OF EVENT TOURISM THROUGH LOCAL COMMUNITY FESTIVAL

The Bradford Festival Mela

The Bradford Festival Mela has been held annually at Peel Park since 1988. An intoxicating festival in its own right, it is the largest outside Asia and a rare blend of party and pleasure trip. The Bradford Festival Mela has created a unique image in the city, over the last 15 years. The Mela perfectly illustrates its unique role in the communities where it brings people from different cultures together, demonstrating various forms of expression. This also brings with it pride and traditional Asian arts to the city of Bradford.

The Bradford Festival Mela attracts more than 100,000 people over two days. This has a huge economic impact on the city of Bradford when local small businesses, in particular, gain vital revenue from the festival. Visitors spend large amounts of money during the duration of the festival and this outweighs the social and physical problems that are encountered by the locals.

Moreover, Bradford Festival Mela brings the local community together to celebrate the diverse cultures within the community. Over the last decade it has become a major multicultural event for the city of Bradford and has dem-onstrated the advantages of cultural diversity to the rest of British society. In addi-tion, the festival has created positive economic impacts for the local community and has enhanced the local businesses that benefit from the actual event.

The Bradford Festival Mela over the years has developed into an interna-tional event that attracts audiences from the UK and throughout the world. Due to the large south Asian community in Bradford, it attracts family and friends from abroad. They often pick festival time to visit family and friends in the city, which increases tourism in the area.

Councillor Margaret Eaton, the leader of Bradford council, stated:

> The Mela really is the jewel in the crown of the International Festival and a high point in Bradford's tourist calendar. It is also a fine example of why Bradford deserves to have its Capital of Culture bid taken seriously and a great chance for Bradfordians of all cultural backgrounds to get together. (*Yorkshire Post*, 2002)

The visitors to the festival provide great financial support for the local econ-omy by overnight stays in the city, which generates direct income from the festival for local businesses. The festival also has a major impact on the host city by creating extra employment for the period leading up to the event and even after the event has taken place. The following data highlight the actual benefits the event brings to the city.

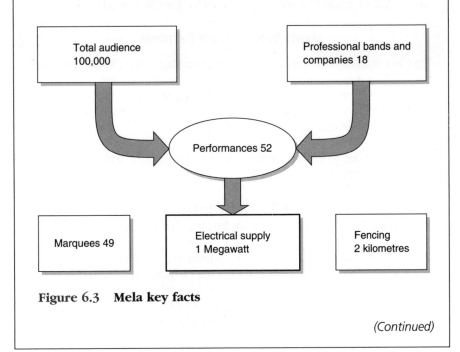

Figure 6.3 Mela key facts

(Continued)

(Continued)

The Bradford Festival Mela has developed into one of the centrepieces of the Bradford International Festival programme. The Mela displays over the last ten years have attracted tourists and built up the image of Bradford. The event itself has changed from a community event into a commercial commodity over the last five years; Bradford city council have given the contract to run the Mela to Scottish firm UZ/ZAP Productions, who were chosen over local company Bradford Festival Ltd to attract more visitors to the city.

The Bradford Festival Mela has developed into a multicultural festival over the years, but it now attracts tourists from different community groups and creates cultural experiences for visitors in a general context. Traditionally, the Mela depended on local visitors. In its early years the Mela attracted over 95 per cent of local people to the festival. This image has changed over the last decade and now 42 per cent of visitors attend the event from outside the city. Some of the visitors come from as far as Pakistan, India and Bangladesh. The festival has created the image among the south Asian communities of Bradford as a city with cultural events. Other cities in England have adopted a similar approach to Bradford to develop cultural festivals to create an enhanced image, reputation and status among the south Asian community to attract visitors to their area.

The festival has become without original intent a PR event for the Asian community and has added an educational focus for other cultures to understand the different aspects of south Asian communities. Finally, Bradford Festival Mela has created an image that enhances tourism for the city of Bradford.

Leeds West Indian Carnival

The Caribbean carnival is an annual event celebrated in the city of Leeds since the 1960s. It is one of the oldest Caribbean carnivals in Europe.

Since 1967 the carnival has created a multicultural spirit that encourages people of all races and nationalities to attend the event during the August bank holiday. Carnival founder Arthur France said:

> This continues to be one of this city's most important and enjoyable family attractions.

> Our events in the run up to Carnival Day provide something for everyone as well as giving the whole city the chance to come together in one big party. (*Yorkshire Evening Post*, 2002).

Originally, the Leeds West Indian Carnival used to go into the city centre, but that tradition changed during the 1980s. The carnival has outgrown the original concept and now it takes place around Chapletown and Harehills.

Behind the colour and music of the carnival there is a deeper meaning that is rooted in the experiences of Caribbean people arriving in England at a time

of great change in the late 1950s and early 1960s. So it was a search for identity, for community and belonging that led to the carnival being developed in
the early 1960s in the Notting Hill area of London.

The carnival has created a platform for Caribbean people to come together
and share their social and cultural differences with the local community from different backgrounds. It is about people coming together and people having fun.

In 2006 over 80,000 people enjoyed the mixture of local and international
talent. Music was mixed with the wonderful smells of Caribbean cooking. In
the afternoon over 100,000 people watched the carnival procession. The
carnival was led by the Lord Mayor of Leeds and, dressed in a traditional
costume, the MP for Leeds North East, Fabian Hamilton.

Carnival day starts early with the J'Ouvert procession at 6.00 a.m. In the afternoon the procession leaves Poternewton Park for three and a half hours of non-
stop dancing around the streets of Chapletown and Harehills. This year 800
revellers joined the procession and two sound systems lit-up Chapeltown and
Harehills, demonstrating a colourful mixture of people from all backgrounds
and different cultures.

Moreover, the carnival creates cultural variety for the local community and
encourages party-goers to enjoy the sights and sounds of the spectacular cos-
tumed troupes, the parade and traditional Caribbean music. It also brings
together people of different races, nationalities, and ages to enjoy the day
with others.

Over the last ten years tourism in the area has grown because the event
attracts those interested in the culture and spectacle created. Another element is the image of the carnival expressing an invisible side of local and international culture, developed by the event over the years to attract more and
more visitors to the area.

The carnival has created a very special image for Leeds, because it has brought
the local community together and has enhanced the local image, attracting
tourism from all over the country and from as far away as the Caribbean itself.

The carnival organisers have suggested that the event is becoming more of
a tourist attraction. This is due to the better press coverage by the local and
national press. Previously the carnival relied on local people, yet recently the
growth and size of the carnival mean it is a major tourist attraction. In return
it has created considerable economic and social impacts on the local community of Leeds. It is now strongly viewed by the local community and small
businesses as a significant element in attracting tourism to the area and they
value the tourist market as a vital tool for the development of the local economy. Therefore, the carnival can be seen as a key development event for a
true tourist attraction, bringing local, national and international tourists to
this unique event.

The Leeds West Indian Carnival is one of the oldest carnivals in the country,
whose image and reputation mean the local area can enjoy cultural and economic
benefits from this the event. Significant audiences and visitors attend the carnival
weekend from all over the country to celebrate West Indian culture.

Managing visitors for events

Hosting and staging events as part of tourism strategies to promote destinations has become an increasing focus for tourism agencies and national governments around the globe over the last decade. From staging international events to promoting community festivals within localities, events can shape tourist perceptions of a region and can shape the geography of the imagination.

By analysing event provision within tourism, insights can be gained into not only as to what a destination wants to present to visitors but also as to what that destination aspires to be. Events thus serve to provide potential visitors and other nations with an insight into a country's vision of their past, present and future.

Community festivals provide displays of local cultures deemed appropriate for the eyes of passing audiences. Mega event hosting can raise the status of a country and offer an opportunity for it to showcase its cultures and aspirations on a global stage. Events have become part of an image-making process, playing a crucial part in positioning destinations against their competitors.

Destinations can position themselves in marketing terms through event hosting and staging to reach niche as well as mass audiences, not simply through increasing visitor numbers at events but by creating powerful associations for the destination in the minds of visitors. These associations may be connected to the nature of events, such as religious festivals, but event associations can also result in an overall perception of a country or locality as 'dynamic', 'youthful', 'historic', 'sporting', 'showbiz', etc.

Cultural and economic impacts

Events can have several types of impact on a host city, ranging from cultural, economic, social and environmental. Events have both positive and negative impacts on their host cities, but the emphasis is often focused on their economic aspect. It is the role of event organisers to focus on impacts other than the purely economic ones that may be created by the event.

The impact of events on host cities is changing in accordance with significant developments in the events market that has developed during the past ten years. Consequently, post-event evaluation is extremely important, not only to review the situation but also to identify and manage the impacts to assist in maximising future benefits. Additionally, events have an important role to play within both the national and local community in the context of destination planning, enhancing and linking tourism and commerce. Some aspects of this role include events as image makers, economic impact generators, and tourist attractions; overcoming seasonality; contributing to the development of local communities and businesses; and supporting key industrial sectors. However, the event manager will put great emphasis on the financial

Host City	Economic Impacts	Political Impacts
Los Angeles	• $9.6b tourism • $225m 'surplus' • Airport construction speeded up • New fiber optics infrastructure ($100m) • Upgraded sports facilities • Amateur Athletics Foundation of Los Angeles Legacy Fund ($90m)	• $145m tax revenues • LA's Mayor presence enhanced • Interlocal cooperation • Mobilised anti-LA sentiment in San Fernando Valley • Public art • Uerborroth picked to head RLA in 1992
Atlanta	• $650m in new construction • $609 in federal funds • 18 companies relocated • $5b in tourism • Expansion of tourism businesses • Chambers expands international sports presence	• CODA, ANDP created • Affirmative action employment and purchasing • Local politics nationalised • Federal empowerment zone • Public art • Downtown QOL ordinances • Liquor store licences not renewed • Centennial Olympic Park
Salt Lake City	• $1.3b in federal funds • $4.5b in tourism (est.) • Expansion of tourism businesses • $40m in legacy fund (est.)	• Enhanced IG lobbying capacity • Conflict over paying for costs in venue communities • $79.5m in tax revenues (est.)

Figure 6.4   Olympic Games political and economic impact

Source: Andranovich et al. (2001, p. 55) 'Olympic cities: Lessons learned from mega-event politics', *Journal of Urban Affairs* 23(2): 113–131. Reprinted with permission from Blackwell Publishing.

impacts of the events and will invariably become myopic concerning other possible impacts that might occur during the event. It is important for the event manager to realise this potential situation, be aware, and identify and manage both positive and negative impacts resulting from the event.

Community festivals now play a significant role in income generation for local businesses and create tourism for the local area. Festivals now attract visitors from all over the country and even further afield. Festival organisers are now able to target wider audiences through the use of technology and media, which has a considerable economic impact on the host community that in turn convinces tourists to visit the area and to stay longer. Getz (1997, p. 6) defines economic impacts as:

> The economic role of events is to act as catalysts for attracting visitors and increasing their average spend and length of stay. They are also seen as image-makers for the destination, creating a profile for destinations positioning them in the market and providing a competitive marketing advantage.

Economic values are often placed on the benefit of publicity obtained for the event, which may occur before, during and after its occurrence. Column inches and advertising costs are used to quantify such impacts.

Undoubtedly, in addition to creating community cohesion, festivals and events potentially give a greater economic life to host destinations, by developing employment, additional trade and business development, investment in the infrastructure, long-term promotional benefits and tax revenues. Events and festivals not only generate significant economic benefits, they also provide host destinations with the opportunity to market themselves nationally and internationally, bringing people from diverse backgrounds to a destination for the duration of an event or festival. As a result, they have the potential to provide host destinations with a high-status tourism profile. The economic impacts of events are the most tangible and therefore are most often measured. Economic impacts can be positive and negative; the positive economic impacts of an event are visitor expenditure, investment in the infrastructure and increased employment.

SUMMARY

Many countries have realised the positive effects that events tourism can have. Countries such as the USA, Australia and China, have all attracted a wide variety of events, for instance the Olympics and 'Incentive Travel', that have been successful in the development of a country as well as improving the number of annual tourist arrivals. Examples such as these have shown that there is a definite link between events and being an effective tool to attract tourists, not only to the events but to the destination as well.

Festivals contribute to the development of events and cultural tourism. Festivals attract events tourists to local community events, promoting cultural exchanges between tourists and residents. Events tourism brings benefits to the cities, but these benefits are not being analysed in greater depth. Tourism festivals have major affects on the local economy directly and indirectly. Spending by visitors on local goods and services has a direct economic impact on local businesses; these benefits pass more widely across the economy and the community.

This chapter has also suggested that events tourism has been increased through the development of local festivals and provides greater economic and cultural benefits to the local area. Visitors are attracted to these festivals from as far away as Europe and the Caribbean. It was found that social and economic factors contributed to events tourism growth in these festivals. The Bradford Mela and Leeds West Indian Carnival have become major tourist attractions to local, regional and international visitors.

Discussion questions

Question 1

Identify and discuss the economic impact of outdoor events on host cities.

Question 2

'Festivals attract culture tourists to local community events to promote cultural exchanges between tourists and residents'.
Critically evaluate the above statement.

Question 3

What are the advantages and disadvantages for destinations in holding major community and cultural events?

FURTHER READING

Dwyer, L. et al. (2000) 'A framework for assessing "tangible" and "intangible" impacts of events and conventions', *Event Management,* 6: 175–189.

English Heritage (2000) *Tourism Facts 2001.* Swindon: English Heritage.

Getz, D. (1997) *Event Management and Event Tourism.* New York: Cognizant Communications Corporation.

Leslie, D. (2001) 'Urban regeneration and Glasgow's galleries with particular reference to the Burrell Collection'. In G. Richards (ed.), *Cultural Attractions and European Tourism.* Oxon: CABI Publishing.

Notting Hill Carnival: A Strategic Review (2004) Published by Greater London Authority www.london.gov.uk

Richards, G. (ed.) (2001) *Cultural Attractions And European Tourism.* Oxon: CABI Publishing.

CHAPTER 7

The marketing process

OUTLINE OF THE CHAPTER

History and theory of marketing

Application of the marketing concept to events

Events marketing research and planning

Consumer behaviour at events

The events consumer and segmentation

The events marketing mix

Positioning events for substantial competitive advantage

Relationship marketing for events

Summary

Discussion questions

Further reading

The aim of this chapter is to apply marketing process models to events from conception to evaluation to examine marketing research, segmentation, targeting, the positioning of specific events as examples and to highlight the application of marketing research. The focus will be on positioning an event favourably in the minds of its target market in order to ensure long-term success.

Introduction

The chapter will begin with a brief summary of the history and theory of the marketing concept, followed by a discussion of the marketing concepts and marketing research in relation to events. The chapter will then examine the behaviour of consumers and how they can be segmented. A detailed discussion will then follow on the marketing mix and its constituents: product,

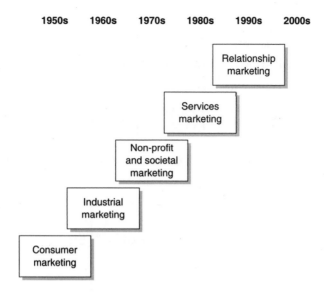

1950s   1960s   1970s   1980s   1990s   2000s

Figure 7.1   The development of marketing

price, place and promotion, as applied to events. Finally, how events could be positioned within the marketplace to compete successfully and how relationship marketing could be applied to achieve repeat visitors and loyalty will be discussed.

History and theory of marketing

The marketing era began in the early 1950s (see Figure 7.1) and the public appetite for new goods and services appeared insatiable. In western markets consumption rose substantially as prices fell. This was also the period when independent commercial television was launched and this became the marketer's most powerful mass market communication medium. The influence of marketing was such that consumer spending doubled during this time (Egan, 2004).

Research in marketing grew in the 1960s and it was during this decade that Borden (1964) introduced the 12 elements of the marketing programme (see Figure 7.2a), which were later simplified further by McCarthy (1978) to what became known as the '4 Ps' of marketing or the marketing mix (see Figure 7.2b).

Application of the marketing concept to events

Marketing is one of the concepts in management that is difficult to define. If you ask people within a business what they understand about marketing

Product planning	Personal selling	Display
Pricing	Advertising	Servicing
Branding	Promotions	Physical handling
Channels of distribution	Packaging	Fact finding and analysis

Figure 7.2a   Borden's (1964) 12 elements of the marketing programme

Product	Price
Place	Promotion

Figure 7.2b   McCarthy's (1978) marketing mix

and the role of the marketing department, you could be expected to get a variety of answers including:

Marketing is about advertising
The people who work in marketing put brochures together
It is the company's sales activities

There have been numerous definitions of marketing and no one definition is correct. They are simply opinions of how people view marketing. Below are just a few of the definitions which have been used.

Marketing is the social and managerial process by which individuals and groups obtain what they need and want through creating and exchanging products and value with others. (Kotler et al., 1999, p. 10)

Marketing is a dialogue. (Mercer, 1996, p. 15)

When looking at the above definitions, they all seem to be different. However, one needs an explanation which will apply to every company in every situation. In the UK the definition given by the Chartered Institute of Marketing is widely accepted:

> Marketing is the management process responsible for identifying, anticipating and satisfying customer requirements profitably. (www.cim.co.uk)

This definition is an elegant description of what marketing means. Of the many definitions that are available it is one of the most succinct. It emphasises the wide scope of marketing, ranging from the initial identification of customer needs by means of research, right through to the eventual, profitable satisfaction of those needs.

Academic research of marketing in events management has been slow to get off the mark as Shannon (1999, p. 517) noted in his article when discussing, in particular, sports marketing:

> **The primary focus of most of the sport marketing publications, to date, appears to be in the marketing communications (advertising/ promotion) and consumer behaviour areas of marketing. There appears to be less research in the pricing, product, and distribution/ place areas of the marketing mix. These areas provide rich research potential for future studies in sport marketing.**

When relating marketing to events management the following definition may be used:

> **Marketing is that function of event management that can keep in touch with the event's participants and visitors (consumers), read their needs and motivations, develop products that meet these needs, and build a communication program which expresses the event's purpose and objectives. (Hall, 1997, p. 136)**

The main reason companies invest in marketing is to make a profit. The customer gets the product, the company gets the money and makes a profit. In order to satisfy the customer an event organisation must identify what business it is in and the purpose it is serving to satisfy customer requirements.

The main marketing principles would include:

Anticipating market needs and opportunities

Satisfying customer expectations

Generating income and/or profit

Maximising the benefits to the events organisation

Managing the effects of change and competition

Coordinating activities in order to achieve their marketing aims

Utilising technical developments

Enhancing customers' perception of the organisation

Enhancing customers' perception of the product.

To illustrate these concepts, the following list shows the number of marketing activities that an event manager should undertake to produce a successful event or festival:

- analyse the target market to establish appropriate event components, or products

- establish what other competitive events could satisfy similar needs to ensure their event has a unique selling proposition

- predict how many people would attend the event

- predict at what time people will come to the event

- estimate what price they will be willing to pay to attend the event

- decide on the type and quantity of promotional activities needed to inform and attract the target market to the event

- decide how tickets for the event can reach their target market

- establish the degree of success for marketing events.

All the above activities are important in the organisation of a successful event. In order to meet these marketing principles, the business would carry out a series of marketing functions, including:

- managing change

- coordinating marketing planning control

- managing the effects of competition

- ensuring the survival of the business.

The term 'marketing concept' is widely used in business circles today. It refers to the adoption of marketing orientation by modern day organisations.
Kotler et al., (1999, p. 19) describe the marketing concept as follows:

> The marketing concept is a management philosophy which holds that achieving organisational goals depends on determining the needs, wants of target markets and delivering the desired satisfactions more effectively and efficiently then competitors.

Marketing can be looked at from three positions in an organisation: strategic, management and operational (Majaro, 1993). One faces the problem of deciding on the vantage point from which the main principles and concepts should be examined. For example, marketing at the strategic levels emphasises directional issues such as:

- corporate mission development

- choice of strategy

- development of a corporate image to match the firm's aims and objectives

- the decision to apply undifferentiated or niche marketing

- product innovation.

On the other hand, marketing at an operational level deals at minutiae levels such as:

- researching markets

- selling

- advertising.

A choice has to be made about whether marketing principles are examined from the top or from the point of view of the detailed methodologies practised at the sharp end of the function.

The success of any business depends on its ability to satisfy the customer. This statement suggests that the main purpose of the marketing function should also be the purpose of other functions within the organisation. The enterprise stands to win or lose by its ability to attain such a goal. To enable organisations to satisfy their customers effectively there are a number of questions which need to be asked.

Who is our customer and what exactly are his or her needs?

Who is responsible for satisfying the customer?

What do we need to 'know' before we can commence the task of planning the process of satisfying customers, now and in the future?

To what extent do our customers expect us to be creative and innovative in whatever we do?

Events marketing research and planning

Marketing research has a specific function, which is to aid effective planning and decision making in markets. It plays an important part in the design and implementation of an effective strategy. There are three areas of activity involved in the successful marketing management of events:

- analysis

- planning

- control.

Analysis

This is a crucial area of marketing. Its aim is to find out about the market in which the company operates or which the company is planning to enter. Through systematic market research, present and future needs can be identified, analysed and evaluated. To gain a comprehensive view of the market, assessments of behaviour and opportunities both qualitative and quantitative should be taken.

Planning

Planning is critical in professional marketing. It follows logically from the analytical approach. From the data derived from the marketing research process, management should be in a position to select markets suitable for exploitation; products and services designed to satisfy the identified needs of specific markets should then be developed. The marketing plan is not separate from the strategic plan but a part of it. Figure 7.3 shows that a sound understanding of marketing principles is essential knowledge for an event manager.

Control

Control is the third area of successful marketing. It is important for the productivity of the business or any type of organisation. Standards of performance need to be set and closely monitored. Marketing management should recognise that success in markets depends substantially on total commitment to management control throughout the business and an awareness of the need for specialists in marketing, design, finance, purchasing, personnel etc., to work together creatively to achieve the objectives of the organisation to which they belong.

There are five sequential stages of the marketing research programme.

Stage 1   Brief research   This stage is the initial stage where clients and researchers can identify a clear indication of the marketing problems. Some areas the company or event manger may discuss are: the industry background and the nature of products made by the company, the proposed topic of market investigation and the extent of market research activities.

This stage is critical because it will determine the type of research and the entire research activities. At this stage the marketing problem must be clearly defined to enable the survey to be carried out effectively.

Stage 2   Research proposal   Information collected from Stage 1 will be studied by researchers who will then submit a detailed proposal to clients for approval. The proposal should be carefully checked before moving on to the next stage.

Figure 7.3   Incorporating marketing into the strategic plan.

Source: Adapted from Morgan (1996) *Marketing for Leisure and Tourism*, Pearson Education Limited © Prentice Hall Europe 1996.

The proposal is likely to contain the following information:

- clear statement of the marketing problems to be investigated
- definition of the product or service to be investigated
- definition of the survey population to be sampled

- major areas of measurement
- methodology
- degree of accuracy of survey findings
- costs involved in the survey
- conditions applying to the research survey
- experience of the researchers.

Stage 3 Data collection Data can be collected using a number of different methods. The two main areas of data collection are primary and secondary. Primary data refer to data collected at first hand such as observations, surveys or questionnaires. Secondary data refer to information which already exists. Secondary research is also known as desk research. This information can be obtained internally or externally. The acquisition of secondary data depends on four factors:

- availability
- relevance
- accuracy
- cost.

Each factor must be carefully assessed to ensure that relevant, valid and cost effective information is obtained in specific enquiries.

Stage 4 Data analysis and evaluation This is one of the final stages of the survey. It involves the editing of survey forms, coding of answers and tabulation.

Stage 5 Preparation and presentation of the report After the first four stages have been completed, the information has to be communicated in an attractive manner. It will take place in the form of a survey report.

Types of marketing research

Qualitative Research

Qualitative methods emphasise producing data that are rich in understanding and that include a depth of information. These methods should also be used to research event motivation. The methods are often carried out on a small group of people and involve in-depth interviews and group discussions. Because the group is small the research can be completed more quickly and be more cost effective.

Quantitative Research

This type of research involves research techniques of representative samples, questionnaires, interviews, etc. These are essential in making it possible to express results quantitatively.

Methods of obtaining first-hand information

Surveys

Questionnaires are often used to obtain quantitative data before an event relating to customer opinion. Research can be carried out by a trained inter-viewer, either face to face or on the telephone, or through self completion by the respondent either on hard copy, or by e-mail or online.

Advantages

Event venues subscribe to an online software system which automatically solicits the opinion of the event organisers on the venue shortly after each event.

It can provide each subscribing organisation with information for competitive benchmarking.

Longitudinal data can be obtained in a survey that is repeated at regular intervals.

Disadvantages

Respondents' reported behaviour and attitudes may be influenced by their knowledge that they are regularly questioned and this variation can be very difficult to recognise and quantify.

Errors can be made in collecting the data.

Focus groups/interviews

This type of method is useful when collecting information on attitudes, opin-ions or motivations. The depth of data obtained from the group discussions or in-depth interviews of participants, local residents, etc., helps to provide the key to problems which may not have been predicted by the researchers.

Advantages

Provides the key to problems which may otherwise not have been anticipated.

The respondents are not forced to make choices.

A useful variation on focus groups is in seeking expert opinion.

A diversity of groups helps to generate different ideas and solutions.

Disadvantages

It is difficult to analyse information due to the richness and unstructured nature of the data gathered.

Groups are chosen on the basis of experience rather than being representative of a larger segment or population. For example, a post-event mixed expert focus group may consist of the event organisers, representatives from the venues involved, local government tourism/event managers and local community representatives.

Observations

Observing consumer behaviour at events can give an indication of how the product is used and may give clues to the benefits gained. It also helps to identify levels of enjoyment or satisfaction.

Advantages

Observing behaviour as it happens provides very reliable information, as it does not depend on a respondent's memory.

The respondent does not have to respond in a certain way.

Disadvantages

Information obtained can be biased.

Information is limited to the event and the type of consumer attending the event and therefore cannot be generalised.

There are two types of observation: participant and covert observations.
   Participant observation is when the observer joins the group being observed. This style of observation has been used to investigate young people's social behaviour as an incentive to developing products such as club nights and promotional events. This – combined with other information – will provide a detailed picture of customer characteristics and their preferences.
   Covert observation of the event experience is a variation on the 'mystery shopper' technique. Here, a trained researcher experiences the event and records the positives and negatives of it. The researcher may play different roles to enable them to carry out the research in different situations.

Estimating attendance and evaluation

Generating accurate estimates of attendance is an important aspect of event evaluation. It is quite simple for ticketed events or restricted number events, but complications arise when the events are open or semi open.
   In Figure 7.4 several sources of information are shown which are needed for an event evaluation.

Consumer behaviour at events

The marketing concept is just as important to the events industry as it is to any other service industry. This is because the service in an event is often intangible, inseparable, variable and perishable.

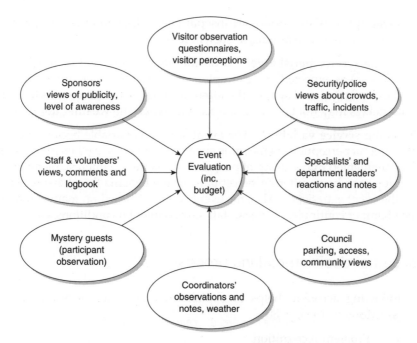

Figure 7.4 Sources of information for evaluation

Source: Adapted from Shone and Parry 2001, p. 221, *Successful Event Management: A Practical Handbook*, Thomson, London. Reprinted with permission.

Why is the service intangible? Unlike buying a product, the customer cannot pick, touch or try it before it is purchased; therefore the customer has to make a decision based on expectations that a need or desire will be met.

Customer expectations may often come from the following sources:

Recommendations from family and friends.

Word of mouth.

Promotional or advertising campaigns from the marketing organiser. For example through posters, television advertisements, leaflets, etc.

The brand image of the event.

Previous experience of similar events Before the event, expectations have a significant impact on the levels of satisfaction and future purchase behaviour. If customers have high expectations of the event, then once they have attended it, and the event does not meet their expectations, then future business may be lost. On the other hand, if an event exceeds customer expectations then event managers would expect to see an increase in the sale of tickets in the future.

Why is the service inseparable? The service the customer receives is inseparable from the consumption of the service. This is because production and consumption of the service are inseparable, unlike purchasing a product from the shops and consuming it elsewhere.

Why is the service perishable? If on the day of the event or festival the weather is not as expected. For example, if the event has been organised outdoors and it is wet and windy, the attendance level would be affected, but unsold tickets may not be sold at a later date when the weather improves.

Why is the service variable? The event service is variable because people have different perceptions of the same event. This is because when markets are tightly segmented into a group of people with a common interest, members of the group may have differing perceptions of the benefits they have received from the event experience. Also, the event service is based on many variables which hamper continuity – artists, staff, environmental conditions, etc.

Consumer decision-making process

The following acronym helps to explain the consumer decision-making process (Morgan, 1996, p. 80).

PIECE: **Problem recognition**
         Information search
         Evaluation of alternatives
         Choice of purchase
         Evaluation of post purchase experience

This process may be used for a consumer making a decision to attend an event.

To influence people to arrive at a decision about attending an event, marketers need to understand the needs, motives and expectations of their potential customers. Many event organisers do not carry out thorough customer-orientated research as they believe in their own ability to know what their customers want, or lack the resources to do it.

Fig 7.5 conceptualises the consumer decision-making process for events. The start of the marketing process is to identify which consumer needs will be satisfied if they attend the event.

A study of customers at a community festival in South Carolina by Uysal et al. (1993) and a study of attendees of a North American hot air balloon festival by Mohr et al. (1993) reported five needs for attending festivals.

1 Socialisation: being with friends and people enjoying the same things.

2 Family togetherness: spending time with the family and doing something together.

3 Excitement: doing something because it's exciting.

4 Escape: having a change from everyday routines and demands.

5 Event novelty: experiencing new and different things.

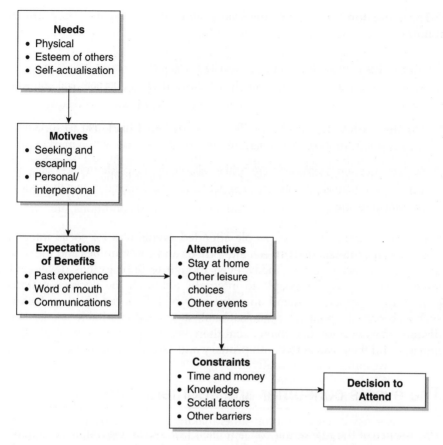

Figure 7.5   Consumer decision-making process for events

Source: Adapted from Getz (1997)

Even though the motivations for visiting the festivals were the same, the order was slightly different. Visitors to the community festivals placed escape at the top of their list, whereas visitors to the hot air balloon festival placed socialisation.

Many choices are available to consumers to satisfy their needs or wants. Events must compete with other forms of leisure and events. There may be barriers which may not allow consumers to take part in the events.

For example:

Personal reasons – time, social influences, money.

Event related reasons – location, accessibility, and cost.

Events are designed to satisfy all levels of need although not necessarily at the same time. People come to events with a variety of motives and expectations but there is no guarantee these will all be met.

There are three types of consumers who attend events. They are as follows:

Allocentrics are more adventurous travellers who prefer to make their own way to events in order to keep away from other tourists. They visit unspoilt and authentic events.

Psychocentrics are conservative, they prefer packaged tours, and go to familiar touristy places. They like to visit mass market events.

Midcentrics are people who are neither allocentrics or psychocentrics. Since the population is normally distributed, most people fall into this group rather than one or the other extreme.

Historically, the main reason people attended events was for social integration, bonding, interaction between individuals and communities and the reinforcement of social norms. Today, even though technology has developed, there is still a need for people to integrate, although the decision-making process for a person to attend an event may be influenced by other factors such as economic, political, organisational, status and charitable needs. This demonstrates that for any given event there is a range of motives and determinants and these can act as both primary and secondary motives.

The events consumer and segmentation

The essence of the marketing concept itself leads to an inevitable consideration of market segmentation. Marketing is about satisfying consumer needs and wants, but it must be realised that even though consumers may have similar need structures, they will not have the same needs at the same time. The majority of events do not appeal to all consumers, therefore when the event organiser is carrying out marketing planning for an event or festival, an understanding of the behaviour of the visitors must be included. This can be done by identifying market segments.

Markets can be segmented by:

1 Geography

2 Demographics

3 Psychographic (lifestyle).

Geographic segmentation

This is to do with where people who are visiting the event reside. For example, a community festival will most likely depend on local residents as a start for their segmentation activity. However, the event or festival may be of interest to other people outside the residential area and the marketing network could be increased to day visitors from outside the area, domestic tourists both local and national, school excursions and international inbound tourists. The chosen geographic segmentation depends on the experience provided by a festival or event.

Demographic segmentation

Demographic segmentation is about measurable characteristics of people. These include:

- age
- gender
- occupation
- education
- income
- cultural economic group.

Another method often used for demographic segmentation is the socio-economic scale based on income.

Men and women have different needs, which some event organisers may arrange to cater for in order to satisfy them. The year a consumer was born can also affect the way they look at life, their attitudes, values and interests. When events are organised they may often be targeted at more then one generation, therefore creating a desire for people to attend events as families and spend quality time together.

What stage consumers are at in their life cycle will often determine the type of event or festival they will attend. For example, empty nesters in socio-economic groups AB will tend to visit cultural events featuring quality food and drink, whereas consumers with families would be more interested in attending events which cater for both adults and children.

Psychographic segmentation

This is another method which event organisers find useful when planning event segmentation. This is based on consumers' lifestyles and their values.

Psychographic segmentation, like personality segmentation, has many limitations for the marketer. One of the main limitations is that it is very difficult to measure life style segments quantitatively. This method can be useful for marketers when trying to identify the characteristics of the target market.

The events marketing mix

The marketing mix is the term used for the four marketing variables the company can control when organising events. The marketing mix consists of the 4 Ps:

- Product
- Promotion
- Price
- Place.

When marketers are deciding on a marketing plan for the event, they can control any of the 4 Ps to enable them to make the event a success. This can only be done when they have carried out some market research and analysed the results to find out who their potential customers are.

Product

Products are usually considered to be tangible. That is to say one can see the product, look at its appearance, touch the product and even try it. However, with events or festivals the product is not tangible. Consumers are not able to do any of these things and have to make a decision whether to attend an event or festival simply by the way the product is marketed.

Often, when choosing an event, consumers tend to look at brand names. This helps them because they will feel more confident visiting events they know will provide them with the product which will satisfy their needs. As with any other product, events also have different stages. This is known as the product life cycle. The stages are as follows:

- introduction
- growth
- maturity
- decline, stagnation, rejuvenation.

For example, an event or festival which is popular today may not have any benefits in the future, unless the event is changed or organised in a different way to enable the consumers to gain benefit and satisfy the motives or needs they initially had to attend a certain event. By making a change to satisfy consumer needs, the event may be rejuvenated.

Another method marketers could use to attract people to events is by launching a new product into the market which would be of interest to them.

In order to bring the new event to the public, there would need to be a variety of advertising campaigns to persuade the public to attend. Once they have attracted people to attend the event they must try their best to satisfy the needs of their customers, in order to achieve an image which will attract consumers to it in the future and even to promote the event by making recommendations to family and friends who may have similar interests.

Promotion

Promotion is taken to mean:

- Advertising
- Sales promotion
- Public relations
- Personal selling.

Advertising includes all types from corporate through product, to point of sale of tickets. Personal selling could include selling tickets on the telephone, intermediaries such as event ticketing agents and merchandising. Sales promotions may include consumer promotions, trade promotions, industrial promotions, trade shows and exhibitions. Public relations means communicating with the event company's publics (e.g., shareholders, workers, suppliers). Often in events, the communication mix is also referred to to mean promotion.

Promotional activities need to be planned and must have objectives that can be achieved within a given timescale.

Price

Events organisers need to set prices for their products, including admission to the event, merchandise, vendor rentals and sponsorship fees. Even events that are normally free enforce a price on customers in terms of travel costs, lost opportunities and time.

Place

Place normally refers to the physical location where the event is held, which could be a building, a set of venues or a space. Within the marketing mix an important part of place also considers the atmosphere and how this may be created through lighting, set and design.

Place could also mean the distribution of event products or how they may be sold to customers.

Positioning events for sustainable competitive advantage

According to Porter (1980), the main aspect of a firm's environment is the industry or industries in which it competes. An event firm can achieve sustainable competitive advantage by positioning itself in any of the three generic marketing strategies: cost leadership, differentiation or focus (Porter, 1985).

Cost leadership

In this strategy a firm sets out to become *the* low-cost producer in its industry. To be profitable as well as cost effective firms must offer customers product quality and features comparable with their competitors, at the same time charging prices about the average for the industry.

A cost leadership strategy may not be applicable if events do not have direct competition with other events, or if they are free. However, adding value to the event experience may be a more likely sustainable strategy.

Differentiation

This means finding one or more unique attributes for which customers are prepared to pay a premium price, and positioning the firm to provide those attributes. Differentiation can be based on the product itself, on the delivery system or the way the event may be marketed. According to Porter, a firm that can achieve, and sustain, differentiation will be an above average performer in its industry.

Focus

In this strategy an event firm may decide to focus on segment or group segments with a view to attaining a competitive advantage by meeting the needs and wants of that segment (or group). A focus strategy can be broken down into sub-strategies; one focussing on obtaining a cost advantage, and the other based on developing a differentiation advantage. Events with special themes and highly targeted benefits may use this strategy.

Porter states that a firm that fails to achieve one or other of the above bases of strategies will not obtain a competitive advantage. It will be *stuck in the middle*.

Once an event firm has decided on which bases to compete in, it then needs to develop a strategic direction. This can be carried out using Ansoff's product-market strategies: market penetration, product development, market development and diversification (Ansoff, 1969).

Market penetration In this strategy an event aims to focus its activities on increasing its market share by exploiting its present offering in its present market. This can be achieved through improved promotions, discounts, increasing sales to special groups or even by providing enhanced value for money.

Product development This means adding or changing the fundamentals of the product offering. For instance, theme parks can add new rides in order to maintain interest, art festivals can enhance the quality of performance or attract big stars.

Market development This strategy involves taking the present event to fresh target markets and thus focussing activities on market opportunities and competitor situations, for example, taking a UK exhibition to other countries.

Diversification This is the most radical and riskiest of all the strategies, i.e., branching out into both new products and new markets. This is very rarely used by event organisers.

Relationship marketing for events

A review of current relationship marketing (RM) literature reveals that a good many definitions have been given to capture the meaning of RM. However, a definition by Grönroos (1994) attempts to incorporate both the transactional and relational qualities of marketing and therefore gains wide acceptance among the RM community. According to Grönroos (1994, p. 4) the aim is for:

> RM is to identify and establish, maintain and enhance and, when necessary, terminate relationships with customers and other stakeholders, at a profit, so that the objectives of all parties involved are met; and that is done by a mutual exchange and fulfilment of promises.

Basically, the idea of relationship marketing is that event organisers will attempt to develop a relationship with visitors so that they will repeat their visit and promote the event to their friends and families. This will result in reduced marketing costs in targeting new customers.

In a general sense, relationships require at least two parties who are in contact with each other. For example, the basic relationship of marketing is that between an event organiser and visitor. Nevertheless, within an event there will be several other players involved and a relationship may need to be developed between the participants in a network. Erickson and Kushner (1999, p. 355) illustrate this with the following network example (see Figure 7.6) when discussing a public event from auto racing.

The authors suggest that the implications found in network theory can be used to better manage public events. They further point out that:

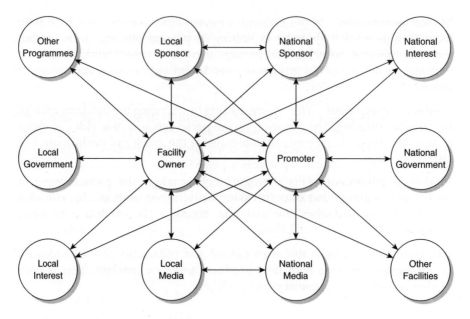

Figure 7.6   The Public Event

> By better understanding what makes a desirable partner in a given network, organizations can more accurately weigh their own attractiveness and that of prospective partners. They can review their own networks with an eye to further connections that may enhance the event or allow entirely new networks to form around additional events. In short, this type of analysis should add to marketing practice by providing a framework for examining these unique organizational structures. (Erickson and Kushner, 1999, p. 363)

Relationship development stages

Dwyer et al., (1987) suggest that there are five stages in the development of a relationship:

- awareness
- exploration
- expansion
- commitment
- dissolution.

In their model Dwyer et al. (1987) see the *awareness* stage where each party recognises that the other party is a feasible exchange partner. No interaction has taken place at this stage but parties may be positioning and posturing to enhance their attractiveness. The *exploration* stage suggests that the parties are weighing up the benefits and drawbacks of getting into an exchange. These may include the psychological and actual costs involved. This stage may also include sub-phases such as attraction, communication and bargaining, the development and exercise of power, norm development (e.g., contractual arrangements) and the expectation development (e.g., trust and commitment). The next stage, *expansion*, represents a period where all parties seek benefits from one another and become increasingly interdependent. The *commitment* stage implies that exchange partners implicitly or explicitly pledge relational continuity with each other. The final stage, *dissolution*, is included in the model to show that disengagement always remains a possibility in any relationship.

SUMMARY

At the heart of marketing is a focus to meet the needs and wants of the consumer. This chapter has demonstrated that marketing is more than selling and advertising, a misconception held by many within the events and festival industry. To summarise the main marketing principles would include anticipating marketing needs and opportunities to stage events, satisfying event visitors' expectations, generating income and/or profit from the event, maximising the benefits to the event organisation and managing change and competition. Furthermore, marketing would involve coordinating activities such as marketing research, planning new product development, pricing, advertising, personal selling and developing relationships in order to satisfy event visitors' needs and at the same time meeting the objectives of the event organisation.

In order to achieve these marketing principles, the event organisation would carry out a series of marketing functions, including: coordinating planning and control, implementing the marketing mix (the right event in the right place with the right promotion at the right price) and ensuring the survival of the business.

Discussion questions

Question 1

Do you think that the customer is always right? Discuss.

Question 2

What sort of internal data might be useful when carrying out a marketing research project for a particular event.

Question 3

In a group or individually try to list some of the purposes of good after-sales service for an event. Some are fairly obvious, others will need a little thought.

FURTHER READING

Ansoff, H.I. (1969) *Business Strategy*. London: Penguin.

Grönroos, C (1994) 'From marketing mix to relationship marketing: towards a paradigm shift in marketing', *Management Decisions*, 32 (2): 4–20.

Kolter, P., Armstrong, G., Saunders, J. and Wong, V. (2001) *Principles of Marketing*, 2nd European edn. London: Prentice Hall Europe.

Porter, M.E. (1985) *Competitive Advantage*. New York: Free Press.

CHAPTER 8

Integrated marketing communications and public relations

OUTLINE OF THE CHAPTER

Events and the concept of marketing communication
What is integrated marketing communications?
Advertising
Sales promotion
Direct mail
Direct marketing
Personal selling
Public relations
E-marketing
Electronic customer relationship management
Viral marketing
Summary
Discussion questions
Further reading

It is important to understand how marketing decisions are made, decisions which will affect the long-term strategy of organisations and the role of events in both promotion and communication. An appreciation of the operational use of marketing communications to make events succeed is needed as well as using each event as a strategic marketing tool.

Introduction

The concept of marketing communication and its application in the events industry is discussed first. This section will cover the marketing communication process and the components of the marketing communication mix: advertising, sales promotion, direct marketing and personal selling. This will be followed by public relations in events continued by a discussion of promotional events as tangibles and intangibles. Finally, the use of modern marketing techniques including e-marketing, ambush marketing and viral marketing will be analysed in relation to events.

Events and the concept of marketing communication

The marketing communication mix is sometimes referred to as the 'promotional mix' within the events industry and consists of advertising, promotion, personal selling and public relations. The marketing communication is an important part of the marketing mix and affects all the other parts of the mix – product, price and place. Therefore, the task of the marketing communications is to present the event in the most appropriate manner.

According to Getz (1997, p. 304–305), event managers have a number of important challenges to take into consideration:

- there is a need for intense, short-term promotion of the upcoming event

- the communication budget is sometimes not appropriate

- many parties must be involved in the event communication mix: e.g., grant givers, sponsors, suppliers, participants, politicians, target markets and volunteers

- the event may be attractive to the media and the event manager may have to deal with reporters from television, the newspapers and magazines

- to maintain a good relationship with the host community public relations may be needed

- sponsorship has the potential to greatly enhance the quality and extend the scope of the communications

- one-time events must manage communications very carefully to achieve early awareness and ensure a peaking of demand as the event nears.

As can been seen above, the role of marketing communications in events management is very important.

What is integrated marketing communications?

The emergence of integrated marketing communications (IMC) has become one of the most significant examples of development in the marketing discipline (Kitchen, 2003). Kitchen and Schultz (2000) have identified four stages of IMC, starting from the tactical coordination of promotional elements, then redefining the scope of marketing communications, to the application of information technology and then financial and strategic integration. They found that the majority of firms are anchored in the first two stages, with some moving into stage three and very few at stage four.

The purpose of marketing communications is to provide a set of information to a target audience in a way that encourages a positive response. Integrated marketing communications emphasises the benefits of harnessing synergy across different media types to establish the brand equity of products and services in achieving that response. Smith et al. (1999) suggest integrated marketing communications comprise three distinguished definitions:

1 Management and control of all market communications.

2 Ensuring that the brand positioning, personality and messages are delivered synergistically across every element of communication and are delivered from a single consistent strategy.

3 The strategic analysis, choice, implementation and control of all elements of marketing communications which efficiently (best use of resources), economically (minimum costs) and effectively (maximum results) influence transactions between an organisation and its existing and potential customers, consumers and clients.

Therefore a definition of marketing communications relating to events can be:

> **It is the process where commonness of thought and meaning is achieved or attempted between an event and its audience.**

In this definition it can be seen that marketing communication is a process, and the audience needs to encompass more than the consumer alone.

But the key question is: how does marketing communications work? There are several conceptual models that are presented in the marketing communication literature but the model put forward in Figure 8.1 perhaps best describes this process. It has eight elements:

- *Sender*: the party sending the message to another party

- *Encoding*: putting thought into symbolic forms

- *Message*: the communication channels which message is sent through

- *Decoding*: the process through which receivers place meaning to the senders' transmitted symbols

- *Receiver*: the party receiving the message (audience)

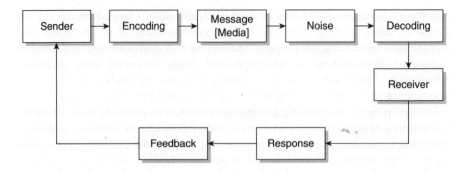

Figure 8.1   Elements in the communications process

Source: Adapted from Yehsin, 1999, p. 7. Figure reprinted with permission.

- *Response*: set of reactions following exposure/reception of message
- *Feedback*: part of the response transmitted back to the sender
- *Noise*: unplanned static or distortion during the process of communication.

In this model the communication is a two-way process as the response and the feedback mechanism are built in and the sender or source may alter the message and media as necessary.

Marketing communications consists of various functions: advertising, sales promotion, direct mailing, direct marketing, personal selling, public relations, e-marketing and viral marketing. Marketing communications works best when these different functions are integrated to achieve the overall marketing goals and thus the corporate goals. In the following sections each function of the marketing communications is now introduced and commented on in relation to events.

Advertising

From its outset, services advertising has been seen as a tool to assist consumers to find their way through a challenging decision-making process. The service cha-racteristics of intangibility, inseparability, heterogeneity, perishability and ownership influence consumer behaviour at a number of levels. First here are the difficulties of searching for information results with the perception of high risk and a reliance on personal information sources (Mortimer, 2002).

Hill and Gandhi (1992) propose that services advertising should contain concrete language to address intangibility, a representation of the service provider and/or customer to address inseparability, documentation to minimise the perception of heterogeneity and a sequence of events to communicate aspects of the service encounter.

Advertising is defined by the American Marketing Association as:

Any paid form of non-personal presentation and promotion of ideas, goods or services by an identifiable sponsor. (www.marketingpower. com)

This definition distinguishes advertising from personal selling and publicity. The purpose of advertising in events is to move the audience along a continuum stretching from complete unawareness of the event to taking action to attend the event.

Advertising communicates information to a large number of recipients, paid for by a sponsor. It has three main aims:

1   to impart information

2   to develop attitudes

3   to induce action beneficial to the advertiser.

For example, an advertisement for a motor exhibition is paid for by the exhibition organisers to achieve a greater number of visitors to the exhibition; a rock group will pay to advertise their concert to sell more box office tickets. It must be remembered that advertising is only one element of the communications mix, but it does perform certain parts of the communicating task faster and with greater economy and volume than other means.

How large a part advertising plays depends on the nature of the event and the number of times it is repeated. It contributes the greatest part when:

1   the event has features which are not obvious to the customer, i.e., the buyer and awareness of the event is low

2   the opportunities for differentiating a particular event are stronger than other similar events

3   event industry sales are rising rather than remaining stable or declining

4   a new product or new service idea is being introduced at an event.

Objectives of advertising

Advertising situations are so varied and unique that it is not possible to generalise about how advertising works. Therefore advertisers should:

• adopt an advertising-by-objectives approach that will it make clear what they are trying to achieve

• determine how they will achieve it

• decide how they are going to measure its effects.

Event organisers often do not give any real scientific thought to exactly what they are trying to achieve through advertising. Clear objectives are required to assist decision making, which include:

1 the amount to be spent on a particular campaign

2 the content and presentation of the advertisement

3 the most appropriate media needed

4 the frequency of display of advertisements or campaigns

5 any special geographical weighting of effort

6 the best methods for evaluating the effects of the advertising.

Planning an advertising campaign

There are six distinct stages in such a campaign:

1 identify the target audience

2 specify the promotional message

3 select the media

4 schedule the media

5 set the promotional budget

6 evaluate the promotional effectiveness.

Identify the target audience

The target audience will be determined by the segmentation that the event is trying to target. Creativity in the ads could be used to highlight mood, atmosphere and environment for brand usage, usually relying on non-verbal communication such as the background setting for an advertisement (indoor/outdoor, relaxed or tense environment, type of music, use of colour schemes, appearance of models etc.).

Specify the promotional message

The intended function of the campaign will determine the promotional message that needs to be specified. This function could be to

1 change perceptions

2 stimulate a desire

3 produce a conviction

4 direct action

5 provide reassurance

6 pass on information.

Each function can suggest an appropriate form for, and content of, the message.

Selecting the media

The media selected provide access to a certain type of audience. The type of media includes national newspapers, regional newspapers, magazines and periodicals, posters and transport advertising, cinema, the internet and radio.

The media selected will be governed by the one that is able to reach the optimum number of potential customers for an event at the lowest price. The choice of medium will depend on who the advertiser wishes to reach with the advertising message.

There are advantages and disadvantages to the various media types. Television is watched by viewers from all social groupings and is the ideal medium for advertising an event targeting mass consumers. Certain mediums may reach audiences with special characteristics: e.g., the cinema is visited mainly by young people, many magazines and local newspapers are read mainly by women and there are trade magazines for certain industries. Events often use flyers and posters which can be mass produced at low cost and widely circulated locally. The size of the circulation for a particular audience is also an important factor in deciding which medium to use.

Another important consideration is the cost of advertising. This consists of:

- the cost of producing the advertisements, and
- the cost of exposure in the media.

The cost of exposure is often far higher than the cost of producing the advert.

Scheduling the media

An advertisement needs to be repeated several times because many of the target audiences will miss it the first time it appears. It has also been found that a large target audience is reached by advertising in several newspapers instead of just one, and in several media instead of just one.

Setting the promotional budget

A budget needs to be set which will meet the objectives for the chosen media to convey the required message. The promotional budget is often linked to sales by using a percentage of:

- the last period of sales

- the target sales

- the target profit.

Evaluating the promotional effectiveness

The problem with evaluating the effectiveness of an advertising campaign is that it doesn't take place in a vacuum. Other factors in the marketplace, such as competing events, changing attitudes, price changes etc., can all affect the advertising effect.

Sales promotion

Sales promotions are largely aimed at consumers, but are also aimed at the 'trade', such as exhibition organisers, wedding planners, festival organisers, the travel industry etc. Sales promotion is a more cost effective way to communicate with the target markets than conventional media advertising.

One important characteristic of sales promotion is its short-term nature. Rarely does a sales promotion last for more than six months, and the majority last for much shorter periods.

Areas of sales promotion generally include the following:

- exhibitions

- contests

- incentives and commissions

- free sampling on sites

- merchandising (demonstrations, auxiliary sales forces, display arrangements)

- display materials (stands, header boards, shelf strips, 'wobblers')

- direct mail (coupons, competitions, premiums).

Sales promotion planning

A full plan is needed to ensure that each stage of a promotion is reached:

1   Analyse the problem task

2   Define the objectives

3   Consider and/or set the budget

4   Examine the types of promotion likely to be of use

5   Define the support activities (e.g., advertising, incentives, auxiliaries)

6   Testing (e.g., a limited exhibition)

7   Decide the measurements required

8   Plan the timetable

9   Present the details to the sales force

10   Implement the promotion

11   Evaluate the result.

Advantages and disadvantages of sales promotions

Advantages

- easily measured response
- quick achievement of objectives
- flexible application
- can be extremely cheap
- direct support of sales force.

Disadvantages

- price-discounting can cheapen the brand image
- short-term advantages only
- difficulty in communicating the brand message.

In general, sales promotion seeks to add value to the decision to purchase or attend, and to communicate a sense of enthusiasm. Two of the most common types of sales promotion, direct mail and exhibitions, are now discussed.

Direct mail

Direct mailing is using the postal service to distribute promotional material directly to a particular person, household or firm.

The usage and acceptance of direct mail are increasing rapidly, and with the growing sophistication of computerisation, this now enables advertisers to segment and target their markets with greater flexibility, selectivity and personal contact.

Direct mail can be used to sell a wide range of products or services, and its uses are also varied.

Consumer direct mail

Some of the most common uses of consumer-targeted direct mail are:

1 **Selling direct**. Direct mail is a good medium for selling a product directly to the customer by a company that has a convincing sales message. It provides a facility for describing the event, fully cutting out the 'middle man'.

2 **Sales lead generation**. Some events need a meeting between the customer and a specialised salesperson, and direct mail can be used to acquire 'qualified' leads. For example, an invitation can be made for a customer to view an exhibition.

3 **Sales promotion**. Promotional messages such as special offers will reach specific targets through direct mail, and in the same way prospects can be encouraged to visit showrooms or exhibitions.

4 **Clubs**. The most popular users of direct mail here are book clubs and companies marketing 'collectables'.

5 **Mail order**. Direct selling and the recruitment of new customers and agents are possible through direct mail.

6 **Fundraising**. It is easy through direct mail to communicate personally with an individual, and therefore it is an excellent method for raising money for charitable organisations. Large amounts of information can be included to induce recipients to make a donation.

7 **Dealer mailings**. Dealers or agents can use direct mail to reach prospects in their own area.

8 **Follow-up mailings**. These help to keep a company's name before a customer following a sale.

Exhibitions

Exhibitions are another form of below-the-line promotional activity. As with many other below-the-line methods they are growing in use and popularity.

Exhibit marketing is a rich and flexible promotional practice that spawns new applications and has the power to adapt to changing situations. A recent example of new exhibit marketing is called the 'pop-up store'. This is a temporary retail set-up that may last a few months and is often used for seasonal products and services. The pop-up store is an unusual and novel idea which generates considerable publicity and promotional value. They can be found in major US cities, malls and airports and include both mainstream retailers and firms with new products to introduce. Pitta et al. (2006).

Exhibitions come in three basic forms:

1 those aimed at the consumer

2 those aimed solely at the trade

3 those aimed at both.

Most exhibitions start off as trade exhibitions and then after the first week or so when all of the 'trade' business has been conducted they are usually open to the public. The public usually pays an entry fee that brings in revenue for the exhibition organiser and helps to pay for the costs of actually staging the exhibition. The general public may have an actual interest in the products and services being exhibited, for example via clothes shows, motor shows and home exhibitions. Sometimes the products and services are of little direct interest to the general public. That is, they are highly unlikely to buy any of the products on show, but nevertheless attendance at the exhibition could be a 'good day out' (e.g., an agricultural show or an air show) and the public is prepared to pay for this privilege.

Direct marketing

Direct mail creates and develops a direct relationship with the event organisers and their consumers on an individual basis. It is a form of direct supply, embracing both the variety of alternative media channels (like advertising) and the choice of distribution channels (like mail order). The direct marketing methods include:

1 **Direct advertising**. This is perhaps one of the oldest methods of reaching the consumer, with printed matter being sent directly to the prospect by the advertiser, often by mail, but sometimes through personal delivery, by handing these out to passersby or leaving them under the windscreen wiper of a car.

2 **Mail order**. Mail order advertising aims to persuade recipients to purchase tickets for an event by post, with delivery of the tickets being made through the mail or another carrier or through a local agent. Thus it is a special form of direct mail, seeking to complete the sale entirely by mail and being a complete plan in itself. Mail order is a type of direct mail, but not all direct mail is mail order.

3 **Direct response advertising**. This is a strategy that uses specially designed advertisements, usually in magazines or newspapers, to invoke a direct response, such as the coupon-response press ad, which the reader uses to order.

Personal selling

A sales force is an important part of the communication mix. They engage in 'personal' selling, as compared with the 'non-personal' selling of advertising and sales promotion activities.

The task of selling involves the following:

- Communicating the advantages of the event to consumers.

- Securing a sale of the event.

- Prospecting for additional customers. This involves searching for prospective customers, perhaps visiting them several times and then making a sales proposition.

- Gathering information about what customers want from an event.

An important decision to make is to decide the possible size of the sales force, which can be increased or decreased depending on the size of the event. However, management need to have an effective, supportive, informative and persuasive communication with the sales force in order to achieve a successful operation.

Public relations

Traditionally, advertising may have been the main communication function in organisations because of budget size. But recently, it has not been too uncommon to find large budgets for Public Relations (PR).

The Institute of Public Relations defines public relations as:

> The deliberate, planned and sustained effort to establish and maintain mutual understanding between an organisation and its public. (www.ipr.org.uk)

Public relations and publicity are sometimes used interchangeably. There is, however, a distinction between public relations and publicity. Publicity may be any form of information from an outside source used by the new media. It is largely out of the hands of the organisation, as the source of the news item will have little control over how and when the story will be interpreted. While public relations may be concerned with publicity, not all publicity derives from public relations. The responsibility of public relations is to create and influence publicity in such a way that it has a positive impact on the event.

Public relations require that organisations relate to the public in some manner. In events, for instance, the public could be the media, event organisers, consumers, financial investors, employees and potential employees, opinion formers and the local community. However, while the type of audience will depend on the nature of the event it is critical that the key audience for a particular event is identified.

Functions of public relations

Public relations encompasses out a range of different functions but the following list identifies a number of these:

- liaising with public officials
- communication policies
- community relations
- media relations
- business sponsorship
- opinion forming.

In some instances events will need to be created to provide an opportunity for 'hospitality', which can be extended to the clients and customers of organisations. At other times they will take the form of participation in conferences and exhibitions, the themes of which are relevant to the functions of a company.

Kurdle and Sandler (1995) outline a number of common events. These include:

- celebrations of the organisation's or event's anniversaries
- launching new events, programmes or attractions
- awards for volunteers, staff, participants, art, etc.
- celebrations when awards are given to the event
- donations to charities (e.g., presentation of the cheque)
- groundbreaking for new developments
- celebrity and VIP visits
- fund-raiser galas
- contests.

E-marketing

It has been widely accepted that the last decade has witnessed explosive growth in internet technology.

The dot.com phenomenon has become a feature of most businesses. Consumers, buyers and suppliers are being connected as a product of the e-business revolution (O'Toole, 2003). Companies can now reach consumers almost anywhere in the world at very low cost, while consumers can easily find product and company information. Some writers have even suggested that the internet and its associated tools have revolutionised marketing, computer, telecommunications and information technology. With all the technological advances, the way business is conducted has been altered dramatically. Hoffman (2000, p. 1) has described the internet as 'the most important innovation since the development of the printing press'.

There appear to be at least three different sources of marketing changes. First, the internet is altering our culture and how customers react to marketing stimuli. Second, the internet is changing the way businesses operate and as a result the speed and style of marketing are changing. Third, this new way of communicating has given rise to e-marketing or internet marketing.

E-marketing can be defined as the use of the internet and related digital technologies to achieve the marketing objectives and to support the modern marketing concept (Chaffey et al., 2003). These technologies include internet media and other digital media such as cable and satellite, together with the hardware and software which enable its operation and use.

Because of e-marketing, the nature of how partners interact has also altered (O'Toole, 2003). Discussing information technology from the point of view of relationships, McWilliams (2000), stresses that it is challenging the power balance in many relationships. For example, the creation of online communities has challenged firms to respond to strong, more vocal, united consumer groups.

Additionally, interactive television (t-commerce) facilitated through new WAP technology is yet another example of the remote interfaces through which customers will be able to interact with their suppliers.

Electronic customer relationship management (e-CRM)

Another way in which the internet can be used effectively is to market an event to loyal customers by using the concept of relationship marketing, as discussed in the previous chapter. By applying the concept of relationship marketing to the internet and associated technologies, event organisers have been able to manage their relationships with customers. This is known as electronic Customer Relationship Management (e-CRM).

One of the most talked about topics of the new millennium, e-CRM has become the number one focus as today's competitive markets are getting more saturated and competitive. Kelly et al. (2003, p. 241) define e-CRM as follows:

e-CRM refers to the marketing activities, tools and techniques, delivered over the internet (using technologies such as websites and e-mail, data-capture, warehousing and mining) with a specific aim to locate, build and improve long term customer relationships to enhance their individual potential.

Much of what is called e-CRM these days is focused solely on improving the functional efficiency of online interactions with customers; indeed, commercial websites are often judged by their functionality. Being inexpensive, efficient, convenient and accessible may have been differentiating factors a few years ago but customers now expect all this as standard and it is difficult to exceed their expectations.

Therefore, according to Brown (2000, p. 161), there are many challenges in moving to a truly electronic customer relationship management environment, including:

- *Consistency*: developing an integrated interaction channel strategy
- *Balance*: getting it right between self-service and agent assisted interaction
- *Technology*: adopting the right technology at the right time
- *Change management*: recognising that there is a radical change
- *Customer expectations*: gauging customer expectations on a web-based service
- *Legacy of the customer care environment*: avoiding building on a foundation of sand.

Brown (2000, p. 185) further warns that merely bolting on a web-based interaction channel to a current call centre operation is unlikely to succeed if customers perceive it as exactly that. Further, unless optimisation of the operation across the board in respect of customer interaction is achieved, then the full benefits possible from e-CRM will not be gained, and indeed a detrimental effect to the customer experience is possible and perhaps likely.

Key analytical CRM applications include:

- *Sales analysis*: offering the organisation an integrated perspective on event sales and enabling the sales function to understand the underlying trends and patterns in the sales data

- *Customer profile analysis*: allowing the organisation to distinguish, from the mass of customer data, individuals and micro-segments

- *Campaign analysis*: providing the ability to measure the effectiveness of individual event campaigns and different media

- *Loyalty analysis*: measuring customer loyalty with reference to the duration of the customer relationship

- *Customer contact analysis*: analysis of the customer contact history of any individual

- *Profitability analysis*: measuring and analysing the many different dimensions of profitability.

As internet usage grows worldwide, the increasing availability of broadband in most homes will mean huge potentials for event organisers to communicate their events in a more innovative and sophisticated manner to an even greater audience.

Viral marketing

Viral marketing refers to marketing techniques that use previous social networks to produce increases in brand awareness, through self-replicating viral processes. This can be through word-of-mouth or online. The internet is very effective in reaching a large number of people rapidly.

Viral marketing on the internet can make use of blogs, chat rooms and websites designed to promote a new event. The purpose of viral marketing is to create media coverage using viral stories that are greater than the budget for advertising an event.

Viral marketing is becoming increasingly popular for the following reasons:

- it is relatively easy to carry out a marketing campaign this way

- effective targeting

- low cost

- the high and rapid response rate.

The main strength of viral marketing is its ability to target a large number of interested parties at a low cost.

Viral advertising assumes that people will share the interesting and entertaining content. This can be achieved through interactive games and images, funny video clips and text.

Through the use of the internet and e-mail advertising, organisations can have a greater impact in acquiring and retaining a large customer base compared to other marketing tools. Unlike spam, viral marketing encourages potential consumers of an event to tell a friend through a positive word-of-mouth recommendation.

SUMMARY

In this chapter the various functions of the marketing communications mix such as advertising, sales promotion, direct mailing, direct marketing, personal selling, public relations, e-marketing and viral marketing have been discussed. When deciding how to properly use the marketing communications mix to meet the marketing objectives, it is important to consider the relative strengths and weaknesses of each component of the mix. It should also be noted that marketing communications is most effective when each of the functions is integrated to achieve the overall aims and objectives of the marketing and thus the long-term goals of the organisation. In addition, the event manager should be knowledgeable about the different marketing communications functions so that he or she can effectively communicate the objectives of an event to the people responsible for the different functions.

Furthermore, the total budget (generally defined in the marketing and/or business plan) needs to be defined first and then the best leverage of the different elements of the mix to maximise the return on event organisation investment needs to be decided. The various parts of the mix should be balanced to not only create an integrated approach to the event marketing communications but also for enough resources to be set for each component to be successful.

Discussion questions

Question 1

Provide at least two event scenarios for your choice where you think integrated marketing communications have been deployed well.

Question 2

Discuss the relevance of PR for events.

Question 3

How can the internet be used effectively to market an event?

FURTHER READING

Hill, D.J. and Gandhi, N. (1992) 'Services advertising: a framework to its effectiveness', *Journal of Services Marketing* 6: 63–76.

Kelly, L.L., Gilbert, D. and Mannicom, R. (2003) 'How e-CRM enhance customer loyalty', *Market Intelligence & Planning*, 21: 239–248.

Kitchen, J.P. (1999) *Marketing Communications: Principles and Practice.* London: Thomson Business Press.

Kurdle, A. and Sandler, M. (1995) *Public Relations for Hospitality Managers: Communicating for Greater Profits*. New York: Wiley.

Mortimer, K (2002) 'Integrating advertising theories with conceptual models of services advertising', *Journal of Service Marketing,* 16 (5): 460–468.

CHAPTER 9

Event sponsorship

This chapter will look in detail at the sponsorship process of events. What are event sponsors seeking to achieve? It will discuss the tendering and pitching of ideas and concepts to secure support, involvement and funding.

Introduction

Essentially this chapter will investigate the relationship between sponsors and the events industry. It will outline the guiding principles for developing and presenting a sponsorship package in line with particular types of events. A clear distinction will be made in denoting the various types of sponsorship levels within a sponsorship deal. The scope required to demonstrate sponsorship within the events industry will be taken from a local, national and international point of view. The chapter will also look at the new and emerging trends in sponsorship allocation across the events sector.

To fully recognise and interpret the context of sponsorship and its role within the events sector, this chapter will attempt to explain the issues with the use of events past and present.

What is sponsorship? Sponsors' objectives

Sponsorship over the years has been developed and is now considered as a specialist area within the marketing framework. Many organisations today employ what is known as a 'sponsorship manager'. This position is taken up by an individual who may also have a team of people who look at supporting events as part of the company's strategic vision. On the other hand, we also have organisations that may employ an individual to acquire sponsorship as part of the event's financial and operational requirements.

Sponsorship comes in many forms and guises. This area is crucial for understanding the type of events one has and the areas that could be covered with goods and services.

Not all sponsorship deals look to increase the market share or competitive edge for the company product or service directly. Indirectly some companies will sponsor to maintain a public image. An organisation may find it necessary to maintain their public image by associating their product/service to a particular event.

However, sponsorship is also applied when an organisation is faced with unacceptable/negative publicity and therefore adopts a strategy to maintain an acceptable level of public image.

Cadbury, the chocolate confectionary company, saw its milk chocolate sales slip 2.5 per cent in 2006 on the back of a salmonella scare, with a recall of 1 million chocolate bars and an estimated £30 million loss to the company. Cadbury's ten year relationship with *Coronation Street* – a British TV series – came to an end in 2007. It was a relationship that had gone from strength to strength and had achieved marked success for both organisations. It was the biggest in financial contribution and the longest TV sponsorship deal in British history. However, what this shows is not a direct cause and effect scenario of negative impact on a business and its decision to relinquish its sponsorship relationship with a TV series, because we do not have the necessary data to make that claim. But there is still room to see a cause and effect situation between Cadbury's relinquishing their deal with *Coronation Street* and a drop in sales due to bad publicity via a food scare in chocolate production. An understanding of the economic landscape through research allows a potential company to be removed as a target for sponsorship for the present.

What this leaves is competition from the big food chains in the UK bidding for the sponsorship rights to that TV series.

With sponsorship we also have ethical and political issues that should also be taken into consideration when researching potential companies.

Sponsorship acquisition in its true form within the events industry looks at seeking out an appropriate sponsor or sponsors to meet the combined strategic vision of the event and sponsoring company, and in particular where financial assistance is a necessary business requirement for the short- to long-term sustainability of the event.

Securing support, partnership and a strategic alliance

The combined strategic vision is the level of knowledge and work required to develop a business partnership. This will be looked at in more detail throughout the chapter. Within this model the chapter will demonstrate how to identify an appropriate company with a particular type of event.

When undertaking any type of sponsorship research it may be prudent to obtain historical data on the type of events previously sponsored by the intended company. One may not be able to obtain the level of financial assistance given to events overall. However, there are some routes where financial information can be obtained. Company accounts, if published via Companies House, could indicate a degree of statistical data on this point. Internal/external newsletters may also carry this information. Company websites along with local or regional newspapers, where the event has a public image, civic pride or newsworthy appeal, might also contain articles with the relevant information. Industry-related trade magazines may also give a specific viewpoint. These are just some of the areas where information can be obtained and may help to build up a picture of the type of events and financial assistance given as part of the sponsorship deal. This invaluable information, when analysed, could demonstrate a profile on events sponsored, the frequency of sponsorship deals, the length of sponsorship deals and any financial assistance given. Where the event draws on local authority resources or is a local authority event, information on it should be in the public domain. The Freedom of Information Act 2000 requires public authorities to disclose information in order to promote greater openness and transparency. Therefore, information should be accessible through the local authority or stored at the local publically-funded library.

This case study will investigate the different types of sponsorship arrangement and the trend towards sponsoring an awards ceremony within a business context.

On the back of London winning the 2012 Olympics in 2005, the office of the Mayor of London set up an event entitled Sport Industry Interviews. This event ran for the first time in 2006. The purpose of the event was to address the UK's the sport industry business leaders and stakeholders on the key milestones, challenges and opportunities ahead.

In the pre-publicity information posted on the web from the Mayor of London's office, a sponsorship package outlined the sponsorship opportunities available for sponsoring the 2006 Industry Interviews.

Within the package it clearly defined the different type of sponsorship levels and the benefits attributable to each option.

This was an invitation-only event with approximately 260 places; it was aimed at CEO/Director-level key decision makers in sport. Part of the event is the sports industry awards, described by the media as the 'Oscars of the sports world'. In previous years the award ceremony received coverage from the BBC, ITV, Sky and national newspapers. This type of extensive media coverage enhanced the sponsorship package on offer.

There are a number of reasons why an organisation would deem this event worthy of sponsorship. To establish the saleability of this event it is necessary to profile its constituent parts from a potential sponsor's perspective.

- It is linked directly to the 2012 London Olympics.

- It is organised and represented by the Mayor of London.

- There is media coverage from three national broadcasters and various national newspapers.

- There are networking opportunities with major decision makers in the sports industry.

- It includes 260 hand-picked delegates attending by invitation only.

- It is an established event with a recognised awards ceremony.

- The awards represent the largest sport business event in Europe.

These seven points are considered to be the sponsorship pitch. This information would be translated via printed media or verbal communication to potential sponsors. Alongside this information the event profile will have a sponsorship package that would outline the different levels of sponsorship deals. These deals are closely linked to the financial commitment from a potential sponsor. The different deals within the package will give an indication of the level of exposure prior to, during and post event. The level of sponsorship is calculated on the cost of hosting the event and the economic value of media coverage in all areas. Levels of sponsorship deal generally fall within three categories. For this particular event there was one headline sponsorship deal and another multi layer of deals for the awards ceremony. As a headline sponsor an organisation can have complete confidence that no other company is competing within the same arena. Exclusivity is given to the headline sponsor. This would be demonstrated by areas within the venue where branding opportunities are given. Press and media coverage would also carry the headline sponsor on all communication associated with the event for a given period of time.

It is essential to remember that each sponsorship document must be constructed around the specific and general opportunities that can entice a potential sponsor. Marketing – advertising along with credible presentation – is what makes the sponsorship package a saleable item. In constructing the package one may wish to consider a particular business sector, with a strategic vision that can propel a company's product/service towards a wider audience through their association with the event.

Major sponsorship deals

Major sporting events such as the Commonwealth Games and the Olympic Games can only occur with a substantial level of financial funding. Financial support for the Olympic Games dates back to Ancient Greece, when prominent citizens gave financial support. The Olympic Games also received funding from the state, as the Games do today when hosted by the world's nations. In 1924 in Paris, advertising hoarding made its first and last appearance. Four years later Olympic rights were extended to other sectors. It is now possible for companies involved in brewing to open bars/restaurants within areas where spectators are. Advertising did return to the Olympic Games but not inside the competition areas. In 1936 at the Berlin Olympics, television made its first appearance. In 1947 at the London Olympics, television rights were assigned for the first time. In 1994, the Los Angeles Olympics were marketed as the beginning of an organised contribution to sponsoring the games by groups of companies. The International Olympic Committee (IOC) set out a marketing plan and divided it into three categories: Major Sponsor, Official and Official Supplier. Thirty-four companies acquired contracts with the IOC as official sponsors, 64 companies acquiring the right to supply and another 65 were granted authority to use the Olympic symbols. The Los Angeles Olympics television rights were bought by 156 countries. At the Seoul 1988 Olympics it was decided to reduce the number of sponsors to increase the value of the rights. The 1992 Barcelona Games continued the reduction of companies acquiring rights. In 1996 the Atlanta Games turned the whole organisational structure upside down. All expenses were covered by private funding, through TV rights, sponsors and ticket sales. Television viewers came from 214 nations and 11 million more tickets were sold than at Barcelona and Los Angeles combined. The Sydney 2000 Games only received 63 per cent of expenses through sponsorship; the rest was provided by the Australian government. It is evidently clear that major sporting events around the globe rely heavily on corporate sponsorship. It also demonstrates that sponsorship over an historical timeframe has developed and become an enormously complicated mechanism in driving a product/service to potential consumers on a global scale or in maintaining the continued presence of a major sporting event. The concepts highlighted earlier for major sporting events have also been grafted onto many of our national and regional events in numerous business sectors: the demarcation of categories within the sponsorship profiles, the selling of TV rights to acquire substantial revenue, funding from regional and central government along with associated agencies. Elements such as exclusivity deals and service deals are now entrenched within many of the sponsorship proposals/packages in the marketplace today.

External influences affecting sponsorship deals

The marketplace for acquiring sponsorship does not operate in isolation and can be very fragile. It is prone to fluctuations and is influenced by geopolitical events. A downturn in the global economy through political or economic market forces will have a direct effect on the stock markets.

Any economic fluctuations, emanating from various parts of the globe can carry a short- to long-term impact on the available financial revenue from corporate organisations listed on the stock markets. The departments within a business most affected by these situations are marketing and advertising, where the revenue spend will be curtailed. A geopolitical event such as the 9/11 attack on the twin towers in the USA in 2001 will have a major negative economic and ripple effect across the world. Due to the robustness of the global market and in particular the US stock exchange the world then did not experience a recession. There was a downturn in stocks for some businesses and the airline industry in particular. Companies laid off staff both at home and aboard and reduced their spending in many territories.

Event companies seeking sponsorship must be fully aware of the economic and political landscape before attempting to approach a business for sponsorship. Research is essential; it will save time and resources, a valuable commodity for most small to medium-sized event companies.

Within this sophisticated sponsorship market, we have what is called 'brand agencies'. Many companies today relinquish the responsibility of placing their product/service in a suitable marketing environment. This approach has been handed to brand agencies, delivered by 'brand managers'. They work on behalf of the client: in essence they become the gatekeeper for managing the product/service. These clearly defined processes require strategies for successful sponsorship proposals to have natural synergy with their intended audience. This must not merely be implied but well documented throughout. Brand agencies – as with clients on the whole – are looking for a return on their investment. Therefore, sponsorship proposals must demonstrate a strategy that communicates across all the communication channels, enabling sponsors to maximise their investment.

Within the events management tool kit for delivering a sponsor's message via a partnership relation, we now have what is called 'new media'. As stated earlier, events companies should look to maximise exposure and the return on investment for sponsors across all communication channels. It is not just a simple matter of branding on a webpage – it should aspire to become a fully integrated and interactive procedure whereby data can be collected and analysed with a view to establishing a method for customer relationship marketing. This will assist the events company and sponsor for future marketing campaigns; where long-term sponsorship deals are in place this method can help to solidify a working relationship.

With this audited data events companies can back up their proposal with facts and figures to attract future sponsors. Sponsorship has its heritage in marketing, advertising and public relations, and this area of business management works well when marketing campaigns fully recognise the target audience. The proliferation of new media has fragmented the consumer market. Therefore, targeting a consumer or potential audience can entail a sophisticated scientific approach. Audience profiles have become expansive with the digital media network through the web, digital satellites, cable TV and digital radio. These communication platforms have provided further delivery portals with the introduction of integrated mobile phones. It is essential for event providers to recognise the changing and developing technological landscape and to use – where appropriate – new media to enhance the event experience and acquire synergy with customers.

Naming rights – part of the marketing mix

Within the sponsorship portfolio are a number of income generating strategies. Naming rights is a concept that has its historical and commercial development firmly rooted in the USA and dates back over 50 years.

In defining naming rights one must look at the process in the first instance from the sponsors' perspective. It is a tool to acquire intangible and tangible benefits by purchasing the space and length of time to apply a name to a facility, and: 'The global market for sponsorship naming rights on venue/stadia is estimated to be approaching $4 billion worldwide, with 75 per cent of the market in the USA' (Sports Business Group, 2001, p. 48).

Naming rights in the UK is a relatively new business concept. There has been a recent introduction in naming rights on sport stadiums within the UK football premier league. Bolton's football ground is called the Reebok stadium. In 1994 BT Cellnet signed a ten-year deal for £3.5 million with the Riverside Stadium, home to Middlesbrough football club. In 2006 Arsenal football club opened their new stadium with a £100 million naming rights deal with Emirates Airways – the largest naming rights deal in the UK at present. With exclusive worldwide rights the new stadium is officially called the 'Emirates Stadium'. This deal will conclude in 2020/21. This deal also includes an eight-year shirt sponsorship deal that began in 2006.

The introduction to the UK of naming rights sponsorship deals has steadily increased over the past ten years. However, the large financial spend is predominantly located within the sports industry.

Academy Music Group (AMG) is the UK's largest owner and operator of nationwide live music venues. This organisation was formally known as the McKenzie Group Limited. The management buy-out of the McKenzie Music Group in 2004 included the promoters SJM Concerts, Metropolis Music and MCD Productions.

Within the AMG business portfolio are a number of live music venues which carry the naming rights of Carling: Carling Academy Brixton, Carling Academy Birmingham, Carling Academy Bristol, Carling Academy Glasgow, Carling Academy Liverpool and Carling Academy Islington. Carling Academy Islington opened in 2003, and it is clear that AMG has a strategic direction to acquire and develop venues as part of their business strategy, with the inclusion of sponsors purchasing the naming rights for a set duration. It signifies a new direction for facilities owners and managers to support their financial business model with sponsorship revenue.

The Department of Culture, Media and Sport (DCMS) estimates the music industry as a whole contributes £5 billion to the UK economy annually. The music industry within the UK is relatively buoyant according to a recent report compiled by the Burns Owens Partnership and published by the DCMS, entitled 'Music Business Growth and Access to Finance 2006'.

> A balance of only 7 per cent of music business made a profit over the last financial year. However, profitability is concentrated within the older business in the survey, and within business involved in performing/composing and arranging/promoting/management. Record labels and publishers struggled over the last financial year, with a balance of 7 per cent these businesses making a loss. (Burns of Owens Partnership/DCMS, p. iv)

There are many factors that have contributed to the fall in profits for some areas within the music sector. The biggest factor can be seen from the digital revolution and in particular across the internet with downloadable music from legal and illegal websites. As is indicated from the report, the live music sector – and in particular management and promoting – is still a profitable business. This can be seen from the strength given to the business model from the three main partners and the offset of financial liability through sponsorship naming rights with Carling Lager, the biggest selling brand of lager in the UK.

Naming rights has also impinged on outdoor live music events over the years. From 1997 to the present day the Virgin brand has been working alongside this dual-sited V Festival. V-festival, Carling festival, O2 Wireless festival and T in the Park are some of the very few events that have effective naming right sponsorship deals in the UK.

Of the 100-plus outdoor festivals that propagate the UK landscape on a yearly basis, less than 5 per cent carry any corporate naming rights sponsorship deals. Evidently there is room for commercial growth in this area along with entertainment facilities.

It has been stated that the USA is coming to maturity as regards naming rights; existing deals have yet to conclude. Therefore, brand managers are looking towards Europe for future sponsorship development. Within the European market it is generally recognised that Germany has the biggest sponsorship market. With that in mind an event provider should be aware of the sea change for corporate sponsorship shifting its focus onto the European and global market, to major sporting events which rotate around the globe such as the cricket World Cup, the European football championship, the rugby World Cup and many more. These events assist in promoting awareness of international brands and the tangible benefits that sponsorship can bring.

CASE STUDY

CASE STUDY: DPERCUSSION SPONSORSHIP PROPOSAL

In 1996 the Provisional IRA undertook a terrorist bomb attack in Manchester, which resulted in substantial structural damage to retail units in the city centre. The result of the terrorist attack meant Manchester had to rebuild the areas worst affected. On the back of that redevelopment the people of Manchester came together a year later via a live music event in Castlefield's outdoor arena. This event was managed and produced by a local events company, Ear To The Ground. The 2007 event celebrated its tenth anniversary. The event is now known as Dpercussion. With that in mind, the event is now going through an internal process of restructuring and seeking financial assistance through sponsorship and government assisted grants. Previously, in the main it was supported financially by Ear To The Ground. As the event has developed and established itself within the city as a free live music event that celebrates the diverse music culture from all areas of Manchester and beyond, it has defined itself within the Manchester calendar of events as *the* free one-day live summer music festival. A number of companies over the years have associated their product or brand with the event, but not enough to secure long-term strategic security.

Ear To The Ground has set out a new process. The organisation has developed a sponsorship package, inviting potential sponsors to consider associating themselves for the long-term sustainability of the event.

Within this proposal they have adopted many of the aspects drawn from the marketing mix. The document began by informing potential sponsors of the history of the event and the potential audience figures for 2007. Specific information about the music content was also included, giving a flavour of the range of musical production. A catalogue of bands was listed who previously had their debut at Dpercussion. Apart from the music, the document also gave a description of the diverse forms of entertainment associated with the event.

Every sponsorship proposal included the audience demographics, a vital part of the decision-making process for any potential sponsor. This looks at age range, along with areas of interest, spending potential and life style, etc.

The attendance figure for each year was given with reference to a sustained incremental rise and the method behind this approach, to demonstrate the continued success of the event in reaching its target audience in Manchester and beyond.

(Continued)

(Continued)

As part of the visual layout to the document and where the event has a historical heritage it could have been considered appropriate to include some visual imagery to enhance the proposal. As indicated earlier in this chapter, when the term 'new media' was introduced, this could be used to explain the technological processes that could communicate the message beyond the usual marketing/advertising channels; within this document the organisation adopted some of the established methods of marketing juxtaposed with new media techniques. For example, the event was given a Myspace.com webpage with a facility to join and become friends of Dpercussion.

With the information from this particular site the events company can build a profile of their audience. Dpercussion also has a dedicated website with a facility to upload personal information. This audited information has ownership with the event provider under the Data Protection Act and is crucial to building a profile of the audience and the advertising campaign if required. It also allows the events organiser to communicate directly through e-mails with the target audience. Customer relationship marketing (CRM) has become an integral element within the tool kit for events organisers who produce and manage their own events.

Exclusivity deals through sponsorship and ambush marketing

The European City of Culture was awarded to the city of Liverpool after a successful bid to the European Parliament. The European Capital of Culture was launched on 13 June 1985. Over the years many cities within the European Union have been given the privilege of having the title of European Capital of Culture. The last time a British city hosted this event was Glasgow in 1990. This particular event is not without its financial requirements. Commercial sponsorship, local government funding, central government and associated agencies all donate financial assistance. The organising committee put together four categories within their sponsorship package, signifying the level of sponsorship and the benefits attributed to each. The first category is Official Partner, this category is limited to 12 companies, and with this a sponsor will receive exclusivity rights across all communication channels, including digital and print media. The Liverpool Culture Company responsible for the sponsorship agreements must ensure that no form of ambush marketing interrupts the sponsors' agreement at any of the events planned for this occasion. Ambush marketing is best explained as a way of usurping another form of adverting or marketing with another product or service without the authorisation or permission of the negotiated client. In essence it is obtaining free marketing/advertising rights. The value of a sponsorship deal is sometimes balanced on how well an organisation can ensure that exclusivity is applied. All major events are susceptible to ambush marketing, given the duration of the event, the scope and audience attendance at various locations. It may become difficult to manage consistently; Adidas achieved ambush marketing at the opening ceremony to the Commonwealth Games at the City of Manchester Stadium, when David Beckham, ex-Manchester United footballer, presented the Commonwealth torch to the Queen in the main arena, wearing a specially made Adidas tracksuit. Adidas was not listed in any format or arrangement within any of the sponsorship categories for the 2002 Manchester Commonwealth Games.

The second category is Official Supporter, and with this an organisation will be given the opportunity to enjoy full involvement in the Capital of Culture programme of events. In the first and second categories (but not the third and fourth), hospitality involvement comes with the sponsorship deal. It must be noted that hospitality has become a major element for any event experience. With some events, it is the integral part of the occasion. It could be supplying beer at an event, or a full three-course banquet as part of the celebration. Where hospitality has a role to play within the event experience, consideration should be given and various opportunities explored for commercial sponsorship. Sponsorship at the level it has been discussed in this chapter carries with it an immense knowledge of contractual negotiation to ensure that both parties are fully represented and achieve their desired outcomes. To present and manage a sponsorship deal, lawyers must continually draft and negotiate to conclude the process.

SUMMARY

The main focus of this chapter has been to illustrate the different types of event and assess the sponsorship arrangements, drawing upon similarities in the sponsorship proposals and how sponsorship can be obtained.

The chapter highlighted major iconic events such as the Olympic Games, and provided an historical journey charting the development of advertising, marketing and sponsorship deals in relation to these events. The chapter also made it clear that sponsorship acquisition and management has become a sophisticated and complex animal. This was indicated by way of presenting case studies around some high profile events, such as the Manchester Commonwealth Games, Liverpool's European City of Culture and a North West regional event titled Dpercussion. Cultural, sporting and music events were selected on the basis of their distinct differences, but illustrating similarities in many areas. One particular similarity was evident in how sponsorship deals are assigned various categories and associated benefits that meet each category. The chapter

(Continued)

> (Continued)
>
> also touched upon the emerging trends in sponsorship and, in particular, naming rights.
>
> An economic viewpoint was highlighted demonstrating the potential for growth within the UK and European market. This was not just connected to sporting and entertainment facilities but included some of the major outdoor live music events within the UK. In closing, the chapter stressed the importance one must place on the area of research, by an individual or an organisation, before approaching a potential sponsor.

Discussion questions

Question 1

Outline and discuss the various categories of sponsorship available within a sponsorship document and explain the need for differentiation in each category.

Question 2

Naming rights is an area within sponsorship that is a recent development within the UK market. What are some of the cost benefits to an organisation when considering naming a live music facility?

Question 3

Explain some of the global impacts that can have a negative effect on corporate sponsorship for major sporting events.

FURTHER READING

'Sport Marketing Around the World', *Sports Marketing Quarterly*, 2006, 15(3): 190–192. Available from Business Source Premier, EBSCOhost. www.ebscohost.com

International Chambers of Commerce, International Code on Sponsorship, prepared by the Commission on Marketing and Advertising 1992 www.iccwbo.org

How to Develop Effective Naming Rights Strategies: Executive Summary. Published by Sports Business Group 2001.

CHAPTER 10

The role of finance as a resource

The aim of this chapter is to provide clear-cut accounting terms for event managers/businesses, enabling them to became familiar with the financial management process. Financial management effectively controls growth and should be carried out by event organisations for the protection of creditors and shareholders and to keep each the company in business.

Introduction

All businesses are started to make profits. The principle of finance is concerned with everything to do with obtaining money for an organisation and recording and controlling how that money is being spent. The principle of financial management is to effectively develop growth and to protect creditors and shareholders by keeping each company in business. Finance is at the centre of every business and at the heart of management. The most important

point to remember for events managers, even if you have no direct responsibility for managing financial resources, is to be aware of the financial procedures that are used in a business organisation, particularly for those items
which cost money or generate cash money for that business.

In order to understand financial accounting, it is important to look at finance
as a whole and to see where it fits in with the organisation as an entire element.
The term 'finance' does not have an agreed definition, but a good definition is
provided by www.tutor2u.net

Financial accounts – a definition

Financial accounts are concerned with classifying, measuring and recording
the transactions of a business. At the end of a period (typically a year), the
following financial statements will be prepared to show the performance
and position of the business; the systematic recording, reporting, and analysis of the financial transactions of a business.

Traditionally, finance is split into four major accounting disciplines.

Traditional accounting disciplines

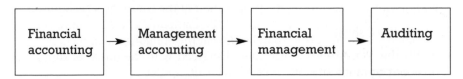

Financial accounting is a technique which involves recording the results and financial
position of a business. Financial accounting reports on how the organisation has performed in the previous accounting period or year. The information is based on what has
already happened. It is only concerned with summarising the historical data that have been
collected over the year. Financial accounting is mainly concerned with financial reports,
which are produced at the end of each period for external users and shareholders.

Management accounting provides information to managers for day-to-day decision making as well as for short-and long-term planning. Management accounting
produces detailed information for each department and is responsible for preparing
budgets and helping the managers and the board to set prices for products.

Financial management is a method used to analyse and predict future trends, to
help managers to make better long-term decisions for the organisation. In addition,
it helps management to decide where to obtain money and how to choose the best
options for the uses of the monies available to the organisation.

Auditing is an evaluation process for an organisation to maintain quality control and
also to provide an assessment of their internal control. The generic definition of an
audit is an assessment of a system, process, product and business. The
role of auditor is to carry out the financial audit as a part of the investigation. The

purpose of an audit is to determine whether financial statements produced by companies are fairly presented in accordance with International Financial Reporting Standards (IFRS), Generally Accepted Accounting Principles (GAAP), or by the individual countries' own legal requirements.

In the UK an audit is carried out under the Companies Acts 1985 and 1989. The annual accounts of a limited company must be audited by a person who is independent of that company. In theory, the company should appoint an independent person or an organisation who is chartered or certified accountants to carry out the annual investigation on accounts prepared by the company. The firm of auditors needs to report at each annual general meeting, stating whether or not the accounts prepared by the company show a 'true and fair view' of the company's accounts for the year end and highlighting whether the financial position is a good one.

Each year the auditor needs to investigate the accounts as prepared by the company and to then complete the report, explaining the work that they have done and the opinion they have formed from the investigation of the annual accounts. If the auditor agrees with the annual accounts, they will state that they carried out the work according to the companies acts' auditing standards and that in their opinion the accounts show a true and fair view. Within accounting terminology this is called an *unqualified audit report* (in other words, a clean report). If the auditor disagrees with the company's board of directors regarding the preparation of the company's accounts, it is the responsibility of the auditor to ask the company's board of directors to make changes and report to shareholders at the annual general meeting, setting out the concerns on which they disagreed with the board of directors. Under accounting terms this is called a *qualified report*.

Under the companies acts, the auditor needs to investigate and compile the report on the following financial statements:

- the Profit and Loss Account for the year end

- the Balance Sheet as at the year end

- the Financial Notes to the accounts at the year end

- the chairman's and directors' report for the audited accounts.

In addition, the auditor's report needs to be included as part of the final annual accounts for the company. Therefore, it is important that the auditor addresses reports to the shareholders, not to the directors of the company or anybody else within the company.

The regulatory framework

In the UK the preparation of financial accounts is governed by the Companies Acts 1985 and 1989, particularly for limited companies. The UK is a member of the European Union and companies need to comply with legal requirements as set out by the EU. The regulatory framework is based on two main accounting laws.

Company law

Company law provides the legal framework within which businesses operate in the UK. The Companies Act 1985 brought together all the previous Acts. This Act was amended on the enactment of the Companies Act 1989. The 1989 Act has repeated certain parts of the 1985 Act and has inserted new sections.

Limited companies are required by law to prepare financial accounts for each financial year for shareholders and other interested groups who are interested in the accounts. Under the Companies Acts, financial accounts need to be registered with the registrar of companies and available for inspection by any member of the general public. The published accounts need to be lodged with the registrar of companies within four weeks after the end of the financial year.

Limited companies are required to keep all accounting records and accounting files for each accounting period with Companies House. Under the Companies Act 1985 company directors are responsible for the preparation of accounts and for ensuring that these are delivered to Companies House within a given time period. If they are not delivered on time, directors can be penalised for late submission.

The annual return, which is submitted by a company, is a snapshot of company information giving details of its annual financial activities and providing information on its chairman, directors, company secretary, the registered office address, shareholders and share capital. Companies House sends an annual return form to a company's registered address each year asking for any changes that have occurred during the year and to check the details. The form needs to be signed-off by the company's secretary and returned within 28 days with a fee.

The legislation also requires directors to produce accounts which show a 'true and fair view' of the company's accounts for the accounting period and that highlight the financial position at the end of the period. The board of directors needs to sign off the annual accounts and the independent auditors will then attach their report. The accounts are presented to shareholders of the company in annual general meetings. Once the accounts have been adopted by members they are sent to Companies House for the registrar to file.

Accounting standards

In the UK, apart from company law, the key principles or regulations which affect accounting procedures are derived from guidelines issued by the professional accounting bodies. The accounting standards were devised in the UK and around the world due to a need to standardise the ways in which a company's accounts are measured. The accounting standards brought change to narrow the areas of difference between each company and their preparation and presentation of accounts, to eliminate any deliberate manipulation of accounts to show companies in a favourable light and to enhance comparability. The Accounting Standards Board (ASB) was set up in 1970 to crack down on the manipulation of published accounts that were being presented to shareholders. This was the first step taken by the UK government and professional accounting bodies to protect investors in the wake of accounting scandals. The Accounting Standards Board (ASB) introduced Statements of Standard Accounting Practice (SSAPs) for companies to follow in 1973.

Accounting Standards consist of the following four accounting bodies, after the recommendations of the Dearing Report 1990.

1 Financial Reporting Council (FRC)

2 Accounting Standards Board (ASB)

3 Financial Reporting Review Panel (FRRP)

4 Urgent Issues Task Force Statements (UITFS).

The financial reporting standards (FRS) are issued by the Accounting Standards Board. The ASB have revised the Statements of Standard Accounting Practice' over the last 15 years to FRS, some of the SSAPs have been superseded by FRSs, and some remain in force. Before 1990, SSAPs were the major accounting standards practice being used by companies. They did have a number of loopholes which were revised by the FRSs. Below are the main FRSs and SSAPs used by sole traders, partnerships and limited companies in the UK.

Financial Reporting standards (FRS)

FRS 1 (Revised 1996) – Cash Flow Statements

FRS 2 – Accounting for Subsidiary Undertakings

FRS 3 – Reporting Financial Performance

FRS 4 – Capital Instruments

FRS 5 – Reporting the Substance of Transactions

FRS 6 – Acquisitions and Mergers

FRS 7 – Fair Values in Acquisition Accounting

FRS 8 – Related Party Disclosures

FRS 9 – Associates and Joint Ventures

FRS 10 – Goodwill and Intangible Assets

FRS 11 – Impairment of Fixed Assets and Goodwill

FRS 12 – Provisions, Contingent Liabilities and Contingent Assets

FRS 13 – Derivatives and other Financial Instruments: Disclosures

FRS 14 – Earnings per Share

FRS 15 – Tangible Fixed Assets

FRS 16 – Current Tax

FRS 17 – Retirement Benefits

FRS 18 – Accounting Policies

FRS 19 – Deferred Tax

FRSSE (effective June 2002) – Financial Reporting Standard for Smaller Entities

FRS 20 (IFRS2) – Share-based Payment

FRS 21 (IAS 10) – Events after the Balance Sheet Date
FRS 22 (IAS 33) – Earnings Per Share

FRS 23 (IAS 21) – The Effects of Changes in Foreign Exchange Rates

FRS 24 (IAS 29) – Financial Reporting in Hyperinflationary Economies

FRS 25 (IAS 32) – Financial Instruments: Disclosure and Presentation

FRS 26 (IAS 39) – Financial Instruments: Measurement

FRS 27 – Life Assurance

FRSSE (effective January 2005) – Financial Reporting Standard for Smaller Entities

FRS 28 – Corresponding Amounts

FRS 29 – (IFRS 7) Financial Instruments: Disclosures

Statements of Standard Accounting Practice (SSAPs)

SSAP 4 – Accounting for Government Grants

SSAP 5 – Accounting for Value Added Tax

SSAP 9 – Stocks and Long-Term Contracts

SSAP 13 – Accounting for Research and Development

SSAP 15 – Status of SSAP 15

SSAP 17 – Accounting for Post Balance Sheet Events

SSAP 19 – Accounting for Investment Properties

SSAP 20 – Foreign Currency Translation

SSAP 21 – Accounting for Leases and Hire Purchase Contracts

SSAP 24 – Accounting for Pension Costs

SSAP 25 – Segmental Reporting

International accounting standards

In 2003 the UK government announced that from January 2005, all UK companies would be able to use the International Financial Reporting Standards (IFRS) as an alternative to the UK's accounting standards. In addition,

European Union law now requires all UK companies which are listed to use the International Accounting Standards (IAS) 2005 act, when preparing their financial consolidated accounts.

Trial balance

Definition

The trial balance is an act of schedule which lists all the ledger accounts in the form of *debit* and *credit balances* to confirm that total *debits* equal total *credits*.

The balance sheet and trading and profit and loss account are prepared from a list of the various balances, which are deduced from a trial balance. Traditionally, the trial balance is derived from the ledger accounts at the end of the financial year or accounting period. These accounts are drawn by the owner or the account for the business. The business accountant records every single transaction that take place in the business during the year.

In reality, the accountant or bookkeeper for the business will use a technique called 'double entry book-keeping' with which to write up individual transactions in the ledger accounts. The accountant needs to enter every transaction over the year twice in the books of annual accounts. This double entry process results in the forming of a trial balance for the business. In return, this equation balances both sides of the trial balance.

Total debit £ amount + total credit £ amount

Traditionally, businesses follow the following principles in preparing a trial balance.

- Find the balance of each account on the ledger account.

- Record the ledger account balances in the right-hand column of the trial balance.

- Once the ledger account balances have been recorded on the trial balance, total up each column.

- Total the two columns of the trial balance and compare then, to see if both totals match up with each other.

- If the totals do match then the book keeper or financial record keeper may have made a mistake in the ledger accounts.

This proves that debits and credits match the ledger accounts and offers the business the opportunity to assess if all individual accounts are correct and

	Dr	CR
Capital		77880
Purchase	51800	
Sales		81200
Motor expenses	800	
Office expenses	1280	
Premises	55500	
Motor vehicles	12500	
Fixtures and fittings	4000	
Light and heat	2880	
Debtors	18200	
General expenses	2100	
Creditors		24200
Bank	8700	
Cash	420	
Drawings	9100	
Stock at 1st Jan 2005	7700	
Salaries and wages	6600	
Rates	1700	
	183280	183280
	9600	

Figure 10.1   Trial balance for a logistic event as at 31 December 2005

accurate. It helps to provide the final accountant with clear and effective proof that the accounting information is correct and efficient for the year. It is vital for businesses that the correct debit balances have been entered into the debit column and the credit balances are entered in the credit column of the trial balance.

The trial balance is used by the accountant to collate the final accounts and at the same time utilises the legal framework to produce the final accounts that meet the requirements of the Companies Act 1985 and 1989. Figure 10.1 shows a worked-out trial balance for a sole trader.

The balance sheet

The balance sheet is one of the main documents to provide information about the financial state of a company. A balance sheet is a snapshot of the company's financial situation at any given moment in time. It is one of the financial statements that limited companies and PLCs produce every year for their shareholders.

Essentially, a balance sheet is a list of the assets, liabilities and capital of a business at a particular moment. In addition, the purpose is to show the financial position of the organisation on a certain date during the year. Under the Companies Acts 1985 and 1989 the balance sheet needs to be produced at the end of a company's financial year.

Fixed Assets	£000	£000	£000
Land and building			xxx
Fixtures and fittings			xxx
			xxxx
Current Assets			
Stocks	xxx		
Debtors		xxx	
Cash in hand	xxx		
		xxxx	
Current Liabilities			
Creditors		xxx	
Bank overdraft		xxx	
Net current assets			xxxx
			xxxx
Long-term Liabilities			
Long-term loan		xxx	
			xxxx
Capital			
Capital as at 1 January 2005			xxx
Profit for the year to 31 December 2005			xxx
			xxxx

Figure 10.2   Balance sheet as at 31 December 2005

Figure 10.2 shows a typical layout of the balance sheet for a sole trader.

Traditionally, a balance sheet is divided into two halves: the top half of the balance sheet shows where the money is currently being used in the business and the bottom half of the balance sheet shows how the money has been raised by the business.

Fixed assets

Long-term assets are known as fixed assets. A fixed asset is an asset purchased for use within the organisation that helps the business to earn income from its use on a regular basis. Examples would be machinery, equipment, computers and so on, none of which actually get used up in the production process.

Fixed Assets = Property + Machinery + Equipment

Current assets

Short-term assets are known as current assets – assets which are used day to day by the firm. In the balance sheet layout in Figure 10.2, the fixed assets are followed by current assets. The current assets are items which are owned by the business. The aim with current assets is to turn them into cash within one year. In addition, current assets are continually flowing through the business at regular intervals. Also, current assets are ones that can be quickly changed to liquid cash. The current assets may include cash-in-hand and in the bank, debtors and advance payment of bills, stock and so on.

Current Assets = Stock + Debtors + Cash/Bank + Prepayments

The current assets are shown on the top half of the balance sheet, and the current liabilities are subtracted from them to show the net current assets.

Long-term liabilities

In a balance sheet, just like the fixed and current assets, long-term liabilities and current liabilities are shown separately. The long-term liabilities are debts which are not payable within the one year period. In the Companies Acts 1985 and 1989, limited companies must show the long-term liabilities by using the term 'creditors' (amounts falling due after more than one year). The amounts can be owed to suppliers, creditors, employees or the government. In addition, if the business receives money in advance of an event taking place, they have a liability to carry out the event or service.

Long-term Liabilities = Bank Loan + Long-term creditors

Current Liabilities

Current liabilities are the short-term debts of the business which are due to be paid within one year. The current liabilities are the bills that are due to creditors or suppliers. In the accounts of the Companies Act 1985 and 1989, limited companies must show the current liabilities by using the term 'creditors' (amounts falling due within one year).

Current Liabilities = Creditors + Accruals

Capital employed

The other half of the balance sheet includes capital employed. Capital employed is the debt owed to the business owners. The three main areas which are shown on the balance sheet under the capital employed are the amount invested by the owner(s) in the business and any profit earned by the business during the year. The final item includes minus drawings; the amount of money which has been drawn from the business by the owner(s) for personal use.

Moreover, capital employed is considered as a liability by company accountants; they treat that money as a liability, because the business owes

Sales		61409	
Less Cost of Sales			
Opening stock		8500	
add Purchases	37302		
less Discounts received	1222	36080	
		44580	
less Closing stock		8800	35780
Gross Profit			25629

Figure 10.3   The trading account

money to the owner(s). Finally, on the balance sheet, the owner(s) equity is shown as a liability.

Assets = Owners Equity + Plus other Liabilities

Profit and loss account

The profit and loss account differs significantly from the balance sheet. The profit and loss account is a record of the firm's trading activities over a period of time, whereas the balance sheet is the financial position at a moment in time. The profit and loss account is broken down into two different sections. In the next section the layout of a trading account for an organisation will be explained.

The purpose of the trading account is to measure the actual gross profit on trading of the business over the last twelve months. This is done by taking the total sales for the year minus the cost of sales (cost of goods sold: see Figure 10.3).

The purpose of a profit and loss account is to define the gross profit of the business by deducting from it all the genuine expenses incurred in running the business over the last twelve months and arriving at a net profit for the given period. There are a number of different types of expenses that are incurred during the year in a business cycle which are deductible from the gross profit.

The profit and loss account looks at how well the firm has traded over the time period concerned (usually the last six months or year). It shows how much the firm has earned from selling its product or service, and how much it has paid out in costs (production costs, salaries and so on). The net of these two is the amount of profit the business has earned. In the next section a profit and loss account will be explained for sole traders.

Historically, the profit and loss section of the trading and profit and loss account shows the net profit of the business for the financial year. The basic principle of a profit and loss account is to show the net profit which is left after all the relevant business expenses have been deducted from the gross profit.

To simplify the concept of a profit and loss account, the following formula can be used to calculate the net profit.

Gross profit – Expenses = Net profit

Gross Profit			25629
Less Expenses			
Lighting and heating	2557		
add accrued electricity	82	2639	
Wages		7565	
Rent and rates	5788		
add rent owing	559		
less rates prepaid	121	6226	
Telephone	223		
add accrued telephone	45	268	
Insurance	483		
less prepaid	56	427	17125
Net Profit			8504

Figure 10.4   **Profit and loss account**

As indicated in Figure 10.4, the expenses in the profit and loss account are the expenses that are incurred in the business over the last 12 months. These are expenses which are not included in the trading account. The expenses for a sole trader are not classified into any category, for the limited company expenses are classified into three main categories:

- Selling

- Administrative

- Distribution.

Figure 10.5 shows a typical layout of a trading, profit and loss account for a sole trader.

Accounting ratios analysis

The ratio analysis is the most essential information contained within financial statements, besides the trading and profit and loss account and balance sheet. The financial position of the business needs to be measured in order that the key stakeholders within the company are able to appreciate how the business has performed during the financial year. The only way you can enhance the understanding of the key stakeholders as to how the company is performing is through ratio analysis.

One of the major principles of ratio analysis is to be able to measure the performance and financial position of a company. Ratio analysis is a technique which compares crucial relationships between numbers in a readily understood form (usually a percentage). It is essential for the events organisation to carry out an evaluation of the performance of the business or event, to compare the profitability, growth, return on fixed and current assets, return

Sales			xxx
Less Cost of Sales			
Opening stock	xxx		
Add Purchases	xxx		
Less Closing stock		xxx	xxx
Gross Profit			xxx
Less Expenses			
Lighting and heating	xxx		
Wages	xxx		
Rent and rates	xxx		
Telephone		xxx	
Insurance		xxx	
Total expenditure			xxx
Net Profit			**xxx**

Figure 10.6 is an actual example of trading, profit and loss accounts and balance sheet, for the Logistics Events Company for the year 2005.

Figure 10.5   Trading, profit & loss account for the year ended 31 December 2005

on equity capital and the general expenses of the business within the industry. This will provide an opportunity for the company to compare the financial performances of the business with other companies in the industry. It is important to understand that ratios on their own are not particularly useful. You need to be able to compare ratios over time or against other ratios to be able to build up a useful picture of the performance of the company.

The ratio analysis is a key technique which compares company financial accounts to generate vital figures by using the following techniques.

- *Performance ratios*: include profit, capital employed and turnover.

- *Liquidity ratios*: concerned with the short-term financial position of the company.

- *Gearing ratios*: focus on the long-term financial position of the company.

- *Investments ratios*: concerned with the return for the shareholder.

Profitability ratios

These ratios help the business and key stakeholders to judge how well the firm's profit has performed over the last 12 months. Profitability ratios are expressed either in terms of the profit earned on sales or profit earned on the capital employed in the business. In addition, profitability ratios relate to a company's ability to earn a satisfactory income, and a company's profitability is closely linked to its liquidity because earnings ultimately produce cash flow. The key profitability ratios are discussed below.

Trading Profit and Loss Account, for the year ending 31 December 2005

	£	£	£
Sales			34949
Less Cost of Sales			
Opening stock		4569	
add Purchases	18422		
less Discounts received	1248	17174	
		21743	
less Closing stock		5721	16022
Gross Profit			18927
Less Expenses			
Lighting and heating	4146		
add accrued electricity	76	4222	
Wages		6947	
Rent and rates	2659		
add rent owing	403		
less rates prepaid	133	2929	
Telephone	176		
add accrued telephone	43	219	
Insurance	956		
less prepaid	65	891	15208
Net Profit			3719

Balance Sheet as at 31 December 2005

Fixed Assets			
Van			3571
Fixtures and fittings			8503
			12074
Current Assets			
Stock		5721	
Debtors		5150	
Cash at bank		6725	
Cash in hand		30	
Prepaid		198	17824
Current Liabilities			
Creditors		3048	
Accrued		522	3570
Working Capital (or Net Current Assets)			14254
			26328
Financed by:-			
Capital		29194	
add Net profit		3719	32913
less Drawings			6585
			26328

Figure 10.6   Logistics events

Type of Ratio	Ratio
Performance	Profit Margin
	Days Sales in Stock
	Asset Turnover
Liquidity & Gearing	Current Ratio
	Gearing Ratio
	Interest Cover
Investments	Earnings Per Share
	Return on Equity
	Dividend Yield
	Dividend Per Share
	Price/Earnings Ratio

Figure 10.7

Profit margin ratios

The profit margin ratio measures the level of profit compared to the sales of the firm for the financial year. It therefore shows the percentage profit on the sales. It can be measured as either a gross or net profit margin.

Gross Profit as a percentage of sales $\quad\quad \dfrac{\text{Gross Profit} * 100}{\text{Sales}}$

Net Profit as a percentage of sales $\quad\quad \dfrac{\text{Net Profit} * 100}{\text{Sales}}$

Return on capital employed ratio

The return on capital employed ratio measures the level of profit of the firm compared to the amount of capital that has been invested.

Return on Capital Employed $\quad\quad \dfrac{\text{Net Profit (before tax)} * 100}{\text{Capital Employed}}$

Liquidity ratios

The liquidity ratios measure the liquidity of the firm. The business needs to ensure that it has enough liquidity in place to meet all its commitments. The liquidity ratios show if the firm has sufficient assets to convert into liquid cash to meet the business commitment for 12 months and it is important for the business to not have all their assets tied up as capital.

Current ratio

The current ratio is calculated by dividing the current assets by the current liabilities:

Current Ratio $\qquad \dfrac{Current\ Assets}{\text{Current Liabilities}}$

Acid test ratio

The acid test ratio excludes stock from the current assets, but is otherwise the same as the current ratio.

Acid Test $\qquad \dfrac{Current\ Assets - Stock}{\text{Current Liabilities}}$

Gearing ratios

Traditionally, all businesses have to borrow money regardless of their size. If a company wants to expand they will often need to borrow money from banks or other financial institutions. In addition, most businesses will fund their investment from profits they have made from business over the years. The other means of investment is met by the issue of shares. In reality most of the investment is met by borrowing money from banks. The only disadvantage of borrowing money for business is that the business has to pay interest on the sum which has been borrowed regardless of whether the investment is a success or not.

The key stakeholders and potential investors will look at a set of accounts to assess how big that risk is, and will use gearing ratios analyses to judge business stability in the industry.

Shareholders' equity ratio

This ratio measures and determines how much shareholders would receive in the case of a company going out of business (liquidation).

Shareholders' Equity Ratio $= \dfrac{Shareholders'\ Equity \times 100}{\text{Total Assets}}$

Interest coverage ratio

This measures how easily the company can pay its interest out of its profit.

Interest coverage ratio $= \dfrac{Profit\ before\ interest\ and\ tax}{\text{Periodic interest charges payable}}$

Investment ratios

The investment ratios are key for current and potential investors and measure a standard return on an investor's equity.

Price/Earnings ratio

This ratio measures the market price per share to earnings per share and is useful for comparing the value placed on a company's shares in relation to the overall market.

$$\text{Price/Earnings ratio} = \frac{\text{Market price per share}}{\text{Earning per share}}$$

Dividend yield ratio

The dividend yield ratio measures the rate of return an investor gets by comparing the cost of his shares with the dividend receivable.

$$\text{Dividend yield ratio} = \frac{\text{Dividend per share}}{\text{Market price per share}} \times 100$$

SUMMARY

In this chapter it has been suggested that understanding finance is vital for events managers. Traditionally, there are three main forms of business organisations that exist in the UK: sole trader, partnership and limited company. The most important point to remember for events managers is to understand the principle of financial statements of a business and legal financial accounting concepts, which are governed by the Companies Acts 1985 and 1989.

The financial reporting standards (FRS) issued by the Accounting Standards Board have been changed over the last 15 years to close the loopholes left by the Statements of Standard Accounting Practice (SSAPs). Over the years financial reporting requirements have become more detailed and so updating is necessary to enhance the structure for large companies to report accurate information.

Finally, the ratio analysis provides comparison for events managers and organisers. The financial position of the business needs to be measured in order that the key stakeholders within the company are able to appreciate how the business has performed during the financial year in line with competitors in the industry. The ratio analysis provides investors with a clear and effective comparison of financial data for the company's financial activities for the year.

Discussion questions

Question 1

The following information was extracted from the books of V-2000 at 31 December, 2000. Prepare a Trading and Profit and Loss Account for the year ending 31 December 2000.

Sales	2,000,000
Purchases	750,000
Vehicle hiring cost	40,000
Trade debtors	23,500
Trade creditors	45,000
Capital	500,000
Security charges	65,000
Salaries	215,000
Lighting and heating	19,500
Stationery	559
Sundry expenses	89,000
Vehicle expenses	9,955
Postage	455
Telephone	5,690
Insurance	6,000
Rent	49,000
Equipment hire	104,500

Question 2

(a) Discuss the difference between 'capital' and 'revenue' expenditure.
(b) Discuss the role of ratio analysis and describe different types of ratios.

Question 3

(a) Explain the difference between financial accounting and management accounting.
(b) Critically outline the role of a balance sheet within private and public limited companies.

FURTHER READING

CAROL website for European, UK and Asian financial reports www.carol.co.uk

Dyson, J.R. (2007) *Accounting for Non-Accounting Students*, 5th edition. London: Pitman.

Fowler, F.J. (2002) 'An Emperical Test of Financial Ratio Analysis for Small Business Failure Prediction', *Survey Research Methods*. London: Sage.

Kotas, R. (1999) *Management Accounting for Hospitality and Tourism*, 3rd edition. London: International Thomson Business Press.

Weetman, P. (1999) *Financial and Management Accounting: An Introduction*, 2nd edition. Harlow: Financial Times.

Wood, F. (2005) *Business Accounting 1*, 8th edition. London: Pitman.

CHAPTER 11

The importance of fundraising and other sources of finance

OUTLINE OF THE CHAPTER
What is fundraising?
The role of fundraising within the events industry
Sources of finance
Fundraising strategies for events organisations
Summary
Discussion questions
Further reading

This chapter will look at the different sources of finance and the wide range of fundraising strategies available to events managers. This should enable events managers to understand, negotiate and make decisions regarding the financial opportunities that may be presented to them.

Introduction

Fundraising is one of the key financial tools which the events manager must adopt in order to survive in the industry. There is a popular misconception that 'fundraising' refers only to raising funds for charity, but it is a vital activity for any business regardless of its size or activity.

Fundraising includes both developing relationships with people who can provide support and ensuring that the event or organisation appeals to a wide range of funders who can finance it in the future. This two-pronged approach is the key to developing strategic, long-term relationships with donors, rather then simply raising funds for the current project or to address an immediate problem.

It is important for events managers to consider how they can raise the profile of an event or company in order to make it easier to raise funds from donors in the future. Donors may include a range of different organisations, such as public funders working to develop communities or private companies wishing to agree sponsorship.

Today's events managers play comparable roles and face similar challenges to those of business managers. They face both an uphill struggle to raise sufficient capital to set up or expand their businesses and to establish a budget for the business unit of their organisations (Goldblatt and Supovitz, 1999). In the UK, most businesses use fundraising techniques to raise the finance to support existing projects and to carry out new projects.

What is fundraising?

Fundraising is about management, ideology and political networking (CCBET, 2004). It requires the ability to sell an idea, and means not only raising money but also identifying people who support the organisation. The US National Society of Fundraising Executives (1996) defines fundraising as:

> **The raising of assets and resources from various sources for the support of an organisation or a specific project.**

Fundraising is undertaken in all sectors and all industries, since every business wants to increase its assets and resources in order to make a profit. Today, fundraising is big business for some people, particularly financial consultants. Financial consultants provide specialist skills and knowledge to small and medium-sized businesses to obtain donations from parent groups, government grants, business angels and boards of trustees or directors.

However, fundraising is itself expensive, since acquiring finance for a business or charity can be a time-consuming and difficult process. Fundraisers must invest time and effort if they are to develop long-term strategic alliances with potential donors. People generally either borrow from the bank or use their own savings to start a business; but it is rarely possible to sustain a business in the long run without a fundraising strategy in place.

The role of fundraising within the events industry

Fundraising plays a major part within the events industry; without it, cultural and corporate events would struggle to exist in the context of extreme competition from others in the industry. Fundraising has two functions within the events industry: it helps businesses to generate income and it also enables events organisers to develop relationships with potential donors and people who can support the organisation, both during the event and in the future.

Fundraising can take many different forms and it is important for event organisations to be familiar with various strategies before planning the specific fundraising activities for an event. The event and festival organiser needs to identify the right funding opportunity for their event and a mix of several strategies will increase the campaign's chances of success. It can take time to raise the profile of an event in order to attract funders. It also requires good coordination, planning and control to bring in the right donors and to create the excellent strategic planning and financial management processes that are necessary to support an event of any size or type.

Sources of finance

Events managers rarely have the pleasure and luxury of sufficient funds to sustain their current and planned business expenditure. However, they need to obtain sufficient funds in order to compete within the industry, and must therefore look to external sources of finance to meet their business obligations. Generally speaking, there are two methods of raising money for business development. First, there is business equity, which covers funds invested by the owner of the business, shareholders and any other interested parties. Second, there is debt, which is generated by borrowing the money through banks, trade credit or leasing. The business needs to pay this money back to the lender at some point in the future.

The most common sources of business funding are outlined below.

Internal sources of finance

Personal savings

Personal savings are most commonly used to raise funds for businesses. The savings invested are normally those of the business owner, partner or shareholder and this type of financing is frequently found in small businesses or businesses which in the early stages of their development. Investing substantial personal savings in a business can help to demonstrate commitment to external finance providers.

Sales of assets

Businesses may decide to sell some of their surplus fixed assets in order to raise funds for current or future projects, to expand the business, or to pay off debts. By selling fixed assets, the organisation can avoid borrowing, which would mean incurring interest charges and increasing the overall liability of the business.

Retained profit

Using retained profit is the simplest method by which a business can finance its own activities. The retained profit is the money which has been generated by the business in the past through net profit and which has not been spent on any other project or activity. Retained profit is typically used by businesses to help them to buy new assets or to expand in other ways. Sometimes business owners save profits to provide security during any difficult periods in the future.

External sources of finance

Bank loans

Borrowing money from the bank is the traditional method used by businesses to raise funds for their current and future projects. Interest must normally be paid on any money borrowed from the bank. There are different forms of bank loan which are available to businesses. It is generally more difficult for new businesses to secure cheaper rates of interest; these are usually only offered to reputable businesses with good track records. The business will need to repay the bank loan in regular instalments, with interest rates being set according to the Bank of England rate. Typically, banks charge businesses interest rates of at least 3 per cent above the Bank of England rate.

There is an endless range of loans on offer, to suit all types of business. These vary according to:

- the amount required by the business
- the length of time over which the business will repay the loan, and
- the type of interest rate being charged by the bank (e.g., fixed or variable).

Choosing the right type of interest rate is very important for the business in the long run. This can be difficult, since both fixed and variable rates have advantages and disadvantages. For example, taking out a fixed rate loan means that the company can accurately predict the size of the monthly repayments. On the other hand, repayments on a variable rate loan can fluctuate if the base rate changes in line with the Bank of England rate. In addition, the banks charge individual customers different rates, usually ranging between 3 and 4.5 per cent on top of the Bank of England rate.

Overdrafts

An overdraft is the most common form of debt available to businesses in the short term. An overdraft is easy to arrange and does not have a minimum borrowing term. It is a flexible method to use in order to finance a business shortfall over a short period. The money can be drawn down by the business fairly quickly and repaid over the period agreed with the bank. Normally, it is a relatively cheap form of finance available to business – though interest rates and the ease of borrowing will depend on the state of a business and on the history of a company. If a company has no previous track record, banks will require some form of security, perhaps involving the assets of the business or the personal property of the owner. Where a business uses its assets to secure an overdraft, this clearly limits its ability to sell these assets or to use them to secure any other sources of finance. However, if the business has a good track record, an unsecured overdraft facility is easy to arrange.

One of the main advantages of this type of borrowing is that the debt can be paid off at any time without incurring a penalty. On the other hand, an overdraft is repayable on demand from the bank. Since overdrafts are given and the interest rate is set according to the status of an individual account, new customers are normally charged more than long-standing customers. Overdrafts are one of the most expensive forms of finance, since the interest rate is usually higher than that set for medium-and long-term borrowing and a business arrangement fee of between 1 and 2.5 per cent of the agreed overdraft facility is commonly charged. It is therefore important to use the overdraft facility for a short period of time only.

Leasing

Leasing is the most common method of obtaining assets, such as back stage equipment, vehicles or computer equipment, without immediate large-scale capital expenditure by the company. Traditionally, the leasing company buys and owns the asset and claims any capital allowances due against them. A number of different types of leasing agreement exist within the market. The two most commonly used by businesses are:

- finance leases, and
- operating leases.

The finance lease is a form of loan repaid by the company in monthly instalments throughout and up to the end of the economic life of the product. An operating lease is an arrangement whereby the product is used by the company for less than its full economic life; the leasing company therefore takes the risk of the equipment becoming obsolete during this period. Normally, the leasing company will pay for the maintenance and insurance of the product.

The main benefit of leasing an asset is that the business does not have to pay a deposit or a large amount of money up front. This allows the finance to be spread over time in monthly or quarterly instalments that are generally fixed and means that costs can be shared with other parts of the business. This can make it much easier for small and medium-sized companies to manage their cash flow and plan their use of capital over the year.

Business angels

Business angels are individual investors who provide finance to support either the start up or further growth of businesses which can demonstrate the opportunity for good future returns. Private investors are usually individuals who are prepared to make a long-term investment of £50,000 or more in promising businesses which are at a very early stage in their development. Business angels usually select local companies or those that are of personal interest in which to invest. Some business angels will also have specific knowledge of a business and can bring a great deal of added value.

Generally, investments by business angels take the form of share capital in exchange for a share of the business and its future profits. It is their intention to help the business develop and they may join the board of directors in order to safeguard their investment and provide support, knowledge and guidance.

Corporate sponsorship

Corporate sponsorship is another method of finance used by events and festivals. It may take the form of cash donations, goods or services from a large corporation in return for specific opportunities to promote their business. These may include using a corporate logo on promotional materials, displaying a special corporate banner at the event or calling an event by a corporate name.

Formal stock markets

The formal stock markets method is the most efficient and proven technique used by large corporations to raise finance. Large organisations have a clear advantage over smaller ones since, once their listing has been established on the stock market, shares in the company can be bought and sold readily and thus become more stable and liquid assets. At the same time, being listed on the stock exchange provides individual shareholders and companies with a better rating on the stock market.

Moreover, once a company's shares are registered and held publicly on the stock market, the stock exchange will impose condition and rules upon the business, which the company's board of directors have a duty to follow by law.

In the UK, various types of stock market listings are available. The type of listing normally depends on the market valuation of the company being floated on the stock exchange. The traditional stock markets are as follows:

1   A listing on the Alternative Investment Market (AIM) for medium-sized companies.

2   A listing on the London Stock Exchange for large companies.

3   A listing on NASDAQ, a US market focused on high growth companies.

4   A listing on EASDAQ, a European market based in Brussels.

Debentures

A debenture is a loan which is given to an organisation for a long period of time by a wealthy investor. Money is lent on a secured basis and with interest rates that may be either fixed or floating. Debentures usually have a number of different conditions attached with regard to interest rates, security and, most importantly, the preferential treatment that debenture holders are given over external shareholders. The debentures are normally rolled over to future periods if the company fails to make a profit, however, even if a company makes a loss, they will still need to pay interest charges to the debenture holder.

Moreover, debenture holders have the right to receive their interest payments before any dividends or interest are paid out to external shareholders. Secured debentures are usually tied to one specific asset like a building or a particular activity, such as a special event.

Share capital

This is the simplest method by which a company can raise finance. However, this option is only open to those companies which are listed on the stock market. This method normally involves a permanent interest-free loan, given in exchange for a part share in the ownership and profits of the business. The share capital scheme is used by investors to buy shares in individual companies through the stock market without stipulating fixed interest rates for their investment. The only payment they will get is their share of the profit, in the form of dividends, at the end of the financial year.

There are a number of types of share capital in each company. The voting rights of shareholders at the end of the financial year are determined by the grade of shares that they own. The ordinary shareholders are the least powerful; preference shareholders have stronger voting rights and also receive their fixed dividend before any other dividends are paid out.

Government grants

Governments are normally very keen to provide support to businesses, both in the form of grants and through the provision of expert advice and information. It is in the public interest that new businesses are started and existing ones developed, since successful businesses provide employment and create wealth for a country by helping the economy to grow. To this end, the UK government has provided finance to companies over the last 30 years through cash grants and other forms of direct assistance.

Government grants have been made available through a number of different initiatives. Over the last decade, the government has created Business Link to help small and medium-sized enterprises with business planning, marketing and legal advice. Government grants are always attached to a specific purpose or project and it can sometimes be difficult for small and medium-sized enterprises to meet the government's criteria. The government applies very strict terms and conditions to all its grants and if a company does not follow the guidelines they may be required to repay the grant immediately. However, the government normally provides clear guidelines and assistance, so companies rarely break the terms and conditions.

Most government grants require businesses to match the public funds they are being awarded. It is important for a business to show that it can provide its share of the total amount before applying to the government for a grant. Businesses normally match funds through retained profits, owner's own funds, bank loans, or through partnership.

Fundraising strategies for events organisations

A fundraising strategy is a plan that sets out the funding need for an organisation, project or event, alongside the identified actions, timescales and possible funding resources to meet this need. (Pembrokeshire Association of·Voluntary Services, 2005).

Fundraising can take many different forms and a mix of several approaches will increase the campaign's chances of success. There are various sources from which an organisation can seek funds to put on an event, including individual donations, grants, corporate and business donations, partnerships or sponsorship.

The majority of contributions will come from individuals who believe in a project or cause. Sometimes a company may ask the relevant private, community and government foundations for a grant. Grants are donations or interest-free loans that are given to groups or projects in accordance with strict standards and procedures. In order to apply for such funds, an organisation must usually submit a formal proposal.

Corporate and business contributions provide the other form of fundraising. Creating a partnership with a business to receive cash, in-kind support, product donations or even employee involvement can be a smart move. Businesses of all sizes have resources to offer, if asked in a proper and timely manner. There are two main methods by which a business may donate funds: corporate underwriting is where a business provides cash to cover a specific item in the budget and corporate sponsorship involves the donation of cash, goods, or services by a corporation in exchange for specific marketing opportunities.

Direct-request campaigns are excellent strategies that can be used both to increase contributions and to spread the word about a project. Recently, the trend in fundraising has changed from individual involvement to mass communication and public participation. As a result, special events, such as parties, royal galas and international sporting competitions, have themselves become important fundraising tools. All of these events involve raising money, conveying the message about the project and, in many cases, they also provide valuable promotional opportunities to donors. However, those who organise such events must undertake a huge amount of planning, pay great attention to detail and put in a lot of hard work (McKoen, 1997).

There is an additional strategy which may be used to approach a different kind of target donor. This is known as an execution strategy and it involves establishing a fundraising committee by choosing people who have different skills and networks, and who will be energised and committed to creating a fundraising plan and calendar. Before drawing on its network of contacts, the committee has to develop a strong case for the event and identify the market segments of the donor base. The committee should devise a strategy for approaching potential donors; this should cover how to make the vital first contact and how to ask for money. The group would then identify possible sources and methods of corporate sponsorship (Michigan Business School, 2004).

Successful fundraising requires a regular programme of communication to keep the company visible to the target audience and potential funders. A range of media can be developed, including news releases, television or radio advertising, e-mail newsletters and a website. Such marketing strategies can have long-term benefits by building a relationship with the public ('friendraising') and saving time later by educating people now about the firm and forthcoming events. A good communication strategy will help a company to focus its energies on raising money (Freedman and Feldman, 1998).

Nowadays, fundraising for events can be a worldwide process, since international mass media enable people of all ages and a wide range of groups and organisations to access both the fundraising programme and the marketing of an event. As a result of this trend, many organisations in both the profit and not-for-profit sectors are turning their attention to the fundraising events business.

Fundraising through sponsorship and ticketing

Sponsorship is a central source of fundraising strategy for many large-scale events. In the last decade sponsorship has become essential to the events industry, providing the means to finance many events. In today's market sponsorship has also become an integral and recognised part of event operations, with many savvied sponsors fully exploiting the marketing opportunity, often through promotional activity, to enhance the consumer's event experience. Sponsorship managers have recognised that they need to adopt a much more hands-on approach.

Lee, et al. (1997, p. 161) define sponsorship as:

The provision of resources (e.g., money, people, equipment) by an organization directly to an event, cause or activity in exchange for a direct association (link) to the event, cause or activity. The providing organization can then engage in sponsorship-linked marketing to achieve either their corporate, marketing or media objectives.

It is very clear that large-scale events, such as music festivals and sporting tournaments like the Olympic Games, cannot take place without the commercial support that comes from sponsorship.

Generating revenue through ticket sales

Ticket sales are one of the major revenue generating strategies for the events organiser to adopt in the modern events market. Ticketing is considered to be the events organiser's main source of income generation at events. Ticketing helps businesses to overcome cash flow problems which are encountered by events. Therefore, selling tickets in advance can provide an organisation the opportunity to raise revenue early on and potentially to ease the short-term cash flow problem. The methods for selling tickets or charging conference fees in advance increase the opportunities for events organisations to take advantage of these for raising funds.

Over the years a number of large-and small-scale events have generated revenue by ticketing events. The following examples show the revenue generated:

- Ticketing at the Sydney Olympic Games in 2000 brought in AU$ 530.3 million in terms of revenue (IOC, 2005).

- The Edinburgh Festival in 2001 earned £1,996,472 in ticket sales (EIF, 2002) which represented 32.57 per cent of the total income of the Festival.

- Of a group of 11 cultural festivals held in the East Midlands in 2002 more than 40 per cent of the overall income generated was through ticket sales and represented over £300,000.

There are a number of difficulties with the ticketing concept, particularly in setting ticket prices. The event's attendees will be attracted to the event for several reasons, but one of the main reasons will depend on the price being charged for attending the event. Therefore, this can cause major problems, especially for the pricing strategies which are set by the events organisers to cover all the costs or to break even. The dilemma for organisers is to attract consumers to the event and at the same time to cover the cost. For this reason it is important for businesses to raise funds from other sources as well. Some of the common sources which can be used to raise funds follow.

Sales of merchandise

Brassington and Petit (2000, cited in Doyle, 2002 p. 262) describe merchandise as

A physical good, service, idea, person or place that is capable of offering tangible and intangible attributes that individuals or organisations regard as so necessary, worthwhile or satisfying that they are willing to exchange money, patronage or some other unit of value in order to acquire it.

Events can provide many opportunities for merchandise sales and this is yet another source of income. The most obvious use of merchandise is to generate direct income for the event through the sale of programmes, for example such as at the Edinburgh Festival. Merchandise sales are particularly popular at events as it is a way of combating their intangible nature. Another benefit of selling merchandise such as programmes is that advertising space in the programme can be sold or offered to sponsors, generating additional funds for the event organisation. A total of £219,164 was raised at the Edinburgh Festival through 'other' methods of income, of which programme sales constituted a large part (Edinburgh International Festival, 2002).

Donations

Donations are sums of money that are given to an organisation which do not require any privilege or service in return. In this way they must not be confused with sponsorship. Obtaining donations can also take a substantial amount of time, effort and resources. Donations often need to be requested, either from existing donors (a database listing previous donors would ease the process slightly), identified targets or the general public. Charities are the normal recipients of donations (Getz, 1997), which means this method of fundraising may not be particularly useful to other types of event organisations. Edinburgh Festival, however, does list donations in the same category as sponsorship in their accounts, suggesting that they do benefit from this area.

Broadcasting rights

Selling the rights to broadcast an event can be a major source of funding for an events organisation, although it is likely only to impact those organisers working on mega, or at least certainly high profile, events. For the Olympic Committee the sale of television rights is the single most important source of funds (Getz, 1997). Indeed, at the Sydney Olympic Games in 2000 the broadcasting rights brought in AU$ 1,132.10 million (IOC, 2005). The growth of internet broadcasting is also likely to create other important sources of income for the events industry (Allen et al., 2002).

There are some dangers, however, with attributing too much importance to broadcasting rights, in that the broadcasting schedule can become the 'master' of the event rather than the needs and expectations of the live audience (Allen et al., 2002; Bowdin et al., 2001).

CASE STUDY

FUNDRAISING FOR THE CHARITY EVENT – CASE STUDY : THE LONDON MARATHON

In 1979, the former British Olympic steeplechase champion, Chris Brasher, first witnessed the unique atmosphere of a marathon as over 11,000 people ran through the streets of New York. He then wrote an article for the *Observer* about the sight of people coming together for such an occasion, concluding with the question of whether London could stage such a festival. (Flora London Marathon, 2006).

Within a few months, Brasher had established a charity committee and the first London marathon emerged. The inaugural London Marathon proved an instant success on 29 March 1981. More than 20,000 people applied to run. Since that time the event has continued to grow in size and popularity, with a capacity 46,500 accepted entrants each year and in 2005 a 20 per cent increase over the previous highest figure with a record 98,500 UK applicants.

The London Marathon is the UK's top one-day charity fundraising event; an estimated £187 million has been raised for various charities since 1981. There is no other marathon in the world that comes close to the London Marathon in its mass appeal as a charity fundraising event. Tens of thousands of individuals, many committed runners, take up the event challenge in order to raise funds for charities close to their hearts.

As a fundraising event, one of the dominant images of the race is that of the thousands clad in fancy dress in support of charitable causes. Since 1981 it is estimated that over £200 million has been raised for charities world-wide.

The London Marathon Charitable Trust distributes all the profits made from the Flora London Marathon and other events to fund and part-fund recreational projects across the capital. Last year alone 37 projects across 28 London boroughs were allocated grants of between £8,000 and £500,000 (Lambeth Council, 2005). Since the first London Marathon in 1981 over £12 million has been given in grants to local community projects. Examples include sports equipment for schools and community groups, ramps and lifts to help disabled people enjoy sports, establishing nature trails and improving existing leisure facilities to meet one of the six objectives detailed by the race's founders, 'To raise money for the provision of recreational facilities in London' (SportEngland, 2006).

Race Director David Bedford said, Running for charity is now a key aspect in the world's biggest marathon. It's not only the runners that add color and excitement to the day; it's also the charity support teams who do so much to make the day as successful as it is. Some of them are on the course at 6 a.m. to get the best cheering points and maximum visibility. This support and everything else they offer their runners is very different to the way it was a few years ago. (RainbowTrust, 2005)

SUMMARY

Finance is vital to the existence of any business in the industry. In addition to bringing in money, fundraising also helps an organisation to develop relationships with the people who can support it. The basic sources of finance for any business include personal savings, debt, grants and earnings from business activities. Few business managers have the luxury of sufficient funds to sustain current and future planned expenditure. The approach to raising funds is not the same for each organisation, and this will vary according to the size and ownership of the business. Generally, the longer the business has been running, the easier it will be to acquire finance for it.

Businesses are funded from two main sources of finance: internal funding streams, including retained profit and the owner's own funds, and banks and other financial institutions, which are the principle source of borrowed money for businesses. These institutions apply very strict conditions before they agree to lend money to any organisation. Other approaches to borrowing include leasing, business angels, debentures and government grants.

Discussion questions

Question 1

Describe and discuss the main sources of financing for capital-investment projects.

Question 2

Discuss and critically evaluate how an events organisation can implement fundraising strategies for their current and future growth and development.

Question 3

'Where (and how) will we make money in the future?'

Discuss this statement by critically evaluating the strategies that have been implemented in the hosting of major events.

FURTHER READING

Brearley, R. and Myers, S. (1999). *Principals of Corporate Finance*, 6th edition. Maidenhead: McGraw-Hill.
Glautier, M. and Underdown, B. (2001). *Accounting Theory and Practice*, 7th edition. Harlow: Financial Times.
Journal of the British Accounting Review

CHAPTER 12

Costing and pricing strategies

This chapter will examine the accounting methods a company uses for its internal reporting and decision-making purposes to give events managers sufficient financial knowledge to manage the company.

Introduction

One of the most important aspects of management accounting is to provide managers and the board of directors of a company with information related to its costing. The costing information system records a lot more than simply who owes what to whom. Costing systems record the reason why money was received and more importantly record the reason why the money was paid out to individuals and other companies. The only way companies can do this is by analysing the cost accounting in a number of different ways to assess the costs. Cost accounting is a vital part of any company, regardless of its size or business activities. The board of directors or managers have the responsibility for planning and controlling the resources used by the company on a daily basis. For this reason it is important to have effective cost accounting systems set by events companies, which analyse the past, present and future data to assess the final results more efficiently.

Costing information is important because it helps managers to understand and know what selling price would lead to a profit. In addition, they must also know which product or service is more profitable than others or which areas to concentrate on to make cost savings in the future and decrease the expenditure on certain products or services. Moreover, cost accounting also provides a basis for managers to take effective action when costs and revenues are being incurred.

Classification of costs

Management accounting is a management information system for managers to analyse past, present and future data for decision making. Cost accounting is defined by the Association of Accounting Technicians (1990, p. 3) as:

> that part of management accounting which establishes budgets and standard costs and actual costs of operations, processes, departments or products and the analysis of variances profitability or dual use of funds.

Traditionally, the elements of costing for events organisations are classified as follows.

- *Historic costs*: these are costs that have already been incurred.

- *Future costs*: these are the costs that are going to be incurred in the future.

The two main methods of costing to divide the company's costs are fixed and variable costs and then between direct and indirect costs.

The organisation incurs a number of different costs when it produces products or carrying service; under the cost accounting system these costs need to be split in various ways. One way is to split them into fixed costs and variable costs.

Fixed costs

Fixed costs are not related to products or services. These costs are totally independent of a company's output. Fixed costs have to be paid out by the company regardless of whether it has produced any activity or not. The

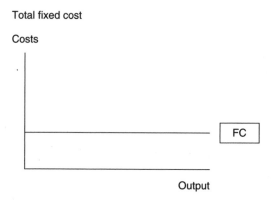

Total fixed cost

Graph 12.1   Fixed cost classification

fixed costs remain fixed for a period and are unaffected by the increases or decreases in the level of activity produced by the company. Fixed costs only change with the time span: as the span increases the fixed costs increase too. It is important for every company to have a successful business, as by keeping fixed costs under control a business can enjoy a very healthy profit and achieve successful development in the future. Graph 12.1 above demonstrates the fixed cost classification.

The most common fixed costs include the following:

- business rates paid to the local authority

- interest paid on bank loans

- rent paid for the use of buildings or venues

- staff costs for permanent members of staff

- company liability insurance.

Variable costs

Variable costs depend on the level of production or service being provided. The variable cost changes with the level of activity being carried out by the organisation. The variable cost is hard to control and is determined by the level of activity being produced or sold. It is important for managers to understand and control the variable cost. By controlling the variable cost it helps the organisation create more effective and efficient products or services. The variable cost for an event organisation will change with the size and type of event. It is important for event organisations to bear in mind that the larger the event or festival, the larger the variable costs will be to control. Graph 12.2 overleaf demonstrates the variable cost classification.

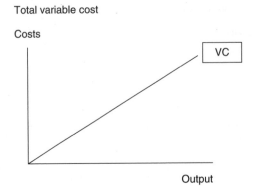

Graph 12.2   Variable cost classification

The most common variable costs include the following:

- hiring the venue
- printing marketing material
- advertising
- guest speakers
- weekly wages paid to the staff working on the event
- gas and electricity bills.

Managers need to bear one important element in mind regarding fixed and variable costs. The clear difference between fixed and variable costs lies in whether the amount of costs incurred will rise as the level of activity increases during the period of the event, or whether the costs will remain the same during the event, regardless of the level of activity.

Traditional cost-accounting concepts

When a costing manager or director looks at individual costs, it is important for the manager to analyse and classify these according to the purpose for which each cost is being used. The following are the most common cost accounting concepts the management accountant and costing managers are concerned with:

1   *Total cost*: the sum of all items of expense which have been incurred in the process of the event or festival or in providing a service to the customer.

2   *Standard cost*: the target or budgeted cost predetermined by the management or business prior to starting the event. The standard cost is estimated by the management

in advance and it is then compared to the actual *results* incurred during the event or activity.

3 *Marginal cost*: determined by the level of activity. The fixed cost under this concept is considered separately.

4 *Direct cost*: the cost which is directly related to the specific event or service cost being determined and assessed. The direct cost is easily traceable within the event cost: for example, direct costs, staff working on the event, security, equipment hiring and advertising for the event.

5 *Indirect cost*: the opposite of direct costs, indirect expenses cannot be traced to the finished product or event. These are costs which are incurred in the business or on the event from the start of the event until its finish . This may include office expenses which are not related to the event, or which may be related to another project or event: for example, salaries of company directors, rent, rates and insurance for the whole year. These cost items cannot be directly related to one particular event.

6 *Functional cost*: the cost which is classified as functional that relates to a specific event or festival and is attached to an area of operations in a business. This could be security, administrative, marketing, personnel and development costs.

7 *Controllable and uncontrollable costs*: the accounting method that provides management with clear guidelines in advance as to which costs are controllable and which are uncontrollable regardless of management action.

8 *Incremental cost*: incurred only when the individual event or project is undertaken. The incremental costs include both additional fixed costs and variable costs arising from the individual event or festival, besides the standard costs that are already being incurred by the business.

Marginal costing

In the marginal costing concept, only variable costs are charged as the cost of sales and contribution will be calculated by accountants. They will ignore fixed costs and overheads. Under marginal costing fixed costs are treated as a period cost and fully charged to the period in which they were incurred. The Association of Accounting Technicians (1990, p. 221) defines marginal costing as:

> **A principle whereby variable costs are charged to cost units and fixed cost attributable to the relevant periods is written off in full against the contribution for that period.**

It is impossible to calculate marginal costing without working out the contribution. The contribution is the difference between the revenue achieved during the event and the marginal cost of the event.

Table 12.1

	Volume	Per Ticket	Total
Sales	100	£30	£3000
Variable costs	100	£20	£2000
Contribution per ticket	**100**	**£10**	**£1000**
Fixed costs			£600
Profit and loss			£400

$$\text{Break-even point} = \frac{\text{Total fixed costs}}{\text{Contribution per ticket}}$$

Leeds Film Festival's break-even point

$$\frac{£600}{£10} = 60 \text{ tickets}$$

> **Contribution per event ticket can be defined as: Selling price *less* Variable costs.**

Total contribution can be calculated by businesses in the following format.

> **Contribution per ticket vs sales volume**
> **Contribution *less* fixed costs**
> **profit or loss**

For example, let's look at the operating statement set out in a marginal costing format. Leeds Film Festival Ltd hosts an annual event in Leeds, which has variable costs and fixed costs.

Moreover, marginal costing is a management accounting system for business managers to analyse the company's individual costs. The marginal costing distinguishes between fixed costs and variable costs and can be compared to the absorption costing method.

The advantages of using a marginal costing for pricing the product or service are as follows:

- marginal costing is simple to understand compared to absorption costing

- it provides managers and boards of directors with information for short-term decision making

- it helps businesses to focus on achieving the break-even point

- it calculates the difference between sales volume and variable costs

- it helps managers to avoid having to make different allocations for fixed and variable costs

- fixed costs are charged fully to the accounting period in which they have been incurred

- under marginal costing, by not charging fixed overheads to the cost of the production or event, the effect of varying charges per ticket is avoided

- marginal costing eliminates large balances overdue in the overhead control account and provides greater flexibility for management to control the overheads.

However, there are disadvantages to using marginal costing methods:

- under the marginal costing method it is difficult for management to raise the prices for event ticketing, if the contribution per ticket is set too low at the start of the event

- the marginal costing method can cause a high risk for management when setting the ticket prices, because it may not recover the company's fixed costs that are set at the beginning

- if the contribution is set very low at the start, it can result in businesses making a major loss at the end of an event

- dividing costs into fixed and variable is difficult to understand and sometimes does provide misleading impressions of the results to management

- the marginal costing concept does take into account stock and works in progress are understated: by not including the fixed costs in the actual event or service it can affect the organisation's profit.

Absorption costing

Absorption costing is the opposite of marginal costing. Under absorption costing the full cost is passed on to the event or service. It does not disregard the fixed cost from an individual event or service. In absorption costing, the fixed cost is included in the pricing of the events or services; under marginal costing the event or service is valued at the variable cost only.

The prime difference between marginal costing and absorption costing is that under absorption costing all the costs incurred during an event are allocated to particular costing areas, for example, direct costs, indirect costs, semi-variable costs and semi-fixed costs, etc. In addition, absorption costing allocates all the indirect costs more accurately to the specific cost area where the cost was incurred during the event or service.

For example, let's look at the operating statement set out in an absorption costing format.

Leeds Film Festival produced 120 tickets for the event
Direct production cost £10 per ticket
Direct labour £10 per ticket
Fixed costs are £600 a month £5 per ticket
Sales are 100 tickets at £30 per ticket

		Per Ticket		Total
Sales		£30		£3000
Cost of sales:				
Direct production cost	£10		£1000	
Direct labour		£10		£1000
Overheads		£5		£600
Total cost of sales	£25		£ 2600	
Profit and loss		£5		£400

The advantages of using an absorption costing for pricing an event or service are as follows:

- Under absorption costing the fixed production costs for events are incurred in order to make an output, therefore it is fair to charge all output with a share of costs that have been incurred during the event production process.

- Absorption costing is the technique which helps management to take into consideration all the costs that have been incurred during the production of an event or service, regardless of its nature. In particular, it takes into account the fixed costs, where marginal costing techniques ignore the fixed costs involved for each event or product.

The disadvantages of using the absorption costing method include the following:

- The fixed cost is carried over to the subsequent accounting period under the absorption costing technique.

- The absorption costing is dependent on the levels of output being put out by the business, which will vary from one accounting period to another.

- This practice does not provide clear and effective cost per unit prices, because it is depends on the existence of fixed cost overheads, which may not be related to the same period.

Contract costing

Contract costing is the name given to job costing where contracts are to be carried out at a sophisticated level between the supplier and customer. The company carries out a formal contract for each large contract work undertaken by the company.

Contract costing provides companies with an up-to-date picture of the expenditure and revenue associated with specific and large-scale contracts or projects. The majority of contracts will be carried out away from a company's head office, therefore it is important for organisations to keep separate records for each individual contract which has been agreed. From the accounting point of view, each contract or project will be regarded as a separate unit or product. Large contracts may take a long time to complete; the time period for large-scale contracts is hard to predict in the initial stages. For this reason it is important for companies to keep individual records for each contract.

However, the problems that may arise within contract costing involve the following:

1 adding overheads

2 identifying direct costs

3 dividing the profit between different accounting periods

4 difficulties of cost control

5 identifying indirect costs.

Therefore, it is important to have some clear guidelines in place and to use documents which can be implemented by the management to record the costs of the each contract. In addition, there are very specific rules laid out by the Companies Act 1985 for disclosing long-term contracts in a company's financial accounts. These rules need to be followed for internal management accounting purposes by management. It is important for any company to keep up-to-date accounts for each contract, as certain contracts may take a long time to complete. Contracts may be spread over two or more accounting periods. Therefore it is important to have a standard structure for each contract.

The structure of a contract

It helps to have a standard contract structure, which can be used by the managers to record the costs of the contract. The following format provides the standard for a normal contract.

• the period of the contract

• the specification of the contract

• the location of the work of the contract

• the agreed price for the contract

• the end product of the contract

• the agreed date for the contract to finish.

Once the structure of the contract has been agreed by both parties, it is important to determine the total cost for the contract. The contract costing can be worked in three different ways:

1 total cost for the project

2 pricing based on the stages of the contract

3 time scales for the contract.

Therefore, the central focus for the costing is to bridge the gap between customer and supplier by providing an up-to-date financial picture of the contract at each stage to both parties. In addition, the contract costing brings together both the financial accounting functions and the operational activities of a business. By anticipating the potential problems action can be taken to rectify a situation.

Contract costing is the main accounting method used by events and festivals organisers to bid for large-scale events or to sub-contract the work out to individual clients. This happens for example where large-scale contracts are undertaken in the events industry, such as the Commonwealth Games, FIFA World Cup, Olympic Games and large music festivals.

Break-even analysis

Break-even analysis is one of the most common techniques used by management accountants. Under this technique the costs are categorised into fixed and variable costs. The break-even analysis technique does not compare the total fixed and variable costs with sales values or the revenue for achievement points at which neither profit nor loss occurs. The break-even analysis is the point at which the sales revenue covers all expenses. At this stage no profit is being made by the festival organisers, but a loss will begin to show as soon as the sales revenue begins to fall below the break-even point. The break-even analysis provides clear and effective information to management about expected future costs and sales revenue for the decision-making processes. This technique is used by management accountants to help managers to plan the budgets for future activities.

The break-even point can be calculated arithmetically by managers or budget planners by using a formula of the number of tickets that need to be sold in order to break even as compared to total costs divide by the contribution per unit. The break-even analysis in formula terms is expressed as follows:

$$\text{Break-even point} = \frac{\text{Total fixed costs}}{\text{Contribution per ticket}}$$

or

$$= \frac{\text{Fixed costs}}{\text{(Selling price} - \text{variable costs per ticket)}}$$

Break-even points can be calculated by representing the figures as a graph. The various cost levels of activity are shown on the same chart as the sales revenue, variable costs and fixed costs. The festival's fixed costs and variable costs will make up the total costs (the straight line parallel with the X axis). The sales revenue will appear on the straight line through the origin of the graph. The graph below indicates the break-even point at the intersection of the revenue and total costs lines, as they appear on the graph.

Graphical approach to break-even

One approach to break-even (graphical approach)
The Real Festivals Limited sells events tickets at £100 each. They pay the festival organisers's company £60 for each ticket.
Office and administration costs are £4000 however many are sold.
With only a little thought we can produce a TABLE like this:

	Quantity	sold
	0	200
Sales (£)	0	20000
Variable costs	0	12000
Fixed costs	4000	4000
Total costs	4000	16000

The next step is to produce a chart from the figures in this table. Graph' demonstrates the break-even chart.

The importance of pricing strategies for events and festivals

In business terms price is a simple expression of the monetary value of a product, service or asset. Price is a very important tool for management and key to the marketing mix of a company to gain a competitive advantage. A pricing policy needs to be in harmony with an organisation's strategic goals and compatible with the market. Economists would argue that the price is an exchange strategy between goods or services that pays for the company's expenditure. It is important for events and festival companies to apply a pricing strategy that is achievable and accepted both by the market and competitors. Another theory of price, as stated by economists and marketers, is that the market price should reflect the interaction between two different concepts. On the one hand the price is determined by the demand consider-ations based on the marginal utility, an the other, the concept of price is determined by the supply considerations based on the marginal cost.

In general, the price is a simple method to calculate and allocate to certain goods or services: in reality it is not simple for companies to manage this.

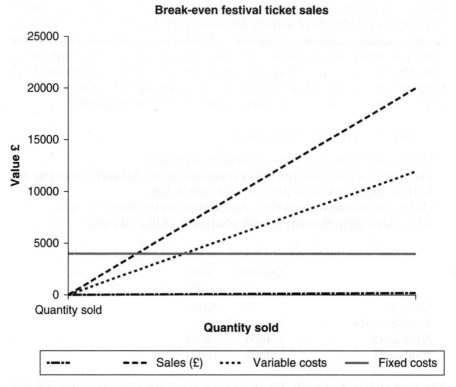

Graph 12.3

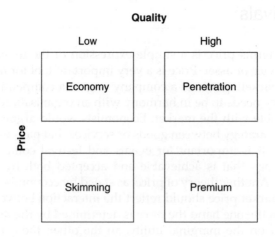

Figure 12.1   Pricing strategies matrix

Therefore, it is vital for events managers to understand and effectively use pricing strategies in order to set the price for events by managing the price in line with the industry.

Pricing strategies

Pricing strategies are an important part of any organisation. Therefore, when a company is managing prices they must keep in mind that the price they want to achieve for an event or service must be in line with their pricing strategy and objectives. An organisation can adopt a number of different pricing strategies, but it is important for them to check that their strategies are based on the objectives set for the given market. Moreover, once the pricing strategies are achieved according to company-set objectives, they must include a number of different segmented pricing strategies on how to gain a competitive advantage over competitors. To gain a competitive advantage companies need to adopt the following essential strategies to determine the actual price for an event or service.

Economy pricing

This method of pricing is known as a low price strategy and is used to attract a high volume of consumers. Under this strategy consumers will respond very positively to down turn prices. This will not work all of the time for a company, because competitors in a similar line will match the price cut, for example, student nights, supermarket brands and cinemas, etc.

Penetration pricing

The price is charged to gain a market share in a new market; once a company has achieved that market share will be, the price will be increased. This is quite common for new companies entering a market for the first time. This approach is used by new organisations, for example, nightclubs, low cost airlines, mobile phone companies, etc. for the following reasons.

1 The market share can be gained very quickly by a company, before its competitors can manage to regroup and launch their own counter attack.

2 It is very difficult for competitors to enter a market, due to the nature of the product or the event's life cycle.

3 A low profit margin will discourage competitors to enter the market. Under this method a company needs to produce a high level product or event, so it can be an uphill struggle for small and new entrants to gain a market share and a low profit margin will deter from competitors entering the market at any stage.

4   The low price will attract consumers very easily, because it will have a very positive impact due to quality/price ratios.

Skimming pricing

This strategy can be used by an organisation in the short and long term. This strategy is applied by organisations that have substantial competitive advantage over their competitors. A high price will be charged for exclusive and unique products, which have added value to the event or service compared with what competitors can offer. The high price is charged in the short term to take advantage of a new event or service being introduced into the market. In addition, a high price will attract new competitors into the market. Once other competitors have entered the market, the price will be reduced. A skimming strategy is then applied to skim off as much profit as possible from the sales at the beginning. There are several reasons for adopting this strategy.

1   The life of the product is expected to be short.

2   The company has a product or event monopoly (e.g., Glastonbury festival, Microsoft Windows).

3   The market segment is very small or very unique and it is not appropriate or profitable for other competitors to enter the market.

4   The company may have cash flow problems, which may require it to recoup cash very quickly to pay off debts.

Premium pricing

The price is set high at an early stage where there is an exclusiveness to the event or service. This method of pricing strategy is applied where a company has a substantial advantage over its competitors. For example, this method of pricing is charged for products or services such as Glastonbury, the FA Cup Final, first class air travel, etc.

However, besides the four main pricing strategies discussed above, there are several other pricing startegies used in the market.

Psychological pricing

A psychological pricing strategy attracts consumers into the market on an emotional basis. This approch is quite commonly used by nightclubs, supermarkets, and low-fare airline carriers to attract consumers.

Promotional pricing

The price is charged for a product or service which offers great value to the customer. This method is quite commonly used by companies to attract consumers to its business, for example, supermarkets, nightclubs, and retail outlets offering buy one get one free.

Exploring pricing methods for events and festivals

Events and festivals are an important part of any community. Besides being very informative, colourful and enjoyable, they provide important benefits to the local and business community. For these reasons, the pricing methods that need to be considered by events and festival organisers include the following pricing strategies, in addition to those above.

Cost-plus pricing

This strategy is used by organisations to calculate the price for an event or product by adding an appropriate profit margin to give the company a base price to charge, which can be altered later to meet the current market. This approach is quite simple to work with, but a company will need to have an appropriate knowledge of the market and management costs. This can be quite demanding for certain companies due to rapid changes in the market, therefore it may not reflect what is really happening to that market. For this reason this strategy can be very risky for new companies. Traditionally, this method is more appropriate for products or events with a stable and predictable demand, where the competitors are well known and are very limited in the market. For this reason it is imporatnt for events organisers to understand what is happening in the industry and to have a very clear and effective underpinning knowledge of costing and competition in the given environment. Finally, this method can only be applied for a short period of time.

Competitive pricing

This method does not always take into account the costing element. Competition plays a major role in determining the price for products or events. Where there is a very high level of market competition, where cost is not considered an important factor, the price will be set according to the nature and extent of the competition. If a company is facing direct competition for an event or product the price will be maintained for a long period of time to gain a market share of the consumers. In addition, if a company is facing indirect competition for its product or service, then there will be more scope for that company to vary the price and apply different marketing strategies to gain a substantial competitive advantage over its competitors.

Therefore, pricing decisions are based on the price set by competitors, and how they price their products or service. This can influence the pricing decision by a company's management: how they set a price for their product. For the management, a competitor's price serves as an important strategic point to determine how to set the price in future, in order to capture a larger market share. For the events industry it is important to determine the product or service price according to the competitor's. An events company can adopt the following approaches in order to address setting their price for the future.

- *Pricing above the competition*: normally companies using this method are perceived as market leaders in the industry, in terms of service quality, product features or quality and brand image, which will support them pricing above their competitiors.

- *Pricing below competition*: under this approach a company tries to keep the price below that of their competitor's, to reach a higher number of sales or output level.

- *Parity pricing*: some companies use this method to set their product or service price at the same level as a competitor's price at the initial stage, in order to capture the market.

These are some of the techniques that will be used by companies to set the price for their event. In the events industry it is important for a company to determine their price according to what its competitors in the market are charging, to maintain a high sales level in the initial stages.

SUMMARY

Cost accounting is a vital tool for any company, regardless of its size or business activities. The main aspects of cost accounting are to provide information which will be useful for the board of directors, managers and employees of the organisation. In reality the majority of them will not be trained economists or accountants. The other reason that cost accounting information is important is because it helps managers to understand and know what selling price would lead to a profit. When a costing manager or director looks at individual costs, it is important for them to analyse and classify the costs according to the purpose for which the cost will be or has been used.

Traditionally, costs are broken into direct or indirect costs. Besides that there are several other ways of presenting the costs. The types of costing classification used by managers depend on the purpose of the exercise. In addition, organisations will also use the marginal and absorption costing methods to calculate the final costs. The marginal costing method only takes into account the variable costing, whereas absorption costing takes into account the total cost.

Another technique which has been explored in this chapter is break-even analysis. This is the most common technique used by management accountants. In this technique costs are categorised into fixed and variable costs. The break-even analysis technique compares the total fixed and variable costs with the sales values or revenue achieved at which neither profit nor loss occurs. The chapter also discussed the strategies employed by companies to set pricing strategies for the future. When a company is managing prices they must keep in mind the price they want to achieve for an event or service and it must agree with the pricing strategy and objectives. An organisation can adopt a number of different pricing strategies, but it is important that these are based on the objectives the company has set itself to achieve in the given market.

Discussion questions

Question 1
Explain and critically analyse the importance of pricing strategies for the Leeds Caribbean Festival and other festival organisations.

Question 2
Discuss and evaluate the essential difference between the marginal and absorption costing concepts.

Question 3
Explain and critically discuss why contract costing is important for events and festival organisations.

FURTHER READING

Burns, P. (2005) *Corporate Entrepreneurship.* New York: Palgrave Macmillan.

Drury, C. (2004) *Management and Cost Accounting,* 6th edition. London: Thomson Learning.

Glautier, M. and Underdown, B. (2001) *Accounting Theory and Practice,* 7th edition. Harlow: Financial Times.

Journal of Business Finance and Accounting

CHAPTER 13

Captial investment decisions

This chapter introduces the relationship between profit and investment expressed through a measure referred to as the capital investment appraisal. Capital investment appraisal methods that consider the rate of return overcome the main weakness of the cost-oriented methods by focusing on profit and taking account of the investment necessary to generate that profit.

Introduction

This chapter provides a background to traditional capital investment appraisal methods. The capital investment appraisal looks at techniques which are involved in the long-term decision-making process. Capital investments appraisals mean that the money necessary for the proposed development or project is required by the organisation to implement at the initial stage. The returns for the project will not be recovered for a long period of time.

At the end of the capital investment's life cycle the assets bought with the initial equity will have little if no value, so the capital employed must be recouped from the returns before any profit is made. This is one of the major differences between investment decisions and financial decisions, which are based on controls and resources already existing within the company as apposed to its long-term future.

The role of capital investment decisions

Capital investment appraisals relate to the future and look at the ways in which an organisation can make a strategic financial decision on whether to invest in or decline a project. They also provide organisations with the opportunity to choose from a number of different projects to invest in. Capital investment appraisal techniques are used by accountants to analyse and collect the information for senior managers to make better decisions. In order to survive and prosper in today's economic market, events organisations must constantly adapt and change to gain a market share.

Events organisations operate in a dynamic environment and must gain a competitive advantage over their competitors through continual improvement. The development of large-scale events will require investments of capital expenditure to meet the demand. The amount of money can vary between businesses, for example it may be thousands of pounds for a small events organisation or millions of pounds for a large-scale events organisation, but the amount will be substantial in relevance to the organisation. This factor dictates that decisions on capital investment should be thoroughly explored and all options and consequences clarified.

Drury (2004) states that the proportion of an organisation's resources committed to an investment are often irreversible, increasing the risk for the organisation and putting a greater emphasis on the need for extensive analysis prior to a decision being made.

Investments usually involve the allocation or reallocation of resources to a project or product which will benefit the organisation. This could involve replacing equipment to improve efficiency or updating it, expanding the existing organisation through, office space or resources, or establishing a new area of business to gain a larger market share. Restricted capital resources will result in strategic business units (SBUs) within the company bidding against one another to have their proposal accepted. A successful proposal will gain not only the investment and development of that SBU, but will lengthen its product life within the organisation. In addition, capital investment decisions will cover a wide range of projects to produce cash flow for years. For example, the main type of projects may include:

- research and development projects
- the replacement of existing assets

- the expansion of existing services and products

- new services and products

- property

- large advertising campaigns

- social and welfare programmes.

Figure 13.1 below shows the four methods used by senior management in the industry. Each method will be discussed and examples will be provided showing how the calculations work and apply to individual organisations.

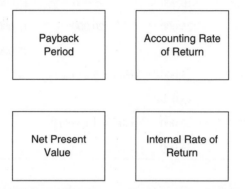

Figure 13.1   Capital investment decision-making method

The payback method

This is a simple method for calculating how long it will take before the cash inflow from an investment is equal to the sum of any costs incurred, including the initial capital investment. This method is the most tried and trusted method among managers and financial accountants. The payback method refers to the initial investment which has been invested in the project and provides analysis to management as to what date the investment will start to make a profit and when projects which meet the payback, in the target period, are accepted.

The payback period is calculated by dividing the total initial investment by the expected annual inflow. For example, if a company invested £100,000 and expected to have an annual income of £25,000, then £100,000 divided by £25,000 would have a payback period of four years.

However, if the cash inflow varies per year, as is likely due to demand, then the payback period is calculated using a cumulative total of cash inflows (shown in Table 13.1). The initial investment is shown as a negative and when the cumulative total turns positive the payback period has been reached. This often occurs part way through a year but the rounded estimation shown in Table 13.1 is acceptable due to the uncertainty attached to the prediction of future income.

Table 13.1 **Payback period calculation**

Year Cumulative		Project A		Project B	
		Annual	**Cumulative**	**Annual**	**Cumulative**
0	Cost	(100,000)	−100,000	(100,000)	−100,000
1	Cash inflow	24,000	−76,000	18,000	−82,000
2	Cash inflow	18,000	−58,000	26,000	−56,000
3	Cash inflow	21,000	−37,000	40,000	−16,000
4	Cash inflow	16,000	−21,000	14,000	−2,000
5	Cash inflow	16,000	−5,000	16,000	14,000
6	Cash inflow	25,000	20,000	11,000	25,000
		20,000		25,000	
	Project A: 5 +	5,000	years = 5.2 years*		
		25,000			
	Project B: 3 +	22,000	years = 4.1 years*		
		24,000			

Table 13.1 indicates a calculated payback period, describing how many years it will take to recover the original investment outlay from the cash flows resulting from an investment project.

The application of the payback period method from Table 13.1 favours the acceptance of Project B as the initial cost would be paid back in less time. However, this method also reflects that the higher total profit gained by Project A is lower than Project B.

Advantages and disadvantages of the payback method

Advantages:

- it is a popular method compared to other methods, due to its simplicity

- managers favour this method, as it is easy to understand and calculate

- it is more objectively based, using project cash flows rather than projected accounting profit

- it favours fast-return projects and reduces time-related risks for the organisation

- it saves management time otherwise spent in calculating forecasted cash flows for the whole of a project or event.

Disadvantages:

- the payback period does not take into account time or the value of money

- under the payback period rule, if the two projects or events are similar, the project or event which has a shorter time period will be chosen

- it ignores the end values of the project, prioritising and wealth maximisation

- it presents the problem of ambiguity: at what point do you start counting the cash flows?

Accounting rate of return

The accounting rate of return (ARR) can be defined as the ratio of average profits of the initial capital invested. The average rate of return also expresses the profit which has been generated from a project into a percentage after taking away depreciation. There is no clear definition for the accounting rate of return (ARR) and different authors will provide different definitions of profits and capital cost.

The accounting rate of return is also known as the 'return on capital employed' (ROCE) or 'return on investment'. These terms can be defined differently, thus causing some confusion.

Pike and Neale's (2006) defininition of ROCE indicates an organisation's efficiency in generating profits from an 'asset base'. ROCE is concerned with the comparison of profitability and capital employed within a single annum. This is likely to fluctuate, increasing in profitability as the project becomes established, whereas ARR finds the 'average rate of return', or annual percentage of profit, over the entire project's life.

In Table 13.2, Project B has a better ARR value than Project A, so it would be the preferred investment. However, Project B has a higher cash flow in the first three years so this would benefit the investor if they had high liabilities, as they could be paid back more rapidly.

The ARR technique has no concept of the life span of the project or its size. If Project B was extended into year seven, yielding a profit of £1,000, this would make the profit seem more attractive. However, the ARR declines from 8.33 per cent to 7.42 per cent as it is the average over seven years as apposed to six years. It also ignores the timing of cash flows as it works out the average profit per year even though the large returns may only occur in the latter stages of the project's life.

The previous examples use the average investment for the proposal, but an alternative ARR technique is:

$$\text{ARR (total investment)} = \frac{\text{Average annual profit}}{\text{Initial capital invested}} \times 100$$

Both are acceptable methods and give appropriate results when applied correctly, yet confusion can be caused if the same equation is not applied

Table 13.2 Accounting rate of return

	Project A	Project B
Accounting Profit	= £120,000 – £100,000	= £125,000 – £100,000
= (Σ inflows) – initial investment	= £20,000	= £25,000
Average annual profit	= £20,000 ÷ 6	= £25,000 ÷ 6
= accounting profit ÷ n years	= £3,333	= £4,167
Average Investment	= (£100,000 + £0) ÷ 2	= (£100,000 + £0) ÷ 2
= (initial asset value + closing asset value) ÷ 2	= £50,000	=£50,000
ARR (average investment)	= £3,333 x 100	= £4,167 x 100
= Average annual profit	£50,000	£50,000
x 100	= 6.67%	= 8.33%
Average investment		

routinely and to all proposals, as the result from each produces wide variations and could lead to a wrong investment decision.

Drury (2004) states that the accounting rate of return method is inappropriate as it is based on profits instead of cash flows and profits are not equal to cash flows because financial accounting profit measurement is based on the 'accrual concept'.

Advantages and disadvantages of the accounting rate of return

Advantages:

- it is easy to understand and calculate
- it is a popular method due to its simplicity
- the accounting rate of return makes it simple for managers and business planners to understand, because it is expressed in percentage terms.

Disadvantages:

- it ignores the time value of the money
- it ignores the timings of inflows and outflows of cash generated from the project

- there is no standard concept of calculating accounting rate of return

- it uses the concept of accounting profit, but profit can be very subjective and is not appropriate for the capital investment decision making, because cash is generated by the project

- it does not help managers to make an investment decision, because it does not give very clear and definitive answers.

Discounted cash flow methods (DCF)

The net present value method

The net present value (NPV) is one of the most important capital investment appraisal techniques being used by the industry. The net present value concept uses the cash flows which have been generated from a project: it is not based on the accounting profit. The net present value is the technique which places the value on cash flows generated from the capital investment project. The NPV applies the present value concept to calculate the cash equivalent of today to a later date when it will be received by the company from the capital investment project.

This concept of present value clearly helps a company to assess the wealth of project at the initial stage, by using the NPV technique to look at the cash flows expected in future years. The value of money varies over periods of time and between different nations. This concept happens due to changes in interest rates and inflation. It is important to understand the concept that the value of £1 in the future will not be what it is now. When calculating the value of capital in future terms, it is important to work out how much present capital will be worth in the future. This method ignores any depreciation as the full cost of the asset is treated as the initial investment so it would mean 'double-counting' the cost.

DCF can be worked out by the following equation:

$$PV = \frac{FV^{\,n}}{(1+r)}$$

PV: Present Value of a cash flow

FV: Future Value of a cash flow

r: The required rate of return/interest rate

n: The number of years until the cash flow takes place.

For example, Project A receives £21,000 in year 4 of the investment, so if this had a required rate of return of 5 per cent then the actual value would be:

$$\frac{25{,}000}{(1 + 0.10)^4} = £20{,}575$$

These manual calculations can become lengthy if the investment lasts for a number of years so discount tables containing annuity factors are produced by HM Treasury in *The Green Book* to simplify the method.

For the previous example, using this table and cross referencing, three years with a discount rate of 10 per cent gives the following equation:

£25,000 × 0.823* = £20,575

The Green Book shows the discount rate for four years at 5 per cent is 0.823.

This published discount rate contains a small margin of error due to rounding off but it makes the DCF method of appraisal a lot more accessible to non-accountants. However, it is advisable that a declining long-term discount rate should be used for investments over 30 years due to uncertainty about the future. These long-term discount rates are also shown in *The Green Book*. In addition, using a higher percentage can be used when calculating high risk investments to give a more cautious present value.

The two main techniques within the discounted cash flow group are: *net present value* and *internal rate of return*.

Net present value

The Net Present Value (NPV) appraisal method utilises discounted cash flow to estimate the current total value of future inflows compared with the initial investment. If – when the total cash inflow at present value is subtracted from the total cash outflow at present value – is negative, then the investment should not be made, but if it is positive an organisation should accept the proposal.

NPV explains whether the capital will be worth more if invested for several years or whether it be beworth more if lent to the capital market. Theoretically, this means if the NPV was zero then the investor should be indifferent.

The formula for calculating NPV is:

$$NPV = \frac{FV1}{1+r} + \frac{FV2}{(1+r)^2} + \frac{FV3}{(1+r)^3} + \ldots + \frac{FVn}{(1+r)^n} - I$$

NPV: Net Present Value

FV: Future value of cash flow

r: The required rate of the return/interest rate

n: The number of years until the cash flow takes place

I: The initial investment.

Table 13.3 Net Present Value with a 4 % discount rate factor

		Project A			Project B		
Year		Amount	Discount Factor 4%	Present Value	Amount	Discount Factor 4%	Present Value
0 80,000	Cost	−80,000	1	−80,000	−80,000	1	−
1	Cash inflow	20,000	0.962	19,240	19,000	0.962	18,278
2	Cash inflow	19,000	0.925	17,575	15,000	0.925	13,875
3	Cash inflow	20,500	0.889	18,225	36,000	0.889	32,004
4	Cash inflow	14,000	0.855	11,970	16,000	0.855	13,680
5	Cash inflow	12,000	0.822	9,864	12,000	0.822	9,864
6	Cash inflow	27,000	0.79	21,330	8,000	0.79	6,320
			NPV = 18,204			NPV = 14,021	

Table 13.4 Net Present Value with a 10% discount rate factor

		Project A			Project B		
Year		Amount	Discount Factor 10%	Present Value	Amount	Discount Factor 10%	Present Value
0 (100,000)	Cost	(100,000)	1	(100,000)	(100,000)	1	
1	Cash inflow	28,000	0.9091	25,455	21,000	0.9091	19,091
2	Cash inflow	23,000	0.8264	19,007	28,000	0.8264	23,139
3	Cash inflow	20,000	0.7513	15,026	38,000	0.7513	28,549
4	Cash inflow	18,000	0.683	12,294	15,000	0.683	10,245
5	Cash inflow	18,000	0.6209	11,176	9,000	0.6209	5,588
6	Cash inflow	35,000	0.5645	19,758	9,000	0.5645	5,081
			NPV = 2,716			NPV = −8,307	

By applying a discount factor of 4 per cent to Project A and B (Table 13.3) both have positive NPVs and should be accepted. When compared with a higher discount rate of 10 per cent, shown in Table 13.4, Project A remains acceptable yet Project B makes a loss. The NPV for Project A, using a discount rate of 10 per cent from *The Green Book* is shown in Table 15.4. The ARR method suggests that Project A would have a profit of £12,000 but the NPV approach shows that in reality the investment would only make a profit of £2,716.

Advantages and disadvantages of the net present value

Advantages:

- NPV allows management to compare and analyse a number of different projects with the same discounting factor
- NPV considers all the cash flows which have been generated from the projects
- NPV takes into account the time value of money
- NPV takes into account the risk of future cash flows
- NPV ensures that the organisation gains maximum wealth from the investment.

Disadvantages:

- NPV is very complicated to calculate and understand
- it is very difficult for senior managers to understand the concept of NPV
- it is difficult to apply the appropriate discounting rates
- NPV is time consuming.

NPV allows a decision maker to compare a number of projects with the same risk factor. A negative aspect is the assumption that the cash flows occur at the end of the year, which is often false. In addition, it is difficult to say that investment appraisal can give a definitive statement to a decision maker as to whether or not to invest in a project. The NPV merely acts as a guide for managers to analyse the future cash flow.

Internal rate of return

The internal rate of return (IRR) is one of the most important methods in investment appraisal techniques to analyse the future cash flow of the project. In other words, it is a capital budgeting method used by companies to make financial decisions about whether to invest in a project in the long run. The internal rate of return is used by managers to assess the positive return from an investment.

The internal rate of return calculates the capital investment return on each individual project. If the project produces a higher IRR than the rate of interest, it will help an organisation to make a better decision when comparing alternative options.

Moreover, the IRR can be defined as the discount rate which gives the net present value of zero to different sets of cash flows. The IRR is a method of working out the discount rate of a project. This can be used when there is a predefined discount rate and the decision maker wishes to know if the project meets or exceeds this target:

If the project's IRR exceeds the comparison rate (cost of capital) accept the investment; if IRR is less than the comparison rate, reject the investment. (Brayshaw et al., 1999, p. 63)

The IRR is calculated by calculating the value of 'r' when the NPV is zero.

$$\frac{FV1}{1+r} + \frac{FV2}{(1+r)^2} + \frac{FV3}{(1+r)^3} + \text{.......} + \frac{FVn}{(1+r)^{\Pi}} - I = 0$$

This equation is simple to work out if the project only lasts for a year by rearranging the equation:

$$\frac{FV1}{1+r} - 1 = 0$$

$$\frac{FV1}{1+r} - 1 = 0$$

$$FV1 - 1 = (1+r) = 1 + 1r$$

$$FV1 - 1 = 1r$$

$$\frac{FV1 - 1}{1} = r$$

FV: Future value of cash flow

r: The required rate of return/interest rate

n: The number of years until the cash flow takes place

I: Initial investment.

If the investment is for a period of two years the equation can be solved using a quadratic equation. However, when an investment is for several years the equation is a lot more complicated.

$$\frac{FV1}{1+r} + \frac{FV2}{(1+r)^2} + \frac{FV3}{(1+r)^3} + \text{.......} + \frac{FVn}{(1+r)^{\Pi}} - I = 0$$

This complex polynomial equation can be solved using computer programs. For example, Table 13.3 shows Project B with a positive NPV, with a discount factor of 4 per cent, and Table 13.4 shows Project B with a negative NPV, with a discount factor of 10 per cent.

Therefore the IRR discount factor must lie between 4 and 10 per cent.

IRR = 4% + (difference between the two discount rates × positive NPV)
$$\text{NPV range}$$

$$= 4\% + (6\% \times \frac{14{,}021}{22{,}328})$$

$$= 4\% + 7.8$$

$$= 7.7\%$$

This shows that for Project B to be accepted the discount rate, or rate of interest, must be below 7.7 per cent. In a stable economy this is possible but risk factors, such as reliance on demand, can be used in conjunction with discount factors. The IRR enables decision makers to calculate the level of interest that a project can withstand and competing projects with the highest resilience will have greater appeal. In addition, the IRR is a very difficult technique to use in the industry, due to the nature of the method and the practical difficulties attached to this technique of investment appraisal. NPV and IRR will usually show the same result when carried out on an investment proposal, and whether it should be accepted or rejected. The IRR, however, as it calculates the average discount per year, does not allow for different discount rates to be used in different years unlike the NPV.

Advantages and disadvantages of the internal rate of return

Advantages:

- the IRR uses the time value of the money
- the IRR is a break-even discount rate used by management accountants to analyse future cash flow
- the IRR method is more popular than the NPV method among managers
- the IRR is a method used by firms to minimise errors in the calculations obtained by using NPV.

Disadvantages:

- the IRR often provides unrealistic rates of return compared to the NPV
- the IRR expresses the return in a percentage rather than forms of currency
- The IRR is time-consuming compared to the payback method and the accounting rate of return
- The IRR ignores the scale of investment, as it only takes into consideration the percentage derived from the project.

Investment appraisal methods used in businesses

Over the past two decades research has shown an increased use in the more sophisticated methods of investment appraisal involving discounted cash flow, NPV and IRR. However, these techniques are still less popular in smaller companies. This may be due to the companies' lack of understanding or because smaller companies concentrate on short-term investments so they do not take account of the difference in the value of money.

Although the payback method ignores profits, it is still widely used in UK industry as it can be a comprehensive, simple argument used by a manager to convince others, who do not have a financial background, that a certain proposal should be accepted. This is emphasised by companies' focus on profits and projects with larger profits despite the decreasing value of money.

The proposed projects for investment can be independent (unrelated to the acceptance or rejection of other projects) or mutually exclusive (precluding the acceptance of one or more alternative projects). As resources are limited, however, projects may have to be adapted as capital is shared: this can endanger the effectiveness of an investment.

Accounting and managerial bodies and experts within financial investment have extensively considered this decision process, however, strategy texts will put a heavy emphasis on past financial analysis instead of ways to direct capital expenditure. Prior to carrying out an investment appraisal there must be a strategic need for the project, so any strategy is interlinked with the investment at all stages of the decision-making process.

The decision-making process in investment appraisals

When any decision is made, be it large or small, it will go through a type of decision-making process. The formality and time taken to carry out this process will vary in accordance to the implications of the decision and the investment required. For a non-biased capital investment decision a formal procedure should be adhered to and applied to each proposal to ensure the correct one is accepted.

Time can be a major factor in how the decision process is carried out. If a company is reactive, then they will want to reach a decision quickly to maintain their competitive advantage in a dynamic environment. However, if an organisation is proactive the time period will be extended as they are predicting changes and planning for them rather than making decisions after the changes have taken place. This is beneficial as they can apply a more extensive decision-making process and ensure that all the proposals are considered equally and any elements of risk are taken into account.

The first stage of the strategic decision process is identification. An organisation must realise the need for investment, which may be instigated through the dynamics of the external or internal environment. Analysis of the organisation and its current strategic position then enables a series of choices to be generated. This includes an analysis which can be used to predetermine how much capital resources the organisation can invest. These choices are developed into proposals by assessing their feasibility and their compatibility with the organisation's strategic direction and culture. After a screening process, a shortlist of proposals is produced that will undergo thorough analysis before a final decision is made and implemented. Capital investment appraisal methods will provide a quantitative analysis, giving a firm logical basis from which a decision can be made. However, it is also important to note that capital investment appraisal methods are only part of the final decision and that other factors must be taken into account as well.

Strategic decisions are subject to external and internal influences. This makes it difficult to come to a non-biased decision but by following a routine process it is more likely that a project that holds the greatest benefits for an organisation will be accepted.

The advantage of capital investment appraisal is that it can enable a company to set benchmarks and have a standard of comparison to help management to make better strategic decisions. This is due to an extensive proportion of businesses using the same investment appraisal techniques to enhance business growth and develop a benchmarking tool to measure the comparison with other competitors and internal managers.

Therefore, strategic management decisions involve making investment decisions by identifying, evaluating and selecting the projects that are likely to help the business to have greater impact and have a competitive edge. Capital investment appraisal can help senior management to make the right decisions and these techniques have been proven successful over the years. As Idowu (2000, p.1) states:

> The question to address is whether or not the future returns will be sufficient to justify the sacrifices the investing entity would have to make.

For this reason strategic investment decisions can help managers in all elements of cost benefit analysis and ensure that future capital can be raised through future returns to invest in the business for future growth. All decision making, be it large or small, demands a process. The formality and time taken to carry out this process will vary in accordance to the implications of the decision and the investment required. For a non-biased capital investment decision a formal procedure should be adhered to and applied to each proposal to ensure the correct proposal is accepted.

Time factors can be a major element for any decision-making process. In the modern events management market, decision making needs to respond quickly in order to prevent competitors from securing a market share, which will result in little benefit for a business. However, if an organisation is being proactive the time period will be extended and techniques like capital investment appraisal can be applied. A successful events company should have processes for both types of decision to ensure resources are allocated correctly, competitive advantage is maintained and future development projects are feasible. Capital investment appraisal can be initiated due to an environmental change or an idea development, so it can be used reactively or proactively. However, due to the nature of capital investments, in which a large amount of resources may be utilised and cost may be recouped over several years, the organisation must go through a methodical process to ensure the correct decision is made.

The identification of an investment need by an organisation is the primary step. This is achieved through a thorough internal and external strategic analysis of that company. A company analysis is an imperative preliminary to the evaluation of investment projects as this will determine the financial and other resources available.

It is important to note that a capital investment appraisal is only part of the decision-making process and other factors must be considered. These are often intangible and more difficult to measure.

SUMMARY

In order to survive and prosper in the economic market, event organisations must constantly adapt and change to gain a market share. Events organisations operate in a dynamic environment and must gain competitive advantage through continual improvement. The development of large-scale events will require investments of capital expenditure to meet the demand. The amount of money can vary between businesses, for example it may be thousands of pounds for a small events organisation or millions of pounds for a large-scale events organisation, but the amount will be substantial in relevance to the organisation. This factor dictates that decisions on capital investment should be thoroughly explored and all the options and consequences clarified.

In this chapter four traditional methods of capital investment methods have been explored and there are similarities between all four models. The NPV and IRR are more sophisticated methods of investment appraisal involving detailed calculations that take into account the time value of the money. However, these techniques are less popular in smaller companies; this may be due to the companies' lack of understanding or because smaller companies will concentrate on short-term investments so they do not take into account the difference in value of money.

Discussion questions

Question 1

Explain and critically evaluate the role of capital investment appraisal methods used in the capital expenditure in decision making.

1 pay back period

2 internal rate of return

3 net present value

4 discuss and distinguish between marginal costing and absorption costing.

Question 2

A company is considering two capital expenditure proposals. Both proposals are for similar products and both are expected to operate for four years. Only one proposal can be accepted.
    The following information is available.

	Proposal A	Proposal B
Initial Investment	46,000	46,000
Year 1	17,000	15,000
Year 2	14,000	13,000
Year 3	24,000	15,000
Year 4	9,000	25,000
Estimated scrap value at the end of year 4	4,000	4,000

Depreciation is charged on the straight line basis.
The company estimates its cost of capital at 20% pa.

	Discount factor
Year 1	0.833
Year 2	0.694
Year 3	0.579
Year 4	0.482

Required

1 Calculate the following for both proposals.

- the payback period

- the average rate of return on initial investment

- the net present value.

2 Give two advantages for each of the methods of appraisal in 1 above, and state the reason for which, if any, proposal you would recommend.

Question 3

What are the advantages and disadvantages of the accounting rate of return method of investment appraisal?

FURTHER READING

Alkaraan, F. and Northcott, D. (2006) 'Stategic capital investment decision making: a role for emergent analysis tool?', *The British Accounting Review*, 38(2): 149–173.

Brayshaw, R., Samuels, J. and Wilkes, M. (1999) *Financial Management and Decision Making*. London: International Thomson Business Press.

Butler, R., Davies, L., Pike, R. and Shaap, J. (1993) *Strategic Investment Decisions*. London: Routledge.

Drury, C. (2004) *Management and Cost Accounting*, 6th edition. London: Thomson Learning.

Lumby, S. and Jones, C. (2000) *Investment Appraisal and Financing Decisions*, 6th edition. London: Chapman & Hall.

CHAPTER 14

Event logistics –
an integrated approach

OUTLINE OF THE CHAPTER

Event logistics
Case study – human resource
External and internal factors affecting event logistics
On-site event logistics
Transportation logistics for events
Logistical challenges for the future
Summary
Discussion questions
Further reading

This chapter introduces the term logistics, and the chapter will give a definition of the term under current academic and industry thinking. The chapter will continue to explore, with examples and case studies, the relationship of logistics within the event management experience. Logistics as a business model will also demonstrate to the reader its direct association with customer satisfaction and its inclusion within the management term, business operation.

Introduction

The chapter will draw upon events across the industry spectrum to create an understanding of logistics' effective application to achieve efficiency and stabilise cost.

Logistics, under current industry thinking, looks at the movement of resources to areas/places where they required. It is the effective forward and reverse flow and storage of goods and services to achive customer satisfaction. Generally, it is explained as a freight management operation. Within this current thinking it has a direct association with supply chain management, inventory management and the supply chain. The chapter will explain these terms as a complete approach to achieving a logistical management framework and control.

Logistics has a direct historical heritage from a military perspective, dating back to the Roman Empire, when resources and people were moved over large geographical regions. However, this term still has usage and relevance within a modern day military framework. Over time there has been a refinement of the process and its adaptation within the business world. The process has now influenced event operations management in teaching and physical application. It is the physical and academic application of this subject area that will underscore the body of this chapter which will demonstrate this process through a representation of events.

To outline and explain this concept the chapter will identify events that have an element of sufficient logistical requirements.

Event logistics

Event logistics can be considered from a number of areas within the event planning process. The event planning process, as indicated in the previous chapter, outlines a horizontal process which includes all the main elements that make up the process for researching, developing, implementing and delivering an event. With this in mind a logistical framework is entwined within the event planning process. An organisation should develop its logistical requirements for the movement of products, plant/machinery, or people to a particular destination/location. This may also require the same identified areas to be stored (inventory) or returned to their original place of departure.

In the process of developing a logistical plan it is paramount to ascertain a number of variables that may have a direct impact on the logistical process. This point will be explained in more detail throughout the chapter. It isn't possible to protect the logistical plan from all the potential problems or issues borne out of unforeseen or completely random circumstances. However, you can manage the logistical plan if sufficient care and attention to detail are implemented consistently throughout, with a review process that allows for a continual updating of the plan.

Most organisations will appoint a logistics manager to develop, maintain control, track progress and amend any problems that arise. The logistics manager must implement a process to obtain information from each of the relevant departments/operational areas to allow for development of the plan. Areas such as financial management, marketing and human resources will become a necessary requirement in the management and delivery of the plan.

The logistical plan should never be considered as an independent operational process disengaged from the entire event planning process. The interconnected relationship between all areas will determine in from large part the success of the logistical plan.

Within the event management setting it has become essential to implement logistics as a management requirement, especially when working on mega events (Olympic Games) or hallmark events (Commonwealth games). The lessons learned and the skills acquired from these events have been well documented within the events management forum.

Therefore, an understanding of how and why logistics decisions are made and their impact on the organisation through the event delivery process will be investigated in this chapter. When developing a logistical plan for an event within an organisation, it is imperative to differentiate between procurement, purchasing and outsourcing within a supply chain management setting. All these aspects are essential elements within the event management process and will have a direct relationship on the success/failure of the plan.

First, we must identify each point and ascertain its relationship on the logistical plan. When an organisation sets out to procure, this involves obtaining goods or services from one location and moving these to another for the purpose of use at the event. The financial transaction around this process may also include hire purchase or lease agreements. It is essential to remember that this particular activity will be replicated a number of times for different goods or services. On doing so, this particular activity will develop into what is commonly known as a 'supply chain'. Often, an organisation will have a number of companies supplying goods or services to an event over a given period of time and each company is thereby connected in creating the supply chain. The procurement process has no definite time span, and for a single event it can be implemented one or two years in advance. With that in mind and long-term planning as a requirement, it is ever-more prudent to negotiate terms well in advance. It is therefore necessary from a financial point of view to establish a method of payment in line with inflation. Once this has been secured from the event management financial controller and the outsourced company it will become a joint operation to ensure that the delivery of said goods or services arrives at the event and, if storage is a requirement, that it remains at the location ready for its intended use. As indicated earlier, outsourcing has become a fundamental business requirement for events companies. Therefore it is necessary to recognise and implement systems that ensure the logistical process does not implode in on itself because of disconnected levels of internal business communication. The logistics manager must secure from the accounts manager/financial controller the required sum of money to intact a process of procurement and payment terms. Service agreements, warranties and insurance, etc., will remain in the area of control of the operational manager and logistics manager. Documentation, as mentioned above, if not supplied prior to solidifying the procurement deal may hinder the logistics process. Other departments within the business should also engage with the logistics process. Human resources may be required at various stages within the procurement, delivery and use.

Where agency staff are required for setting up a particular product the event company must ensure that the correct levels of staffing have been sourced/ requested and that the level of competencies for staff is in place to carry out the intended tasks over a particular staffing period in line with employment and health and safety laws. As the events sector continues to grow, staffing has and will become a bone of contention for many event providers. This is more so the case when sourcing staff from employment agencies. The availability of trained/competent staff and, in particular, at peak season will impact on an event if not considered at a very early stage. Where staff are required to work over a period of more than one day adequate accommodation should be booked in advance and payment terms with that accommodation agreed prior to arrival. This type of forward logistics planning allows the event manager to deliver the event as planned. The human resource issue will have a major impact on any event if this is not requested and sourced prior to the role of the logistical plan.

Purchasing within logistics has two main functions, consumption and resalable items. The purchasing of goods on behalf of an event can relate to the amount of people who may attend the event. This can be calculated on pre ticket sales, the capacity of the venue, and a previous knowledge of similar events. If potential customers are purchasing tickets on arrival the logistics manager will consult with the marketing team and investigate the strategy for customer awareness of the strategy. The latter is a less accurate method to calculate purchasing. However, if this is the only method available, a sale on return of goods if non perishable could be part of the purchasing deal. The operations manager, in association with the logistics manager, could also look at suppliers within the supply chain who are able to work on quick delivery on fluctuating demand (just-in-time). Demand base management where customer needs are reflected by the staffing requirement throughout various stages of the day and the different periods of the event.

The final game for the Cricket World Cup 2007 will have seen an increase in ticket sales, a demand in customer consumption of a perishable good. It is evidently clear that an increase in staffing procurement is essential to meet customer satisfaction. The ratio of staff and the number of potential customers for the sale of goods at key demand base moments will give a greater return on sales to the organiser and thus greater customer satisfaction.

Outsourcing at a logistics level has now developed to where a deficiency exists within the business/organisation or it is cheaper and more efficient to outsource. The International Cricket Council for the West Indies has nominated GL events as the official supplier for temporary structures and for all plant and machinery to erect, decorate and maintain for the period of the event. GL events is a UK-based company with an international profile in many areas of event management with a specialist knowledge, developed over time, in delivering corporate hospitality environments through the use of temporary structures. This gave them a market position to secure a working relationship with the ICC West Indies Cricket World Cup 2007. As part of delivering this event the ICC had to enact a number of outsourced requirements to meet the projects deadline. Each organisation will therefore have their own logistical issue to arrange in line with the event planning process.

CASE STUDY

CASE STUDY – HUMAN RESOURCE

Events such as the 2007 Cricket World Cup in the West Indies have many logistical human resource issues to cope with to deliver the event on time and to the requirement of the client, event organiser and consumers. This event was held over five islands throughout the West Indies. Apart from the overall management team with the core contingent from the five islands, resources for specialist skills in other areas had been brought to the event. Security, media, and event management, alongside a large contingent of local crew and voluntary workers, became the foundation by which the event developed in the pre event stage. With this model of human resources for the event, training with the adequate management of staff enabled the event to be completed and opened on time. This type of event resource would have been undertaken with the assistance of local knowledge by way of employment agencies and previous events held in the islands. This type of forward planning to meet the event schedule for erecting temporary structures primarily for hospitality use was carried out four months in advance.

As outlined earlier, the supply chain becomes the cornerstone of the logistics process and in particular where long-term event planning with suppliers is a necessary requirement. Therefore supply chain management, the control process to enable the supply chain to function without too much difficulty, must also be an integral part of logistics. In developing long-term business relationships with suppliers, the current industry trend looks towards a supply partnership. This particular thinking encourages suppliers to have a vested and shared interest with the client's strategic vision for a sustainable working relationship. Within a logistics framework this is an encouraging situation, where the long-term benefits to both parties can emerge over time. Procurement deals with third party suppliers will smooth over internal and external factors affecting both organisations. The Confederation of British Industry and the Department of Trade and Industry are now working closely to bring about supply partnership as a business philosophy across all industries both large or small.

External and internal factors affecting event logistics

The industry of event management has many business products within the entire field. We shall identify some events and assess the logistical factors that may have an impact on planning and delivery.

In some areas of the event management field, and in particular outdoor music festivals, logistical issue are based around seasonality factors, competitive pricing for suppliers, a high demand in the transportation network, and increased marketing strategies to bring about consumer awareness including temporary staff who are both qualified and non qualified.

The adaptation of a business to enact long-term partnership relationships to meet demand on a seasonality basis becomes a strategic function of the event planning process. Contractors are sourced at least a year in advance or are negotiated on a rolling contractual basis. This allows the main contractor if necessary to implement a supply chain to meet the clients' needs. These logistical supply chains are found at many large-scale outdoor events. Where one company is overstretched in the supply of goods or services in high season, the movement of goods and services via transportation networks becomes an essential logistical issue. Where goods may have been used prior to their arrival at the intended site, contractors may be required to undertake an inventory of goods at a designated location before sending them out again. Upon arrival at the location, if the turnaround did not allow for a full and complete inventory at the original place of exit, there must be a key representative on behalf of the company to assess the goods before transferring them to another event provider. Time allocated for drivers on the road, maintenance of vehicles to meet industry regulations, travel routes to ease traffic congestion, all become part of the logistics criteria.

Within a highly competitive industry some suppliers operate a fluctuating price strategy in line with demand and seasonality differences. This price strategy is also related to the fixed cost of the business along with replenishing old stock and ongoing maintance/repairs. Music festivals by design function within a high demand seasonal window. Therefore a higher cost for goods and service becomes the mainstay of the business relationship. In this type of environment it may be a necessity to develop supply partnership arrangements. In the long term this could stabilise costs and achieve continuity throughout.

On-site event logistics

This section will look at the specific elements that make up event logistics. It will assess the interconnected relationships on each management area for the delivery of a safe and successful outdoor event. Event logistics should be explained as on-the-ground activities in meeting event and customer expectations.

Communication, emergency planning, fire safety management, crowd management, on-site transportation management, waste management, venue site design, medical facilities/welfare, barriers and fencing; all these will be applied to an outdoor event.

On the selection of a suitable site for an outdoor event, there are many logistical issues to take into consideration. Site access for all emergency vehicles must be the first consideration. If the site is within a residential area consideration should be given to the local community in order not to disrupt local traffic where appropriate. If necessary the event provider should apply for road closure to those roads immediately adjacent to the site, with access allowed only for local residents and event traffic, to be applied and enforced for the duration of the event.

The event provider should also look at car parking for customers and staff. Where the event provider can negotiate deals with public transport suppliers bringing customers to the event, this should be considered: it will reduce carbon emission, lowering car transportation with ultimately fewer vehicles on site. National, local bus, rail and coach companies are the preferred options. Car parking on site should be outsourced, if affordable to an on-site traffic management company. They will have an obligation to liaise with the police, the highway agency and the local authority in developing a traffic management system for customers and staff.

When developing an emergency evacuation plan, of primary importance is the safety of customers attending the event. The plan should be constructed taking into account all the possible scenarios that could have a negative impact on customers. For instance, adequate evacuation routes must be clearly marked with stewards/security positioned at those exit points at all times during the event. Those routes must also be kept clear at all times. The emergency evacuation plan will be allied to the fire safety management plan. An emergency plan must also look at vehicle access to the site for all emergency vehicles. An evacuation zone should be located so that customers and staff have a safe place to relocate.

As stated, fire safety is closely linked with the emergency evacuation plan. It therefore concludes that all site layouts must have fire accessibility around and on the overall site.

Crowd management can be developed from a number of standpoints. First, one should develop crowd management strategies in line with the intended capacity and location. Further development will be consistent with amenities and basic facilities, such as toilets and food concessions. Areas of entertainment which make up the major part of the event must be given serious consideration. Where one has a main stage on site due diligence should be paid to the area immediately in front of the stage, with a considerable viewing area allowing access for emergency staff and security. Beyond that there must be enough square footage for more than 60 per cent of customers on site. However, this should take into account the other activities also running concurrently with the entertainment on the main stage. Therefore, scheduling activities throughout the site must allow for the movement of large numbers of people from one location to another, without adding to bottlenecks or congestion points. The free flow of people throughout the site will be a test of the scheduled entertainment within the main arena. The location of basic amenities will assist in this process. During the closedown of the main arena further announcements should be made via display screens if available or by strategically placed stewards/security staff to clearly direct customers to designated exit points.

On-site transportation, as opposed to using a traffic management company, should have sole responsibility for car parking. Traffic on site requires some special measures to remove potential harm to staff and customers. The first restriction should be an overall speed limit for all vehicles. Where the event runs for over one day due consideration should be made for the movement of non essential vehicles at night. If there is a high volume of customers at any given time throughout the event an announcement should be communicated to all personnel who have control over vehicles. A vehicle curfew should be announced and monitored for its duration. Where camping on site is part of the event entertainment, specific access to emergency vehicles with the demarcation of fire lanes should run throughout the campsite. Each campsite should be identified by large signposts for customers, staff and emergency operatives. Observation towers may also be of a benefit within the campsite, as they should have a strategic location to assist in the movement of campers and a vantage point for staff and emergency vehicles as they move around the location. To complement this process fencing around the site and along walkways throughout the campsite will assist in the flow of customers. To ease the movement of traffic and customers throughout the site at night, floodlighting should be placed at all entry and exit points, near food concessions, observation towers and main walkways around the site. If an event has an arena and overnight camping, a clean sweep of the arena is required to remove all customers. At this point the waste management systems can come into operation. All waste vehicles should be allowed into the arena area for the collection of human waste from sanitation areas and consumable rubbish. This can only take place once the arena is closed or a section is closed off to all customers. The event provider must ensure that all vehicles working at night use hazard warning lights when moving around and keep to the speed limit. All personnel working within that area must also remember to wear high visibility attire at all times.

In the management and moving of all vehicles and personnel associated with each management system around the site, a map with grid references is the desired approach. Clear communication channels should be in place and an appointed individuals must be charged with the responsibility of delivering communication messages throughout the site. A site map with grid references should be distributed to all emergency services and non essential services prior to their arriving on site.

To assist in the traffic management of vehicles coming to and already on site, an accreditation system for all vehicles must be part of the overall management. Vehicles should display a valid vehicle entry pass at all times. Passes should denote areas of access and limited access. If the site is fortunate enough to have a number of ingress and egress points they should be ear-marked for contractors arriving at or leaving the site along with other event traffic. While the event is up and running specific notification must be made to ensure that designated points of arrival are clearly signposted. Public transport, taxi collection and drop off points must be kept clear at all times. Roads leading to the site should take into account the heavy volume of traffic, with diversion routes if appropriate. In collaboration with the highway agency and local police, overhead motorway traffic information boards should warn other road users about the event in advance and while the event is underway. Monitoring of the major road networks to the site and around the site is also the domain of the event provider: this should be done in collaboration with the highway agency and the police. If traffic accidents occur on the road network and have a significant impact on event traffic, the event provider must have measures in place for communicating this information to customers.

Disability access, the location of amenities and viewing platforms must also be given sufficient consideration at outdoor events. Where appropriate, the location of viewing platforms must take into consideration access for emergency vehicles. Disabled toilets and car parking must also reflect accessibility at all times during the event. Designated staff and on-site vehicles may also be required for transporting disabled and vulnerable adults throughout the event.

First aid, welfare and medical provision should have a strategic location on site available on a 24 hour basis. Access to these facilities, must again take into account emergency vehicle egress and ingress. Customers should also be able to access the facility without too much difficulty. Therefore, all on-the-ground security staff and stewards must have a clear understanding of the exact location.

It is evident here that all three emergency services must be given full consideration when developing the logistical movement of people and traffic to and around the site. When applying for a temporary outdoor entertainment licence under the Licensing Act 2003, the police service as required for the event must take specific instructions from the event licensee as to the movement of police vehicles on site. The police must also follow vehicle curfews unless they are responding to an emergency situation. This also applies to fire and ambulance services.

Transportation logistics for events

If an organisation is delivering any type of goods there are a number of factors to consider. Consideration must be given as to the nature of the product that needs distributing – is it perishable, chemical, expensive, etc? If your goods are of a chemical nature, they must meet the requirements for packaging, labelling, and the training of drivers. Further advice can be obtained from the Department of Transport Dangerous Goods Branch.

There are some items within the logistical framework that may require the service of couriers, hauliers and freight forwarders. Couriers are normally used for small goods. Couriers specialise in swift, secure deliveries and they can do so nationally and internationally. It is worth nothing that couriers only deliver packages up to a certain weight.

Hauliers, on the other hand, will collect goods from your premises and deliver them to your chosen destination. This type of arrangement will be done by road and could prove to be expensive if your goods don't fill up the entire vehicle.

Freight forwarders specialise in 'consolidation'. They combine your goods with other consignments in a single container or vehicle, thereby reducing the cost. Due to the nature of their business and international logistical operation, they can generally offer related services, e.g., organising the paperwork for export. They can also manage the entire transportation process, track goods, and provide warehousing and local distribution centres if necessary. For further advice the British International Freight Association (BIFA) can assist with many of the logistical requirements.

With so many event companies working internationally, an understanding of the available services has become an important part of event logistics. With all these service providers there are ultimately pros and cons with each mode of transportation.

Some of the pros and cons can be identified, however this will depend on distance, destination, volume and type of goods. Here are some of the general pros and cons associated with each service.

- Road *advantages*: cheap, convenient, flexible, private.

- Road *disadvantages*: noisy, pollutes the environment, less safe than alternatives, stressful for drivers, potential delays, congestion road charges.

- Rail *advantages*: fast, safe, more environmentally friendly, does not add to congestion.

- Rail *disadvantages*: limited routes, inflexible routes and timetables, expensive and sometimes unreliable.

- Air *advantages*: fast for long distance delivery, safe.

- Air *disadvantages*: expensive, unsuitable for some goods, limited routes, environmental pollution, airport taxes.

- Sea *advantages*: cheap for large volumes.

- Sea *disadvantages*: very slow, relatively few ports, inflexible routes and timetables, port/duty taxes.

It is clear that before developing a logistical plan you should decide whether you require the services of companies that specialise in this sector. Sufficient forward planning is essential to develop a mix of services that best meet the requirement of the event profile. As with all event planning processes it is also essential to attach a credible contingency plan: one that looks at all the potential variables including weather-related impacts.

Logistical challenges for the future

Logistics as an automated service has been instrumental in improving operations and reducing the cost to businesses. This does not mean that event providers should adopt an expensive automated service to achieve better cost benefits to the business and customers, however, there are aspects that can be highlighted and if appropriate could be deemed a successful addition to meet future challenges.

Many companies today that have a large geographic area to cover will set up local distribution centres to meet customer demand. Event providers should actively seek, where appropriate, distribution centres or contractors in close proximity to the event. This helps to save travelling time, reduce the cost and where perishable goods are required allows local produce to be utilised.

Contractors who supply equipment to events can also look at the labelling and security tagging of their goods prior to leaving a facility for intended use and returning to the original location. A sufficient method of inventory is therefore essential at both locations to meet supply and demand.

The fundamentals of a supply chain have not changed greatly over the years, as it is still based around planning procurement and outsourcing. However, the scope and control around this will continue to change and develop. As pointed out earlier, supply chains will continue to grow in length due to demand and at peak season.

An interesting feature of the future is the reduction in HGVs but an increase in smaller (low) goods vehicles (LGVs), due to predictions on transportation congestion and in particular urban delivery vehicles throughout the UK.

Future industry trends suggest consolidation on transportation, the polarisation of different supply chain strategies, and better collaboration between event providers and suppliers. Where goods and services follow a similar continuity, duality could be a solution.

Procurement delivery to site is as that seen within the construction industry, where construction materials are cut and delivered to order. Translating this to the event industry is acceptable in some sectors such as exhibition design and build. This could help to reduce the overall cost, human resources and time.

With the Far East becoming a major source for imported goods, traffic at ports will also become a congested area in the future. Cities outside of London have implemented or are thinking of implementing congestion charges for road users.

SUMMARY

The chapter has highlighted the significant use of logistics within the event management framework. It has shown how the process has been developed into a credible business model. Further development of the process has shown its flexibility in applying the process to on-site event logistics. This process and application has synergy with all type of events and their location. It has shown that logistics for event managers is not only a business requirement but has methodologies that translates to pre-event, during and closedown. This has now become paramount when applying for an entertainment licence under the Licensing Act 2003. Licensees have a duty of care to ensure that customers leaving the event have appropriate access to transportation, without causing harm to themselves or others in the process.

A report was compiled by the Health and Safety Executive (HSE), 'Management Standards for Workplace Transport', published in 2006. In this document there are some alarming statistics which relate to transportation injuries and fatalities.

> On average, annually there are around 70 fatalities related to workplace transportation (in 2003/04, 57% were 'struck by a vehicle' and 7% were 'falls from vehicles'). (p. 1)

These statistics exclude transportation by rail, public highway, and water.

This has given rise to a whole new conceptual model for managing outdoor events. Logistics for this chapter was taken out of its recognisable setting of transportation logistics. The term logistics was presented alongside and partnered with a number of operational management processes. Supply chain management, demand management and inventory management were all discussed Case studies were presented to show the diverse application of logistics in the overall business of running an events company and event.

Discussion questions

Question 1

Demonstrate your understanding of the business relationship between event logistics and supply chain management; outline your concept within an event management context.

Question 2

Outline two challenges that will face event organisers in the future when developing their logistical transportation plan.

Question 3

Demonstrate how seasonality issues within the outdoor event sector can have a negative impact on transportation logistics for event providers.

FURTHER READING

Getz, D. (1997) *Event Management and Event Tourism*. New York: Cognizant Communications Corporation.

Goldblatt, J.J. and Suprovitz, F. (1999) *Dollars and Events: How to Succeed in the Special Events Business*. New York: Wiley.

Shone, A. and Parry, B. (2001) *Successful Event Management: A Practical Handbook*. London: Thomson.

CHAPTER 15

Events production and equipment design

How to identify and select the appropriate equipment for a particular event, in association with venue facilities and performers, will be addressed in this chapter, in terms of legal requirements, contractual responsibilities, regulations, policies and procedures. The understanding for this particular approach should be aligned to industry standards and best practice. Comparisons will be made with distinctly different venues to establish commonalities in equipment specification and usability. The international perspective will be determined with the universal equipment chosen by an events producer when touring internationally. In reflecting this approach technical procedures will also be redefined to allow for changes in the regulations.

Introduction

This chapter will define the term 'production' as both a process and a business entity within the very wide spectrum of organised events. It will illustrate some of the key working practices, legislation, guidance and codes of practice from a European and UK perspective. To supplement the term production this area will be looked at as an outsourced requirement for developing aspects that are generally associated with the finer points of live performance/entertainment, where static, mechanical or electrical equipment and certified and trained individuals are a requirement. The chapter will provide a minimum working standard and develop a framework that gives events management companies the ability to engage in a business relationship that is mutually beneficial to both parties. It is for organisers (who will know what they expect to receive), the production company (who will know what they expect to provide) and associated agencies that are also connected with the production process.

Production within the events industry has many specialist roles and responsibilities. Principally, the majority of the working practices are governed by the Health and Safety at Work Act 1974 and the numerous UK and European regulations attached to this. Production management and control as a business entity also covers many areas within the events experience.

First, this chapter will outline the different types of events covered by production and identify some of the specific areas within events that are relevant to it. Through this process we will build a clear understanding of the integral role of production in enhancing the quality of the events management experience.

In today's global business environment 'production' can be located in many events. The corporate sector of events management has remained at the leading edge of technological advancement through its use of ground breaking multimedia equipment. Where a corporate event has a speaker or performance demonstrating a product or a service to an invited audience over a given time span, to engage and focus the attention of the audience and enlarge the physical presence of the presentation a large video wall, plus satellite links with live feedback or pre-programmed information accompanied by laser, amplified sound and lights are a combination generally employed to achieve a memorable and powerful experience. Alternatively, single elements may be selected or further combinations, perhaps including static or mechanical equipment, which may be specifically designed to generate a memorable and visual impact.

Exhibition and production

The exhibition industry has a far reaching and global appeal with many internationally recognised venues throughout the UK, such as Earls Court London and Birmingham's NEC. Exhibitors are constantly developing ways of competing within a closed environment, on a designated floor space to a trade or consumer audience. Where budgets are sufficient, exhibitors may employ professional production personnel to create an element of excitement and visual presence. This type of marketing strategy is sometimes carried out with the company's corporate colours displayed using lights and gobos (a metal stencil attached to a light fitting that enlarges and projects an image over a surface or distance). The exhibition environment may also employ the use of moving images projected and displayed strategically on the walls surrounding the designated area. An ambient use of amplified sound may also be used within a semi- or fully-enclosed area of the exhibition stand. Exhibition stands are essentially constructed to carry a marketing message so production equipment will usually serve to expand on and amplify the company image.

Commercial music events and production

Music events, both in closed venues and outdoors, are probably one of the biggest exponents of light, sound and stage equipment, since these are the core elements that create a powerful and dominating atmosphere. There are many possible combinations; generally determined by the budget, the performers and the creative production team. All this must be closely monitored in line with fire regulations, health and safety and UK and European regulations. At music events professional sound engineers have a duty to amplify sound in a way that both meets the artist's/band's requirements while giving the audience audible sound. They are also required to work within the licensed agreement on allocated hours for the performance and the decibel level. Professional lighting engineers at large outdoor music events can sometimes be working with up to 30–50 individual lighting units arranged on a lighting rig above the stage and performers. The lighting rig supported above the stage can be static or mechanically operated. It is the responsibility of the lighting engineer to pre-programme the rig and lights to work in tandem with the music and performance. Today's technology allows lighting and sound engineers a greater degree of flexibility in achieving artist and customer satisfaction. Sound and lighting desks at live music performances can be operated manually or can be pre-programmed at source with an option to store the information on a CD or disk, thereby enabling pre-programmed information to be transported electronically across international boundaries. Again, we can draw comparisons with many other areas of the events industry and begin to build on our knowledge and understanding of the use of production, equipment and personnel.

Live public events

Events that involve the use of lasers, fireworks, strobe lights and outdoor bonfires are regular features within the UK calendar. These events have additional regulations and guidance for their safe control, use and management when used at public events. Fireworks must comply with the Fireworks (Safety) Regulation 1997 and British Standard 7114; 1989. Supplementary

Figure 15.1   Millennium Square, Leeds: a demonstration of sound and lighting equipment, and high powered lasers

guidance is provided in The British Pyrotechnics' Association and Explosive Industry Group Firework Handbook 2000/01. Firework operators at public events must work with the local authority to establish the safe storage, safe fall-out area for projectiles and the amount of explosive intended for use at the event. Certification should be forwarded to the local authority and event organiser for personnel handling fireworks. Laser operators who are not fully conversant with their equipment should obtain guidance from the Entertainment Laser Association. Laser operators under the HSE have a duty of care to the people who are exposed to lasers, be they customers or operators. This is also the case for strobe lights, which can induce fits in people with epilepsy. Clear information must therefore be included in pre-event publicity and before entering venues/sites. Information should also be displayed throughout the venue and announced through an amplified sound system if one is available. Such procedures enable the events manager to operate with due diligence under the Health and Safety Act and to create a safe environment for employees and customers. With production equipment that has the potential to cause harm or injury to customers or employees, event managers have a responsibility to limit, reduce or remove the risk of injury or harm. This can be done though information, public announcements, or by limiting exposure over a given time span.

So far this chapter has introduced events of a different size, audience profile, location and content. What is constant and apparent is the use of production personnel and equipment.

Production equipment may include mechanically operated machinery designed for its purpose and assembled on site, or an integration of special effects such as lasers, fireworks and strobe lights. Multimedia technology is used to enhance customer enjoyment by creating a memorable experience. This is also the case at large-scale music events where amplified sound and light become the driving force behind presenting and promoting a live stage performance.

To gain a greater understanding of the production process and the procedures that support the successful integration of these elements within the events management experience, we must first illustrate the working principles of a production house and its personnel. A production company located within the events industry is generally operating as a specific and specialist supplier of equipment and trained/qualified personnel. On the whole, event management companies outsource to production companies when required. The working relationship between the events management company and the production company will be critical to achieving a successful outcome.

Developing a business relationship with a production company

A reputable production company will pride itself in the first instance on its key personnel who are able to translate ideas into a working solution on time and within a budget. It must also maintain high standards, which must be demonstrated through inspections and the production of certification documents. These companies may be affiliated to a UK association recognised by the industry as acceptable. They will also have trained and qualified personnel (if required) who are responsible for the maintenance and use of a particular type of equipment. Depending on the exact nature of the work undertaken by these companies, it may be necessary for them to show permits and certification before any work can proceed. The production company, in agreement with the organiser, the local authority and suppliers if required, will assess the type of activity and assign a particular type of equipment and personnel to complete a task.

It is the responsibility of an organiser to request (if not presented with) certification and permits for activities/equipment that are to be used both at the pre-build stage or during the event itself. It is necessary to obtain this information as the event insurance liability cover may be invalid if work is carried out without clear supervision, certification or a permit if required. Insurance therefore becomes a significant issue for all production companies and the event's organiser should request a copy of the insurance cover from the production company before any work commences. Insurance liability cover for equipment and personnel will fluctuate from company to company. Mechanical machinery and flammable substances that are used either to generate power or to install and erect both off-the-shelf and specifically designed equipment should have a premium cover that is commensurate with the type of activity. Individuals who carry out a particular task on behalf of the production company, whether freelance or employed directly, may also require significant employee insurance liability cover and a permit to work if the activity or task has been assessed as potentially hazardous to health. This is sometimes the case for people who work at height. If an event is held within a venue and the venue has the structure to allow working at height, the venue manager should insist that people wear a harness when working above head height. Again, if this procedure is not adhered to the venue insurance cover could be invalidated along with the insurance cover held by the production company, including the venue licence in some cities and venues in the UK.

Within the production company armoury there are a number of operational procedures that require validation and support.

A health and safety policy/statement, risk assessment and method statement are fundamental operational procedures for production companies. If they are to fall in line with the Health and Safety at Work Act and the numerous UK and European regulations, while also safeguarding their insurance liability, adherence to these procedures must become the common working standard.

It is necessary to establish what a health and safety policy is and why it is needed. A health and safety policy is a document that sets out a clear working standard for all employees while working on behalf of that company. This document should be written with direct reference to the Health and Safety at Work Act 1974. The policy will set out the company's duty to ensure that individuals carry out their tasks in a safe environment. It will also specify what is acceptable for employees while undertaking their particular tasks. Acceptable measures may also state that training is to be provided before undertaking a particular activity or using equipment. The document may also be supported with guidance notes that will give an employee further information before commencing a task and regulations to which an employee must adhere when 'completing a task' or 'before commencing a task'. If protective clothing is essential to a particular activity it will be indicated in the document as a necessity. An event manager should request a copy of the heath and safety policy from the company by way of ensuring that hazardous activities are governed appropriately and safety is paramount.

Risk assessment has been given a significant amount of attention within the business environment in all industries. For all events it is essential that the principles of risk assessment are applied. The heath and safety executive's guiding principles are:

1 Look for the hazard

2 Decide who might be harmed and how

3 Evaluate the risk and decide whether the existing precautions are adequate or whether more should be done

4 Record your findings

5 Review your assessment and revise it if necessary.

Threat Level

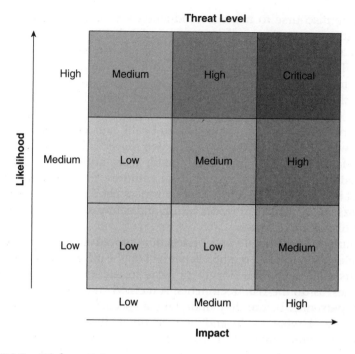

Figure 15.2   Risk matrix

Risk assessment is a legal requirement in the UK in order to execute the 'Duty of Care' under the Health and Safety at Work Act 1974. It is essential that a risk assessment is fully presented as part of the production process. The risk assessment should be formulated in line with the five key steps set out above. Upon identifying the activity or task, it is necessary to look at ways of limiting exposure, removing, controlling or transferring risk. In some documents you may also find a risk rating, which gives further information about the likelihood of the risk accruing and the impact of the risks to person(s) in the immediate vicinity.

By using a matrix, a priority can be established. If likelihood is high, and impact is low, it is a medium risk. On the other hand if impact is high, and likelihood is low, it is high priority. A remote chance of a catastrophe warrants more attention than the high chance of a hiccup.

The risk matrix is a more scientific method of developing risk control measures. The document should also highlight who has responsibility for monitoring and controlling the identified risks. For more complicated or hazardous production processes, further guidance will be required by the production company and associated agencies.

Risk assessment is not to be confused with risk management, which should be regarded as any other management function. It should involve the identification, analysis and control of risk which has the potential to threaten assets or the enterprise. The risk assessment document, when presented to the venue, local authority and event manager, allows all parties to engage in reasonable discourse to manage production safely. Within the production process it is also essential to document injuries that have occurred as a direct result of any of the risks identified in the risk assessment or the management thereof. The documentation should be in a separate incident log book. In regards to regulation, registration and inspection, events companies must register their business if they have ten or more employees with the Social Security Claims Payment Regulation 1987. When a business falls under leisure and entertainment, inspection for health and safety/risk assessment will be with the local authority. However, the HSE have the authority to inspect fairgrounds. On the other hand, local authority events can be inspected by the HSE if they are on local authority land. Therefore, jurisdiction will be with the HSE. If the event business has fewer than five employees there is no requirement under health and safety to produce a health and safety policy for employees.

To improve operational and production procedures, many production companies also include a method statement on the information they can give to events managers. This document aims to ensure the duty of care for employees, as do the risk documents. A method statement is given to production personnel before they undertake a specific task to ensure they are fully aware of what to do and how to do it. It sets out a step-by-step approach to completing a task, especially where equipment is required to complete a task or is the finished article. If technical illustrations are required, they must also accompany the method statement. A method statement should either be prepared by the production manager or should accompany the equipment. It should also identify all of the tools and supplementary equipment to be used in order to create a safe working environment from which to carry out work. There should be a method statement for each task or operation and copies should be held at the production office on site. This document can also create a safe working environment and safeguard employees against insurance claims.

Where an organiser has arranged for an event to be held, whether inside a venue or outdoors, it is essential to obtain electrical test certificates for electrical equipment powered by fuel or a mains supply. This process of testing electrical equipment is called a PAT test (portable appliance testing) and it must be signed off by qualified electrical engineer. It will give a degree of assurance to organisers, venue managers, licensing authorities and production personnel that electrical equipment has been tested and is ready for use. It is not possible to provide complete assurance of the electrical stability of the tested equipment but this process will go some way to ensuring that equipment is safe for its intended use.

From the information presented so far, we can see the fundamental relationship between the production company and the event organiser. Each has a direct responsibility to ensure that individual employees are given sufficient training, information, certification, a method statement, insurance, permits, protective clothing and well maintained equipment to carry out each specific task. All this information should be written down and given to the event organiser and the associated agencies (which may include the fire service, the local authority and the police) in the pre-planning stage of the event.

When the production company is satisfied with the information they have in turn obtained from the site/venue, an official undertaking to commence work will be ordered. Any sub-contracted companies must also adhere to all the agreed documentation and regulations, in accordance with the requirements set out for the main contractor for whom they are working. If sub-contracted production companies have any special requirements, all new details must be forwarded to the relevant organisations.

What the production company needs

An order to commence work on the site/venue can resemble a logistical and military operation. The production manager will draw up a checklist and site supervision order. It is the responsibility of the production manager to appoint roles and responsibilities for all personnel and any sub-contractors. The production manager will set up a method for communicating with all production personnel and appointed sub-contractors and will compile an emergency procedure plan if one is not already available. This document must be verbally announced and/or given to all personnel before they commence work. The emergency procedure should conform to the health and safety policy.

The production manager may be required to set up an office on the site/venue if one is not already available. The office is where all the documentation and agreements pertaining to the production set-up should be held. If any inspecting organisation or authorities (fire officer, local authority operative) make an appearance on the site/venue, information should be made available to them. If an inspection is carried out by any expert adviser, or agencies or departments from the local authority, documentation relating to that inspection should be documented and held with the production manager on site. If erecting a temporary structure outdoors for a commercial or public event under licence, it is advisable for a fire officer to inspect the structure before allowing the public admittance. A fire certificate will be presented to the production manager stating the fire regulations for that structure and its readiness for use.

The production manager should also appoint a site supervisor if the type of event requires a considerable number of sub-contractors, personnel and equipment over a lengthy time period. This division of labour allows the site supervisor to deal with site deliveries, construction requirements and on-the-ground health and safety issues. This may include monitoring the working procedures of each contractor on site. Large-scale events like outdoor festivals catering for between 20–200,000 plus people will require all of the above production personnel with the possible addition of an appointed health and safety officer. This type of arrangement is common at large-scale air displays (e.g., Farnborough Air Show in England), where a safety officer is appointed by the event organiser to monitor all the contractors on site.

If the production site/venue requires mechanical handling equipment, there is a legal responsibility for each production manager to ensure that contractors provide adequate and proper training for the use of cranes and lifting appliances in accordance with the manufacturer's test certificate and the load test certificate. All this information should be made available for inspection on request.

Security at a production site must be considered a necessity, especially if working outdoors. It should rest with the event organiser to appoint an accredited security firm to monitor security on site. Accredited security guards should wear distinctive markings or uniforms in line with the Security Act 2002.

Final handover

A final checklist should be used by the production manager to bring any out-standing issues to the attention of the event organiser, inspecting officer or associated agencies. This part of the production process can act as an official handover once the checklist is completed and the organiser and authorities are satisfied. The official sign-offs for the production can then take place and full responsibility for the event reverts back to the organiser.

Production managers have a great deal of documentation to process prior to and during an event. The Event Safety Guide for Pop Concerts and Similar Events (known as 'The Purple Guide') published by the HSE has been designed in part with this process in mind.

Associated agencies and organisations

So far in this chapter we have touched briefly on the relationship of 'production' with associated agencies. There are a number of regulated agencies and organisations that have an integral part to play within the production process. We will now consider how legislation under governance and agencies sit within the production process and allow production managers expediency in delivering an exciting and memorable element to an event.

When developing a production process that has a direct relationship to an entertainment licence (under the 2003 Licensing Act) of some description, a production manager must take considered or specific instructions from that licensing authority. Where an event has a public audience, the onus will be placed on the organiser and production manager to demonstrate that elements of the event that have a risk attached have been investigated adequately and constructed to fit the intended use, without causing harm, injury or disturbance to the audience, workforce or resident community.

A number of stipulations regarding the use of equipment prior to and during the event may thus be inserted into the licence agreement. For example, a road closure order may be required where large vehicles are supporting the set-up process for the event delivering equipment and the event is located in a residential or business area that has a high throughput of traffic. Such an order can be obtained from the local police station in advance of the vehicles arriving. The licence agreement may also indicate that machinery that might disturb local residents can only be operated within agreed times. Where an event (be it indoors or out) has amplified music that might cause a disturbance to the local residents, a decibel level could be set in place by the local authority or venue. Checks are sometimes carried out by the licensing authority to ensure that the event does not break any of the conditions set. As an events manager, it is vital that any such conditions are brought to the attention of the production manager and sound engineer.

The testing of sound equipment will be allowed only within permitted hours as in the agreement. Any public entertainment licence obtained from a local authority will have a number of conditions set, which may either be statutory or specific to the location/venue and community. Breaching these conditions may risk the licence being revoked or a fine being levied against the organiser. Once the local authority licensing department has granted a licence, the organiser must appoint a licensee approved by the local authority to take full responsibility for the licence.

In addition to the local authority, another key associated agency is the fire service clearly having a principal responsibility for fire safety. They will have the authority for full access to the venue/site at all times. An appointed officer from the local fire service will be given the authority to check that any electrical equipment, material or environment temporary or otherwise meets with fire regulations. They will check that appropriate fire fighting equipment, exits and signs are available, and if any flammable substances are being used at the event that they are stored and managed as prescribed by the regulations.

SUMMARY

In this chapter it has been demonstrated that production companies, when working alongside an events organiser, have a very dangerous and sometimes specific undertaking. It has been revealed that clear processes, instructions and documentation are required from both parties to achieve event satisfaction. Where a licence is required or governed by one it must be a fundamental requirement.

A great deal of responsibility will rest with both companies to maintain the industry standard and a safe working environment for all. Therefore, the chapter has highlighted some of the many regulations that may fall under this specific task. It has also demonstrated that production personnel working for production companies, be they freelance, temporary or directly employed, may require training, certification, permits and a level of competence before they can undertake any particular type of work. The chapter has also indicated how insurance for events and production companies is closely linked. This was highlighted through the articulation of risk assessment.

Discussion questions

Question 1

Outline your understanding of a 'method statement' and it's relevance within the production process.

Question 2

Outline two methods available to the licensing authority if an organiser breaches the sound amplification level agreement stipulated in the licence condition.

Question 3

Within the 2003 Licensing Act there are statutory requirements attached to the licence, including conditions on how to apply and control the licence within any given local authority. Describe why local authorities are able to make specific recommendations within the licence condition when referring to their local area.

FURTHER READING

'Introducing standards raising standards worldwide'. British Standard Institute (BSI) www.bis-global.com

'Use of contractors a joint responsibility'. Published by the Health and Safety Executive (2002).

'Health and safety law: what you should know'. Published by the Health and Safety Executive (2006).

'Consulting employees on health and safety: a guide to the law'. First published by the Health and Safety Executive (2006).

CHAPTER 16

Lights and associated equipment in common usage at venues and events

---

OUTLINE OF THE CHAPTER

Lighting equipment: the industry standard
Venue requirement for lighting and associated equipment
Rigging equipment for different venues and outdoor events
Performer's requirement and musical arrangement
Operational management for lighting personnel
Summary
Discussion questions
Further reading

Theoretical understanding with a practical approach to applying lighting at events and venues will also be outlined as per current industry practice. The atmospheric and psychological approach to lighting at events to achieve customer satisfaction will also be discussed. Health and safety regulations will be presented alongside lighting equipment and technology to achieve management and operational control. International standards on equipment specification and associated products for touring events will be examined.

Introduction

Apart from the documentation and legislation accompanying the area of production we also have sound and light. These two particular aspects to the event experience have become a fundamental element in creating a memorable and lasting impact. This section will highlight the benefits of sound and light equipment, and its specification and implementation within the production process.

Alongside this, it is essential to organise a setup procedure. This will involve a full list of equipment and personnel with a production schedule that demonstrates the full implementation process of all equipment to a designated location. This information is crucial as most production managers are working to a deadline. Within the production schedule it is also necessary to include rehearsal time for performers.

When working with amplified sound it is essential to assess the type of venue in relation to the overall floor size, the internal material finishes, the audience capacity, the venue's proximity to other buildings or adjacent rooms, the type of performance and the number of people performing. Apart from the areas mentioned above the venue may have other areas that could impact on the type of sound system that is required for use within a chosen venue. There may be a restriction on decibel level set by the local authority, particularly if the venue is located in a residential area. Other restrictions might apply, such as hours within the day or night that amplified music can be played or the type of performance allowed within any particular venue. To accompany this there is also a HSE regulation on the Noise at Work Regulation 2005. This regulation does not apply to members of the general public who make an informed choice to enter noisy places, but to employees who work in a noisy environment.

With this regulation it is necessary to highlight some of the specific areas that must be taken into consideration for employers: to undertake a risk assessment, provide hearing protection, look at ways to reduce noise level, limit the time spent in a noisy area, check that suppliers are aware of their duties and keep records of your decision process to help show that you have met your legal duties.

Amplified sound operates within a frequency range of high to low frequency. A qualified sound engineer can set the frequency range as required for the performance or venue.

Within the production process it is essential to delegate and communicate with a qualified sound engineer, where sound equipment will be brought into a venue to meet the performance and audience requirements. A sound engineer can determine the type of equipment to achieve the set outcomes. As sound propagation can be a very personal experience, it is essential to monitor sound levels throughout the venue and in particular when the full audience capacity has been reached. This can be done by the sound engineer or any member of the event team. The golden rule is that if you can't hear it there is a good possibility that your audience is having the same difficulty.

Therefore, when selecting a sound system it is essential to have a clear idea about the type of performance. In creating the right type of audible sound, various speaker systems and their arrangement will go far in setting a quality sound and atmosphere. The most common type of speaker arrangement in cabinets is designed for all types of sound. This method is commonly used in home hifi systems. Each cabinet could have a three band arrangement of low band, mid band and high band; this will be the frequency range emanating

Figure 16.1   Virgin Festival 2002 – main stage speakers

from the speaker cabinet. Or all three bands could be separated within individual speaker cabinets.

When operating within a closed environment such as a school hall or medium-sized music venue with a capacity of approximately 1000, the entertainment will be positioned at one end of the venue on a stage/platform. Speakers should be placed where they can provide a good distribution of sound across the venue. If speakers are placed on a platform/stage or suspended from the ceiling, better distribution of sound will be achieved within the venue. Speakers suspended above head height and positioned to direct sound into the audience is commonly applied to larger venues such as arenas, sport stadia and outdoor live music festivals. This is appropriate in a large venue with a high audience capacity, where sound must travel over a greater distance and maintain its frequency range along with clarity of sound. All this can be achieved by a competent sound engineer.

There is also another method for setting up speakers to reach a large audience, and again this can also be found in arenas, sport stadia, concert venues and outdoor live music festivals. Delay speakers – as the name suggests – allow music to be heard at a greater distance from the stage with the same frequency range and clarity. As sound travels over a greater distance it can be interrupted and become unintelligible.

To achieve consistency with the music coming from the stage speakers, delay speakers are set with a minimum delay to coincide with the performance on stage. Any member of the audience standing in the locality of the delay speakers should hear an audible and clear sound. The average speed of sound is 340 metres per second. This depends on wind speed, humidity and air temperature. The equation for setting the delay time is the distance in metres from the stage divided by 340 and multiplied by 1000, which equals the time in milliseconds. From the information presented thus far it should become clear why a competent sound engineer is required when selecting and setting up sound systems. So far we have only just touched upon some of the elements associated with sound systems. Apart from a sound engineer it is essential to have a qualified electrical engineer available at all times. This individual, apart from ensuring the power distribution is commensurate with venue supply, must also give their approval as part of the final handover process. Once the setup/installation has been achieved to meet the legal standards of health and safety and fire risk assessment, handover to the event manager is the final stage.

When you have a live music performance with individuals performing with musical instruments, it is essential to work with a sound engineer if the final outcome is to be quality sound. This individual will have control over what is called a 'sound desk', and this allows music to be mixed and distributed appropriately through the speakers within the venue. The sound engineer (generally positioned at the front of house, i.e., some distance back and facing the stage) can also mix the music for the performers on the stage. This process enables the band to have an indication of the quality of sound produced, if they are playing in time with each other, or if they only wish to hear themselves or another member of the band. To achieve this, each performer on stage must have their own independent mix via a microphone which in turn is linked back to the sound engineer at the sound desk/ front of house desk.

To achieve sound quality that is commensurate with the status of the performers (see Figure 16.2), sound equipment is on stage to mix the sound that is produced by the performers. Once this process has been achieved it is distributed automatically to the front of house sound desk, where it is then channelled into the speakers and then to the audience. The sound desk on stage is called a monitor desk. The monitor operator can mix the sound for all the performers on stage. It can be channelled to each independent performer via a wedge monitor speaker (Figure 16.3), which is located in front of each performer.

Within the collection of sound equipment to achieve quality sound, a sound engineer must also work with power amplifiers, graphic equalisers and an arrangement of effects racks, enabling the sound engineer to stabilise and deliver quality and audible sound. The effects rack, along with the power amplifiers, has a similar heritage to a quality home hifi system. A stacked home hifi system comes with an independent amplifier and graphic equaliser. However, the amount of equipment required and cables to set up a quality sound system at events can be delivered within a truck. Therefore a crew should be made available to unload this equipment at the designated location.

As touched upon earlier, sound equipment can create a memorable experience. To enhance that experience sound engineers can also work in partnership with lighting engineers. This joint partnership is also carried forward with the performers who will communicate to a large extent the type of lighting arrangement that is required.

Figure 16.2   Millennium Square, Leeds – demonstration of sound equipment on stage with effects rack

Figure 16.3   Millennium Square, Leeds – demonstration of sound equipment with five wedge monitor speakers for each performer

Figure 16.4   Vodkafields outdoor music event, Bramham Park, Leeds, 2001 – moving light attached to a truss

A lighting designer, just like a sound engineer, can undertake a number of courses in developing their skills. But on-the-job training is the true test of any lighting designer. In today's environment the majority of lighting desks are pre-programmable. This allows the lighting designer to work from a lighting arrangement stored on a disk. It also allows the lighting engineer to have a degree of flexibility with each performance on stage. In association with that process there may be a requirement to interpret a lighting plot. A lighting plot will enable a lighting designer to have a clear idea about the amount of trusses needed, with cabling required for patching into the dimmer rack.

There are common features that have been translated into the events and entertainment industry from the theatre sector, such as chalk positions on stage to help follow spot operators, performers and the positioning of stage equipment, and equipment brought in from the truck to be colour coded and located on stage (stage left and right or front of house).

Lighting arrangements on stage come in two basic formats, fixed and moving lights. To accompany this there is also special effect lighting, such as strobe lights and lasers. Moving lights (see Figure 16.4) can be controlled via the lighting desk as designed by the manufacturer. Fixed light can be controlled by (the lighting desk) adjusting the intensity of the light, which is sometimes covered with a colour filter.

The distance to which each lamp can illuminate an object or area without losing intensity is governed by the inverse square law: as the distance between the

Figure 16.5   Taking Liberties, Vodkafields outdoor event, Bramham Park, Leeds, 2001

light/lamp is doubled the light intensity is reduced to one fourth of the original. Even though you may achieve a greater spread of light over a surface the optimal range from that light will diminish as the distance increases. Therefore, it is necessary to know the optimal working range for each light fitting.

Lighting on stage can have an adverse effect on performers; the intensity of light is far greater than that used within the home or the working environment (Figure 16.5). The average bulb or lamp as it is called within the trade could be 1000W. There is no particular legislation or regulation that determines how many light fittings can be positioned on stage, and this also applies to the amount of light emitted from each bulb.

Each performance determines the lighting arrangement. There are many different types of light fittings, with the most popular used across all types of performances, venues and events being Par cans. They come in a range of sizes with the largest labelled as par 64. Working as a lighting engineer requires a good degree of creativity in the selection, arrangement and interpretation of the performance to the audience. When setting up a lighting arrangement, venues may have the facility to hang lights from a roof structure. This structure is generally called a lighting truss; it may be fixed to the ceiling or have the capability to be lowered to floor level. The lowering of the truss allows easy access for connecting the light fitting to the structure.

Production personnel will attach chain supports to a triangular truss before lifting it above the stage (Figure 16.6 and 16.7). Prior to the truss being fully raised the Par can 64 in a bank of six together with colour filters will be attached

Figure 16.6   Ear to the Ground outdoor live music event (Dpecussion), Castlefield Arena, Manchester, 2006

to the truss. Before lifting commences all the lamp connections will also be checked. The truss will also be checked for tightness and safety. Once the truss has been lifted into position it must be checked to make sure that it is level, otherwise undue stress on the structure can cause it to fail.

When it comes to connecting a light fitting to a structure one should have a rigger who has their own insurance and permit to undertake a job of work.

An outdoor music event that runs into the late evening must look at installing independent general lighting at strategic areas throughout the site. Portable lighting units can be powered independently by using an internal generator.

As sound and lighting equipment has a tendency to consume a large amount of power, it is essential when selecting a venue to ensure that independent power units can be are available to run the sound and lighting equipment separately. The amount of power for a lighting system depends upon the number of lamps and their wattage. The power for a sound system is calculated by the amplifiers driving the speakers. If too much power is drawn from a venue the result will be a blown fuse or a blackout. To operate a sound and lighting system for a live music concert in a stadium or arena type venue, a three phases and a single phase independent power unit are required.

Apart from having lights fixed to the stage via a lighting rig or trusses, some performers may request a spotlight, commonly known as a follow spot, that requires an operator who will follow the performer on stage as and when the cues dictate. A follow spot is a very powerful light unit and should only be operated by a trained individual. Part of the process of lighting is the amount of cables needed. Cables that are used for lighting at events should

Figure 16.7   Ear to the Ground outdoor live music event (Dpecussion), Castlefield Arena, Manchester 2006 – portable lighting units

never be left tightly wound. The cables have the potential to create an enormous amount of heat and thus can burn the cable's outer casing. Cables should never be restricted en route, or be strung up above fire exit doorways or run through a duct. The electrical connection process is as follows: lamps, dimmer rack, then power with the lighting desk connected to the dimmer rack. The dimmer rack's main purpose is to vary the amount of electricity sent to a lamp thus controlling the brightness. This process is no different to a common dimmer on a house light. Theoretically a dimmer does not switch off therefore keeping both efficiency and heat at a low level. To conclude the operational process there needs to be a level of communication between lighting personnel. The front of house lighting operator will need to communicate with operatives on the stage or riggers attached to the truss. An intercom system not only allows the team to set the lights as required, it also enables communication to continue throughout the performance.

Regulations, legislation and standard documents explained

As stated earlier in this chapter, the Health and Safety at Work Act 1974 is the overarching legislation, and therefore covers all areas of production within the UK. Many regulations come directly from Europe but not all are embedded in UK law. Compliance by employers and employees is sometimes questionable across various industries. It requires robust monitoring and evaluation from the Health and Safety Executive and its regional offices, that trade unions and their representatives uphold and ensure that employers and employees understand and implement regulations throughout, and with appropriate reporting of incidents to their regional office and the local authorities working directly with the HSE and employees to raise working standards.

It has also been mentioned that UK and European regulations can have a major impact on production equipment and personnel. Therefore, to continue and give a more in-depth understanding, these two specific areas will be developed further. Prior to the European Parliament announcing new regulations for all new member states, it was the domain of the UK government to update the working practices by way of regulations. The Working at Height Regulations started life as a UK regulation; it consolidated the European Council Directive 2001 and replaced all the previous regulations. The Health and Safety Executive has reported that in 2003/04 there were 67 fatal accidents and 4000 major injuries in the UK's workplaces. This particular regulation was brought about to prevent the deaths and injuries caused each year from working at height. The translation of this regulation is crucial within the event production field. Working at height can relate to anyone up a stepladder, suspended from a fixed roof truss, climbing a scaffold structure or operating an extendable mechanical cherry picker. These are just some of the areas associated with this regulation. Within events production, be it exhibitions, conferences or outdoor live music events, there will be some aspect of working at height. As stated earlier, some venues throughout England do not allow working at height unless a permit has been applied for with the local authority and the person also has adequate personal insurance including a recent risk assessment. If an individual is employed directly by an organisation or event production company, it becomes the responsibility of that company to ensure all the documentation supports that particular task. The 2005 regulation sets out employers' responsibilities, and it must be stated that these responsibilities have to relate to the type of activities undertaken. The general responsibilities as stated in the Work at Height Regulation 2005 offer a brief guide.

> Avoid work at height where they can; use work equipment or other measures to prevent falls where they cannot avoid working at height; and where they cannot eliminate the risk of a fall, use work equipment or other measures to minimise the distance and consequences of a fall should one occur. (p. 3)

It may also be a requirement to have a qualified professional to inspect an area or structure before allowing any personnel to carry out work. This method is far more acceptable where one has erected a stage/platform or a temporary tented structure. The risk transfer and liability will rest with the professional upon completing an inspection and signing the documentation (fit for purpose).

As indicated earlier there are numerous regulations – the Health and Safety Executive website gives a full catalogue of regulations applicable to various types of industries and working conditions.

As mentioned previously we have a set of regulations that will cover most industries. The 'Six Pack' regulations were introduced in 1993, primarily for the management within the Heath and Safety at Work Act 1974. The six regulations are:

- Management of Health and Safety at Work Regulations

- Manual Handling Operations Regulations

- Display Screen Equipment Regulations

- Workplace (Health, Safety and Welfare) Regulations

- Provision and Use of Work Equipment Regulations

- Personal Protective Equipment Regulations.

When working within the field of production it is essential that whoever has operational/health and safety responsibilities must understand and implement where necessary those regulations listed above.

It is very common that regulations one, two, four, five and six will have a universal application on most sites/venues where production equipment and personnel are required to undertake a degree of physical work.

Occupational health has become a major and significant area of understanding for all industries. For the production industry it must be given significant representation. The Health and Safety Executive report from 2004, entitled 'Thirty Years On', looked forward to the development and future of the health and safety systems in the UK.

> One of the trends that has been increasingly evident in our work is the growing emphasis on occupational health matters. (p. 6)

Occupational health assessors are becoming a common feature of many industries and in particular the public sector. Companies assess the health of a new and existing employee before allowing them to undertake a particular task. The method of assessment must also become the standard practice for production companies: if not applied appropriately, cases may be subject to industrial tribunals or legal proceedings, if negligence of non compliance to assessing the health risk associated with employees at work is found. Therefore, when developing a health and safety policy, occupational health assessments must take centre stage.

> In 2004 more than twice as many people suffer ill health as a result of their work as are injured in accidents. Musculoskeletal disorders and workplace stress account for over half of all cases but the total includes diseases ranging from asthma and dermatitis to infections and deafness. (p. 7)

SUMMARY

In this chapter the production process has been identified from a particular point of view, it has also been illustrated with a number of relevant regulations and legislation appropriate to achieving successful outcomes within the area of sound and light. Not all regulations have been identified in this chapter. Thus it requires an individual to research the HSE website to gain a full and complete understanding of all the regulations associated with this particular area. A great deal of the focus has hinged upon health and safety as the main driver for successful event producers within today's climate. It has given the reader an insight into the very complicated area of work within an aspect of event management. It has also shown how integral the working relationship of various skilled individuals is necessary to achieve a quality production. This chapter was not written to enable an event manager to become a sound or lighting engineer or even a production manager. It was developed so that a level of communication and understanding could occur between two parties who are ultimately working towards the same end. Further reading and training is therefore suggested if one desires to obtain a knowledge and understanding in this particular field. There is one highly recognised trade organisation within the UK that represents production personnel. The Production Service Association is a trade organisation with a website that gives help and guidance to people within the industry. It has a database of members and a resource of information on training courses along with recruitment, plus general news within the sector.

The chapter presented some of the issues that are the mainstay of any lighting and sound engineer working for a production company at an event.

It gave an insight into some of the aspects related to their job of work and in particular where it would have an impact on regulations and legislation. A diluted approach was outlined demonstrating some of the equipment and processes required to achieve quality live music at events. The chapter informed the reader that seeking out supplementary information, and guidance from credible published books and organisations will go far in developing a greater understanding of production personnel and equipment.

By the very nature of the work that is carried out within and on behalf of the production industry we are able to extrapolate that 'production' contributes to the HSE statistics. To better equip an organisation with the necessary knowledge, this will be a vital test for this long-term success and growth within the events sector.

Discussion questions

Question 1

Production managers working at events with special effects lighting have the potential to cause harm or injury. Describe the measures that should be taken to limit or remove risk to customers.

Question 2

Outline your understanding of the term 'rigger' and describe the documentation required by that individual before he/she can commence work.

Question 3

Outline your understanding of a lighting plot and discuss some of the key attributes of supplying a lighting designer with said lighting plot.

FURTHER READING

Professional Lighting and Sound Association www.plasa.org
Guide for the Operation of Lasers, Searchlights and Fireworks in United Kingdom Airspace. Published by the Civil Aviation Authority December 2003 www.caa.co.uk

---

References

Books

Allen, J., O'Toole, W., McDonnel, I. and Harris, R. (2000) *Festival and Special Event Management*, 2nd edition, John Wiley & Sons, Milton Keynes

Allen, J., O'Toole, W., McDonnel, I. and Harris, R. (2002) *Festival and Special Event Management*, 3rd edition, John Wiley & Sons, Milton Keynes

Association of Accounting Technicians (1990) *AAT Study Text: Cost Accounting and Budgeting Paper 10* (Paperback), BPP Publishing, London

Ansoff, H.I. (1969) *Business Strategy*. Penguin, London

The Business Tourism Partnership (2006) British Tourist Authority

Blyton, P. and Turnbull, P. (1992) *Reassessing Human Resource Management*. Sage, London

Boella, M. and Goss-Turner, S. (2005) *Human Resource Management in the Hospitality Industry*, 8th edition, Elsevier Butterworth and Heinemann

Bowdin et al. (2001) *Events Management*, Butterworth Heinemann, Oxford

Brassington, F. and Pettit, S. (2000) *Principles of Marketing*. Prentice-Hall, London

Brayshaw, R., Samuels, J. and Wilkes, M. (1999) *Financial Management and Decision Making*. International Thomson Business Press, London

British Tourist Authority (2007) *An Overview of the UK's Business Visits and Events Industry*, http://www.businesstourismpartnership.com/news/BusinessTourism Briefing.pdf [Accessed 12 August 2008]

Brown, A.S. (2000) *Customer Relationship Management – A Strategic Imperative in the World of e-Business*. John Wiley & Sons, London

Butler, R., Davies, L., Pike, R. and Shaap, J. (1993) *Strategic Investment Decisions*. Routledge, London

Canadian Coalition of Community-based Employability Training (CCBET) (2004) *Leadership, Fundraising and Resource Development*

Carrell, M.R., Elbert, N.F. and Hatfield, R.D. (2000) *Human Resource Management: Global Strategies for Managing a Diverse and Gobal Workforce*, 6th edition. The Dryden Press: San Diego.

Chaffey, D., Mayer, R., Johnston, K. and Ellis-Chadwick, F. (2003) *Internet Marketing– Strategy, Implementation and Practice*. Prentice Hall, Harlow

CIMA Study Systems (2006) *Management Accounting Fundamentals*. Elsevier Butterworth Heinemann, Oxford.

CIPD (2007) http://www.cipd.co.uk/subjects/dvsequl/general/divover.htm? IsSrchRes=1 [Accessed 12 August 2008]

Dessler, G. (2000) *Human Resources Management*, 8th edition. Prentice Hall International, London

Doyle, P. (2002) *Marketing Management and Strategy*. Financial Times/Prentice Hall, Harlow

Drury, C. (2004) *Management and Cost Accounting*. 6th edition. Thomson Learning, London

Egan, J. (2004) *Relationship Marketing: Exploring Relational Strategies in Marketing*, 2nd edition. Financial Times Press, Prentice Hall, Harlow.

Freedman, H.A. and Feldman, K. (1998) *The Business of Special Events: Fundraising Strategies for Changing Times*. BookCrafters, Michigan.

Getz, D. (1997) *Event Management and Event Tourism*. Cognizant Communications Corporation, New York.

Goldblatt, J.J. and Supovitz, F. (1999) *Dollars and Events: How to Succeed in the Special Events Business*. John Wiley & Sons, New York

Goss, D. (1994) *Principles of Human Resource Management*. Routledge, London

Hall, C.M. (1997) *Hallmark Tourist Events: Impacts, Management and Planning*. Belhaven, London

Health and Safety Executive (2006) *Health and Safety Law: What you should know*.

Idowu, S. (Aug 2000) *Capital Investment Appraisal: Part 1*. Association of Chartered Certified Accountants, London

Kandola, R. and Fullerton, J. (1998) *Diversity in Action: Managing the mosaic*. Chartered Institute of Personnel and Development, London

Key Leisure Markets (2001) *Tourism in the U.K.* MarketScape Ltd: London.

Keynote (2004) *Market Report 2004: Corporate Hospitality*, 4th edition. Hampton, Middlesex, Key Note Limited.

Kitchen, J.P. (1999) *Marketing Communications: Principles and Practice*. Thomson Business Press, London

Kotler, P., Armstrong, G., Saunders, J. and Wong, V. (1999) *Principles of Marketing*, 2nd European edition. Prentice Hall Europe, London

Kurdle, A. and Sandler, M. (1995) *Public Relations for Hospitality Managers: Communicating for Greater Profits*. Wiley, New York

Mabey, C., Salaman, G. and Storey, J. (1998). *Human Resource Management: A Strategic Introduction*. Blackwell Publishers, Malden, MA

Majaro, S. (1993) *The Essence of Marketing*. Prentice Hall, London

McCarthy, E.J. (1978), *Basic Marketing: A Managerial Approach*, 6th edition. Richard, D. Irwin, Homewood, IL.

McKoen, S. (1997) *Successful Fundraising and Sponsorship in a Week*. Cox & Wyman, London

Mercer, D. (1996) *Marketing*, 2nd edition. Blackwell Business, Oxford

Michigan Business School (2004) www.bus.umich.edu

Morgan, M. (1996) *Marketing for Leisure and Tourism*. Prentice Hall, London

Mullin, R. (1976) *The Fund Raising Handbook*. A.R. Mowbray & Co. Limited, Oxford

Mullins, L.J. (1999) *Management and Organisational Behaviour*, 5th edition. Financial Times/Pitman Publishing, London

National Society of Fund Raising Executives (1996) *The NSFRE Fund-Raising Dictionary*, John Wiley, New York

Pembrokeshire Association (2005) *Developing a Fundraising Strategy*. Pembrokeshire Association of Voluntary Services, August, pp. 1–2

Pike, R. and Neale, B. (2006) *Corporate Finance and Investment: decisions and strategy*, 5th edition. Pearson Education Limited, Essex

Porter, M.E. (1980) *Competitive Strategy*. The Free Press, New York

Porter, M.E. (1985) *Competitive Advantage*. The Free Press, New York

Shone, A. and Parry, B. (2001) *Successful Event Management: A Practical Handbook*. Thomson, London

Smith, P.R., Berry, C., Pulford, A. (1999) *Strategic Marketing Communications*. Kogan Page, London

Stone, R. (1998) *Human Resource Management*, 3rd edition. John Wiley & Sons, Brisbane

Watt, D.C. (1998) *Event Management in Leisure and Tourism*. Pearson Education Limited, Essex

Yehsin, T. (1999) *Integrated Marketing Communications*. Butterworth Heinemann, Oxford

Yeoman, I. et al. (2004) *Festival and Events Management*. Butterworth Heinemann, Oxford

Journals

Alkaraan, F. and Northcott, D. (2006) 'Strategic capital investment decision-making: a role for emergent analysis tool?', *The British Accounting Review*. Vol. 38(2) pp. 149–173

Borden, N.H. (1964) 'The concept of the marketing mix', *Journal of Advertising Research*, Vol. 4 pp. 2–7

Dwyer, F.R., Schurr, P.H. and Oh, S. (1987) 'Developing buyer-seller relationships', *Journal of Marketing*, Vol. 51, pp. 11–27

Erickson, G.S. and Kushner, R.J. (1999) 'Public event networks: an application of marketing theory to sporting events', *European Journal of Marketing*, Vol. 33(3/4) pp. 348–364

Foote, D.A. (2004) 'Temporary workers and managing the problem of unscheduled turnover', *Management Decisions*, Vol. 42, pp. 863–874

Grönroos, C (1994) 'From marketing mix to relationship marketing: towards a paradigm shift in marketing', *Management Decisions*, Vol. 32(2) pp. 4–20

Hanlon, C. and Jago, L. (2004) 'The challenge of retaining personnel in major sport event organizations', *Event Management*, Vol. 9(1–2) pp. 39–49

Hill, D.J. and Gandhi, N. (1992) 'Services advertising: a framework to its effectiveness', *Journal of Services Marketing*, Vol. 6, pp. 63–76

Hoffman D. L. (2000) 'The revolution will not be televised: Introduction to the special issue on marketing science and the internet', *Marketing Science*, Vol. 19(1), pp.1–3

Hoffman, D. and Novak, T.P. (1996) 'Marketing in hypermedia computer mediated environments: conceptual foundations', *Journal of Marketing*, July, pp. 50–68

Kelly, L.L., Gilbert, D. and Mannicom, R. (2003) 'How e-CRM enhance customer loyalty', *Market Intelligence and Planning*, Vol. 21, pp.239–248

Kitchen, P.J. (2003) 'Critical times; an integrated marketing communication perspective', paper presented at the First International Conference on Business Economics

Kitchen, P.J. and Schultz, D.E. (2000) 'A response to "Theoretical concept or management fashion"', *Journal of Advertising Research*, Vol. 40(5), pp. 17–21

Krulis-Randa, J. (1990) 'Strategic human resource management in Europe after 1992', *International Journal of Human Resource Management*, Vol. 1(2) pp. 131–139

Lee, M.-S., Sandler, D.M. and Shani, D. (1997), 'Attitudinal constructs towards sponsorship: scale development using three global sporting events', *International Marketing Review*, Vol. 14(3) pp. 159–69

Maslow, A. (1943) 'A theory of human motivation', *Psychological Review*, Vol. 50 pp. 370–96

McWilliams, G. (2000) 'Building stronger brands through online communities', *Sloan Management Review*, Vol. 41(3), Spring. pp. 43–54

Mohr, K., Backman, K., Gahan, L. and Backman, S. (1993) 'An investigation of festival motivations and event satisfaction by visitor type', *Festival Management and Event Tourism*, Vol. 1, pp. 89–97

Mortimer, K. (2002) 'Integrating advertising theories with conceptual models of services advertising', *Journal of Services Marketing*, Vol. 16(5), pp. 460–468

O' Toole, T. (2003) 'E-relationships-emergence and the small firm', *Market Intelligence and Planning*, Vol. 21(2), pp. 115–122

Pitta, D.A., Franzak, F.J. and Flower, D. (2006) 'A strategic approach to building online customer loyalty: Integrating customer profitability tiers', *Journal of Consumer Marketing*, Vol. 23(7) pp. 421–429

Pitta, D.A., Weisgal, M. and Lynagh, P. (2006) 'Integrating exhibit marketing into integrated marketing communications', *Journal of Consumer Marketing*, Vol. 23(3) pp. 156–166

Raj, R. (2004) 'The impact of cultural festivals on tourism', *Journal of Tourism Today*, Vol. 4, pp. 66–77

Shannon J.R. (1999) 'Sports marketing: an examination of academic marketing publication', *Journal of Services Marketing*, Vol. 13(6)

Stiernstand, J. (1996) 'The Nordic model: A theoretical model for economic impact analysis of event tourism festival management and event tourism', *Festival Management and Event Tourism*, Vol. 3 pp. 165–174

Uysal, M., Gahan, L. and Martin, B. (1993) 'An examination of event motivations' *Festival Management and Event Tourism*, Vol. 1, pp. 5–10

Websites

Andranovich, G., Burbank, M.J. and Heying, C.H. (2001) Olympic Cities: Lessons learned from Mega Event Politics [Internet], California State University, Los Angeles, Available from: www.blackwellpublishing.com/images/Journal_Samples/JUAF0735-2166~23~2-079/079.pdf [Accessed 20 March 2007]

www.accountancyage.com/accountancyage/features/2141181/[Accessed 12 December 2006]

www.barmitzvahs.org/[Accessed 12 April 2006]

The British Conference Market Trends Survey 2001 [Internet] Available from *The Business Tourism Partnership (British Tourist Authority, 2006) www.businesstourismpartnership.com/research* [Accessed 12 April 2006]

www.britishmotorshow.co.uk/[Accessed 12 April 2008]

The Review of Bradford Mela (2000), Bradford Festival 2000 Review. Bradford Festival. [Internet] Available from www.bradfordfestival.yorks.com [Accessed 20 December 2006]

The Bradford Festival (2002) www.bethere2002.com/links.html [Accessed 2 December 2006]

Canadian coalition of community-based employability training-CCBET (2004): "Leadership-Fundraising and resource development. http://www.savie.qc.ca/Ccocde/An/AccueilPublique.asp [Accessed 2 April 2007]

The Chartered Instituted of Marketing (www.cim.co.uk) [Accessed 2 April 2007]

Chartered Institute of Personnel and Development (2005c) 'Reflections on the 2005 Training and Development Survey', CIPD, London. www.cipd.co.uk/guides [Accessed 3 March 2006]

Department for Culture Media and Sport, www.culture.gov.uk/ [Accessed 28 April 2007]

Edinburgh International Festival (2002) www.eif.co.uk [Accessed 3 January 2007]

Flora London Marathon (2006) www.london-marathon.co.uk [Accessed 3 January, 2007]

The Football Association Premier League www.premierleague.com [Accessed 30 November, 2007]

Health and Safety Executive (2004) http://www.hse.gov.uk/aboutus/reports/30years.pdf [Accessed 30 April 2007]

ICOMOS www.icomos.org/tourism/charter.html/ [Accessed 12 December 2006]

www.ipr.org.uk [Accessed 9 March 2007]

Health and Safety Executive www.hse.gov.uk/ [Accessed 30 April 2007]

Keillor, G. (1995) [Internet] Available from www.nasaaarts.org/artworks/ct_cotents.shtml [Accessed 14 December 2006]

Liverpool's Matthew Street Festival Available from: (Liverpool Culture Company) www.liverpool.gov.uk [Accessed 3 November 2006]

London Borough of Lambeth (2005) www.lambeth.gov.uk/NR/rdonlyres/7B786033-45F8-4ECE-A13C-E597A5F3F9DB/0/CPA2005scorecard151205.pdf [Accessed 3 January 2007]

www.marketingpower.com [Accessed 10 March 2007]

Michigan Business School (2004) Fundraising [Internet], FACUM. Available from www.aactmad.org/ppts/fac_UM_fundraising_slides.ppt#31 [Accessed 11 March 2007]

Music Concerts and Festivals, Mintel Report August 2004, www.academic.mintel.com [Accessed 30 April 2007]

Production Services Association, www.psa.org.uk/ [Accessed 30 April 2007]

RainbowTrust (2005) www.rainbowtrust.org.uk/subpage.cfm [Accessed 12 December 2006]

Sport Buisness Group www.sportbuisness.com/ [Accessed 3 March 2007]

Sport England (2006) www.sportengland.org/index/news and media/commonwealth games 2006.htm [Accessed 12 December 2005]

The Saudi Arabia Information Resource, www.saudinf.com, the Saudi Ministry of Culture and Information website and official News Agency of Saudi Arabia.

White Book (2006) White book directory (online database) www.whitebook.co.uk/about/default.aspx [Accessed 12 December 2006]

UNEP (2002) [Internet] Available from www.uneptie.org/pc/tourism [Accessed 29 November 2006]

U.S. Department of Labor, Bureau of Labor Statistic: www.bls.gov/home [Accessed 3 March 2006]

T in the Park www.tinthepark.com [Accessed 3 November 2006]

Yorkshire Evening Post (2002) available from www.thisisleeds.co.uk/ [Accessed 29 December 2006]

Index

Please note that page numbers relating to Figures and Tables will be in *italic* print; titles of publications beginning with 'A' or 'The' will be filed under the first significant word. References to summaries will have the letter 's' following the page number, while references to cases will have the letter 'c' following